MAS

GLOBAL MASCULINITIES

Edited by Michael Kimmel and Judith Kegan Gardiner

Michael Kimmel is Professor of Sociology at the State University of New York at Stony Brook. He is the author or editor of more than twenty books, including: *Men's Lives, Guyland: The Perilous World Where Boys Become Men, The Gendered Society, The Politics of Manhood*, and *Manhood in America: A Cultural History*. He edits *Men and Masculinities*, an interdisciplinary scholarly journal, and edited the *Encyclopedia of Men and Masculinities* and the *Handbook of Studies on Men and Masculinities*. He consults with corporations, NGOs and public sector organizations all over the world on gender equity issues, including work-family balance, reducing workplace discrimination, and promoting diversity.

Judith Kegan Gardiner is Professor of English and of Gender and Women's Studies at the University of Illinois at Chicago. Her books are *Craftsmanship in Context: The Development of Ben Jonson's Poetry* and *Rhys, Stead, Lessing, and the Politics of Empathy*. She is the editor of the volumes *Provoking Agents: Gender and Agency in Theory and Practice*; *Masculinity Studies and Feminist Theory*, and a co-editor of *The International Encyclopedia of Men and Masculinities*. She is also a member of the editorial board for the interdisciplinary journal *Feminist Studies*.

Published by Palgrave Macmillan:

Masculine Style: The American West and Literary Modernism
By Daniel Worden

Men and Masculinities Around the World: Transforming Men's Practices
Edited by Elisabetta Ruspini, Jeff Hearn, Bob Pease, and Keith Pringle

Constructions of Masculinity in British Literature from the Middle Ages to the Present
Edited by Stefan Horlacher

Becoming the Gentleman: British Literature and the Invention of Modern Masculinity, 1660-1815
By Jason D. Solinger

Men and Masculinities in Irish Cinema
By Debbie Ging

The History of Fatherhood in Norway, 1850-2012 (forthcoming)
By Jørgen Ludvig Lorentzen

Masculinity and Monstrosity in Contemporary Hollywood Films (forthcoming)
By Kirk Combe and Brenda Boyle

MASCULINE STYLE

The American West and Literary Modernism

Daniel Worden

palgrave
macmillan

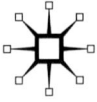

First published in hardcover in 2011 by PALGRAVE MACMILLAN® in the United States—a division of St. Martin's Press LLC, 175 Fifth Avenue, New York, NY 10010.

Where this book is distributed in the UK, Europe and the rest of the world, this is by Palgrave Macmillan, a division of Macmillan Publishers Limited, registered in England, company number 785998, of Houndmills, Basingstoke, Hampshire RG21 6XS.

Palgrave Macmillan is the global academic imprint of the above companies and has companies and representatives throughout the world.

Palgrave® and Macmillan® are registered trademarks in the United States, the United Kingdom, Europe and other countries.

ISBN: 978–1–137–36069–4

The author gratefully acknowledges permission to publish portions of the manuscript that have appeared, in earlier forms, in the following publications:

"'I Like to be Like a Man': Female Masculinity in Willa Cather's *O Pioneers!* and *My Ántonia*," *Willa Cather Newsletter & Review* 49.2 (Fall 2005).

"'I Like to Be Like a Man': Female Masculinity in Willa Cather's *O Pioneers!* and *My Ántonia*," *Violence, the Arts, and Willa Cather*, edited by Joseph R. Urgo and Merrill Maguire Skaggs, Fairleigh Dickinson University Press, 2007.

"Masculinity for the Million: Gender in Dime Novel Westerns." Reprinted from *Arizona Quarterly* 63.3 (2007), by permission of the Regents of The University of Arizona.

The Library of Congress has cataloged the hardcover edition as follows:

Worden, Daniel, 1978–
    Masculine style : the American West and literary modernism / Daniel Worden.
        p. cm.—(Global masculinities)
    Includes bibliographical references.
    ISBN 978–0–230–12031–0
    1. Masculinity in literature. 2. American fiction—19th century—History and criticism. 3. American fiction—20th century—History and criticism. 4. Sex role in literature. 5. Social role in literature. 6. West (U.S.)—In literature. 7. Modernism (Literature)—United States—History. 8. Masculinity—United States—History. I. Title. II. Title: American West and literary modernism.
PS374.M37W67 2011
813'.509353—dc22   2011009535

A catalogue record of the book is available from the British Library.

Design by Newgen Imaging Systems (P) Ltd., Chennai, India.

First PALGRAVE MACMILLAN paperback edition: October 2013

CONTENTS

ILLUSTRATIONS

Note from the
Series Editors

In Sweden, a "real man" is one who does childcare for his own children, and liberals and conservatives argue not about whether there should be government-mandated paternity leave but about the allocation of time between new mothers and fathers. In China, years of enforcing a one-child rule have led to a population with a vast demographic imbalance in the number of males over females, with consequences yet to be determined. In Iran, vasectomy becomes increasingly popular as men seek to take more responsibility for family planning in an atmosphere of restrictive gender roles. In the Philippines, government-supported exports of women as nurses, maids, and nannies to first-world countries alters the lives of boys and girls growing up both at home and in the developed countries, and Mexican-American men adapt to their wives' working by doing increased housework and childcare, while their ideology of men's roles changes more slowly. And throughout the world, warfare continues to be a predominantly male occupation, devastating vast populations, depriving some boys of a childhood, and promoting other men to positions of authority.

Global Masculinities is a series devoted to exploring the most recent, most innovative, and widest ranging scholarship about men and masculinities from a broad variety of perspectives and methodological approaches. The dramatic success of Gender Studies has rested on three developments: (1) making women's lives visible, which has also come to mean making all genders more visible; (2) insisting on intersectionality and so complicating the category of gender; (3) analyzing the tensions among global and local iterations of gender. Through textual analyses and humanities-based studies of cultural representations, as well as cultural studies of attitudes and behaviors, we have come to see the centrality of gender in the structure of modern life and life in the past, varying across cultures and within them. Through interviews, surveys, and demographic analysis, among other forms of social scientific inquiry, we are now able to quantify some of the effects of these changing gender structures. Clearly written for both the expert and more general audience, this series embraces the advances in scholarship and applies them to men's lives: gendering men's lives, exploring the rich diversity of men's lives—globally and locally, textually and practically—as well as the differences among men by social class, "race"/ ethnicity and nationality, sexuality, ability status, sexual preference and practices, and age.

MICHAEL KIMMEL AND
JUDITH KEGAN GARDINER

ACKNOWLEDGMENTS

I have had the pleasure of circulating in a number of academic communities while working on this book. Caren Irr and Michael T. Gilmore worked with me during the early stages of this project, and their guidance has been invaluable to me. I also learned a great deal from John Burt, Patricia Chu, Eugene Goodheart, Thomas King, Susan Lanser, Paul Morrison, and Mark Sanders at Brandeis, and my work on this book has been enriched by conversations with and comments by Christine Bold, William Handley, Melissa Homestead, Victoria Lamont, Marilee Lindemann, Sean McCann, Alan Nadel, Forrest Robinson, Ann Romines, Merrill Maguire Skaggs, Joseph Urgo, Michael Warner, and Nicolas Witschi. I would also like to thank Ross Barrett, David Bottorff, Max Brzezinski, Danielle Coriale, Melanie Doherty, Geneva Gano, Jason Gladstone, David Greven, Shannon Hunt, Holly Jackson, Doug Kirshen, Mikel Parent, Jordan Stein, Erica Still, and Dan Stout for reading and helping me to think about this project.

My colleagues in the Department of English at the University of Colorado at Colorado Springs have been supportive of my work in every possible way, as were my colleagues in the Department of English at Wake Forest University. I owe a special note of thanks to the Georgia O'Keeffe Museum Research Center, where I worked on this project as a scholar-in-residence. Barbara Buhler Lynes, Heather Hole, and Eumie Imm-Stroukoff made me feel at home and gave me the space and time needed to read, write, and edit. Ondine Chavoya, Pat Hills, Lois Rudnick, and Sue Taylor provided welcome intellectual company during my stay in Santa Fe. I was able to conduct archival research with the help of an Ernest Hemingway Research Grant from the John F. Kennedy Library, a travel grant from the American Heritage Center at the University of Wyoming, a Robert Preyer grant from the Brandeis Department of English and American Literature, and two Provost's Dissertation Awards from Brandeis University. The generosity of these institutions has contributed greatly to my archive and my work. I owe many thanks to the librarians at Brandeis

University, the John F. Kennedy Library, the American Heritage Center at the University of Wyoming, the Center for Southwest Research at the University of New Mexico, and the University of Colorado at Colorado Springs. Thanks to Brigitte Shull, Jo Roberts, and Richard Bellis at Palgrave for enthusiastically ushering this book into print.

My family has been supportive of this work in innumerable ways. Thanks to my Mom and Dad—or, Brenda and Dan Worden—and Cory and Jessalynn Worden. The Worden and Jones families have always supported me, and this means more than I can put into words here. While working on this project, I also joined another family; many thanks to Diane and Peter Vennema, who make Santa Fe feel like home, Peter Zuromskis, who keeps Massachusetts feeling like home, John, Tamara, and the Biscuit.

Last, my deepest thanks to Catherine Zuromskis, for so many things.

Masculinity, Modernism, and the West

Masculinity is not a thing but a history. Actions, bodies, styles, texts, images, publics, and politics compose this history. One does not "possess" masculinity, in the sense of having a penis, a gun, or a rugged leather jacket. Instead, one acts masculine, and this acting involves negotiation of a complex set of signs. The often-voiced commands to walk, talk, act, and take it "like a man" make clear that masculinity does not reside in a male body but instead in a series of performative gestures and public presentations. Being "like a man" has little to do with possession and everything to do with performance.[1]

In *Masculine Style*, I analyze masculinity's role in literary modernism by focusing on the American West, and in so doing, I chronicle how texts performatively produce masculinity rather than merely represent it as an object possessed by particular figures. Masculinity is multiple, historical, and social, and *Masculine Style* traces masculinity as a mode of stylization, self-fashioning, and inscription in American literary culture from the late nineteenth century to the Cold War. My study begins with and insistently returns to the frontier and to a form of "cowboy masculinity," not often linked to modernism due to the frontier's associations with nostalgic regionalism and modernism's congruity with cosmopolitan, urban aesthetes. Despite this apparent contradiction, it is my contention that the American West, as imagined in dime-novel Westerns and works such as Owen Wister's *The Virginian* and Theodore Roosevelt's *An Autobiography*, provides a space for the reinvention of the self and social relations central to even the "highest" of modernisms. A gender historically saturated with privilege, masculinity is a site for modernist writers to produce new visions of social belonging, though these visions often contain the very structures of dominance that they purport to subvert. Because it is bound to everyday life, masculinity is a site where aesthetic concerns become social, and the American West offers an ideal setting for the exploration of masculine performativity in late nineteenth- and twentieth-century American culture. From the "closing of the frontier" with the 1890 census to the emergence of the "organization man" and the ubiquitous genre Westerns of the 1950s, American masculinity has undergone a series of shifts that are registered in and facilitated through literary texts about the West.[2] By analyzing American literature from this period, I chart the contours and shifts in Western masculinity as it is detached from rigid class associations after the Civil War, remade as a normative requirement for national belonging at the turn of the century, articulated as a mode of aesthetic embodiment in modernist texts from the 1910s to the 1930s, projected as a mode of enigmatic activism during the Great Depression, and contained as a threatening force during the early years of the Cold War. Masculinity is multiple in American modernism.

The crucial first step for thinking of masculinity as both an aesthetic and social project, and, more specifically, as a potentially utopian mode of self-fashioning is to delink masculinity from a necessary connection to dominance and conservatism. In the introduction to the anthology *Male Trouble*, Constance Penley and Sharon Willis critique the common construction of masculinity and patriarchal power as "seamless and monolithic" and the presumption that "any approach…that would study masculinity as a split and contradictory construction, and would cast patriarchal power as uneven and sometimes unsuccessful in its effects represents a dangerous digression from 'properly' feminist projects."[3] As Penley and Willis point out, masculinity tends to be stabilized by an association with male dominance, patriarchy, masculinism, machismo, heterosexism, or heteronormativity. The coupling of masculinity with a distinctly monolithic politics has been reinvigorated by recent work on American imperialism that links masculinity to nativism and social Darwinism. Gail Bederman's *Manliness and Civilization*, for example, charts how "hegemonic discourses of civilization explained precisely the connection between the male body, male identity, and male authority."[4] Bederman's work is one text among many that link late nineteenth- and early twentieth-century American manhood to hegemonic politics.[5] This scholarship rarely looks at modes of masculinity apart from the imperialistic, jingoistic, chauvinistic, and nativist drives of dominant manhood.[6]

In contrast, Judith Halberstam argues in *Female Masculinity* that there are other ways of approaching masculinity than through the lens of dominance: "Masculinity in this society inevitably conjures up notions of power and legitimacy and privilege…But, obviously, many other lines of identification traverse the terrain of masculinity, dividing its power into complex differentials of class, race, sexuality, and gender."[7] While Halberstam goes on to focus on female masculinities, *Masculine Style* builds on her methodology by focusing on both male and female masculinity.[8] Drawing from this scholarship, I argue that masculinity—even masculinity that *is* male—contains, in whatever ultimately compromised form, the possibility to critique social conventions and produce alternative modes of social belonging. Masculinity has no necessary relation to dominant politics, be they imperialist, patriarchal, or heteronormative. Instead, it is historically linked to these modes of power, and in this book, I make the case for thinking of masculinity as only contingently connected to dominance, and, therefore, also a vehicle for other aesthetic, political, and social projects. In American modernist literature particularly, masculinity often offers a site for protest against the dominant, a way of channeling power into unconventional publics and subjects.

Even when theoretically detached from its normalizing associations with patriarchy, masculinity is still not entirely malleable. As Judith Butler is careful to point out in *Bodies that Matter*, thinking of gender as performative does not mean that any individual has the agency to choose, create, or revise gender wholesale:

> The reading of "performativity" as willful and arbitrary choice misses the point that the historicity of discourse and, in particular, the historicity of norms…constitute the power of discourse to enact what it names. To think of "sex" as an imperative in this way means that a subject is addressed and produced by such a norm, and that this norm—and the regulatory power of which it is a token—materializes bodies as an effect of that injunction.[9]

Masculinity's fixity—its seeming objectivity in lived experience and culture—is the product of this performativity, this discursive history that is brought to bear on a subject in each gesture, utterance, and act. Butler's theory of gender performativity accounts, though, for gender's ability to morph over time, as signifiers emerge and recede from repertoires, and attention to masculinity's fluidity is crucial to exposing the historical gestures, acts, and styles that constitute gender as a social reality. Understanding gender as historical in and of itself is central to *Masculine Style*, which is an attempt to recover a particular history of masculinity in American literary history. Butler's theory of gender performativity informs my readings of masculinity in American literature. Throughout *Masculine Style*, I focus on how texts stage masculinity as a performative gender, a cluster of norms concretized through iteration. These performative masculinities critique and rework norms by attaching masculine styles to unusual bodies or developing new political valences for masculinity. One of the implications of gender performativity is that masculinity cannot be easily divided into the binaries of "hegemonic" and "alternative." Instead, it is itself uneven, saturated not just by patriarchal citations but also by sentimental, collective, queer, effeminate, and butch masculinities, masculinities that are not outside of "sex" but revisions, reappropriations, and rearticulations of masculinity. My interest in literature stems from its ability to imagine "liveable lives" that differ from our own immediate social conditions, and "cowboy masculinity," precisely because it fixates on such tropes as individualism, sentimentality, ruggedness, and violence, and offers a unique site to interrogate the ways in which literature remakes masculinity rather than takes it as an object of representation. Like all masculinities, the literary masculinity I examine in this book is imaginary; it is endowed with a charisma and power that often exceeds the material conditions of actual lived experience. It is important to remark, though, that I am not claiming that authors such as Cather or Hemingway fashion masculinities from scratch. Instead, their texts reproduce, with a difference, masculinity as a discourse, on an imaginative plane that does not have the same material constraints as lived experience. This ability of literature to imagine rearticulations of gender stems not from some humanistic conceit about imaginative power but instead from the recognition that power has no center. The very unevenness of discourse allows literature to intervene, to act. From dime novels to *Shane*, the works that I analyze here imagine potentially unrealizable masculinities, and in that imaginative work there is potential for emergent lived masculinities that are more heterogeneous than those we encounter in our everyday lives.

If masculinity is heterogeneous, then its politics and social roles must also be multiple. As Wendy Brown explains, "the feminist critical theory of the liberal, capitalistic, bureaucratic state" does not necessarily limit one to the view that all masculinities are bound to patriarchy. Instead, she argues that feminist views of the state focuses selectively on the power relations that constitute male dominance:

> The elements of the state identifiable as masculinist correspond not to some property contained within men but to the conventions of power

and privilege *constitutive* of gender within an order of male domi-nance. Put another way, the masculinism of the state refers to those features of the state that signify, enact, sustain, and represent mascu-line power as a form of dominance.[10]

One implication of Brown's account of patriarchy is that masculinity exceeds male dominance. Power is not entirely consolidated within the state, nor is masculinity entirely consolidated within state power. Instead, the state co-opts and produces forms of manhood to serve as emblems of citizenship and models of proper behavior. However, in doing so, masculinities fall outside of its overt control. Butler claims in *Bodies that Matter* that the law—and here one can read the state as one particular institution of the law—never completely interpel-lates its subject: "the performative, the call by the law which seeks to produce a lawful subject, produces a set of consequences that exceed and confound what appears to be the disciplining intention motivat-ing the law."[11] If "the law" attempts to produce bodies of intelligible gender and sex, then it seems that masculine interpellation holds out a promise of reversing the call of the law. Are there masculinities that do not claim dominance? What about masculinities that do not emphatically endorse the autonomous individual but instead strive for forms of collective belonging? What about masculinities that actively resist patriarchy and male dominance? These masculinities that stand apart from male dominance, while often uninterrogated by gender theorists, occupy a central place in American culture. Masculinity reflective of frontier mythology was so often cited, experimented with, and imitated in American modernism precisely because of its excessive heterogeneity, pliability, and style.

My understanding of masculinity synthesizes theoretical work on gender, literature, and culture by Butler, Fredric Jameson, and Eve Kosofsky Sedgwick. Following Fredric Jameson's proposition in *The Political Unconscious*—"history is what hurts"—I want to emphasize that masculinity exists outside of any individual embodi-ment of masculinity and, by implication, necessarily frustrates radical self-fashioning.[12] However, and precisely because masculinity merely seems natural but is in fact performative, it is also malleable, especially in literary texts, sites of the imaginative reworking of social life. As Jameson remarks, "the effectively ideological is also, at the same time, necessarily Utopian."[13] Masculinity's utopian promise is precisely what its ideological function denies: individual freedom to refash-ion the self and live as an equal among others. The texts studied in this book demystify masculinity as neither individually liberating nor egalitarian yet also envision utopian masculinities that would realize the promise of individuality and equality. In the interpretations that follow, I make the critical wager that cowboy masculinity in modernism exceeds dominant constructions of manhood, even if modernist masculinity is ultimately flattened and streamlined into hegemonic channels, either by narrative structures that force a conventional ending onto otherwise unruly texts or hegemonies that eventually contain alternative masculinities within racist, patriarchal logics.

Of course, there are many masculinities, and I should clarify that I am indeed dealing with a particular historical range of masculinities. I focus here on a style of masculinity that emerges in late nineteenth-century America and thrives in the works of American modernist writers such as Willa Cather, Ernest Hemingway, and John Steinbeck. This modernist masculinity is a style of self-presentation that insists on the mobility of hierarchical signifiers. It is this emphasis on mobility that gives masculinity such power in American culture and, at the same time, endows it with the promise of resisting the very hierarchies that it signifies. By contesting the conventions that govern selfhood, intimacy, and sociability, this form of masculine self-fashioning promises to inaugurate new publics, formed around alternative systems of belonging.

This book will explore the possibilities unleashed by masculine performance in American literature from 1860 to 1952. I interrogate the association of nineteenth- and early twentieth-century masculinity with dominance by looking back to dime-novel Westerns as well as turn-of-the-century writing about the frontier and its expansion to places such as San Juan Hill in Cuba during the Spanish-American War. Then, I turn to the modernist prose of Willa Cather, Ernest Hemingway, and John Steinbeck. American modernist literary culture is preoccupied with masculinity as both a subject matter and a mode of authorial self-fashioning, and I argue that this fixation on masculinity is crucial to the aesthetics and politics of modernism. In so doing, I advocate for an alternative history of masculinity that accounts for both masculinity's power to not only repeat but also rework social conventions. In this book, I seek to construct an account of masculinities that revise conventions, refashion the self and its relation to others, and serve as crucibles for the emergence of new possibilities for subjectivity, embodiment, and action as they emerge in the aftermath of the "closing of the frontier" through the "containment culture" of the Cold War.

Understanding masculinity's role in American modernism demands the complication of the masculine/feminine binary.[14] As Eve Kosofsky

Sedgwick argues, "masculinity and femininity are in many respects orthogonal to one another."[15] That is, valuation of masculinity in a work of literature does not necessarily entail denigration of femininity. The persistence of the masculine/feminine binary often obfuscates masculinity itself. For example, in *The Gender of Modernity*, Rita Felski remarks that for all of the modernist dandy's play with femininity, he nonetheless devalues the female body. She concludes her reading of feminized masculinity with this claim: "To dematerialize the 'natural' by insisting on the totalizing power of the textual may thus be to echo rather than challenge a long-standing aesthetic tradition which has sought transcendence through a denial and erasure of the female body."[16] Felski analyzes masculinity, ultimately, through its implications for femininity or femaleness. This insistence on the binary and fixed relationship between masculinity and femininity—that any masculine cause has a feminine effect and vice versa—results in the conceptualization of gender less as a malleable cluster of conventions than as a stable structure. Departing from the binary conceptualization, I wish to study masculinity itself, and I hope that this method will bring to light not how masculinity affects femininity—a model that assumes patriarchal privilege and results in a logic of victimization—but how masculinity works in multiple registers.

Another integral facet of my argument is the complication of traditional accounts of modernism and its "high/low" divide between literature and popular, or mass, culture. There have been numerous convincing arguments for the displacement of the "high/low" divide as a fiction developed in the postwar period, yet many works about the division between "high" modernism and "low" culture merely complicate and never fully do away with the divide.[17] As Michael North argues in *Reading 1922*, late twentieth-century critiques of modernist elitism, canonicity, and masculinism have done little to diminish the monolithic concept of modernism as separate from culture in general:

> Though the prestige of Eliot and Pound, if not Joyce, has been considerably diminished since the days in which the whole of the literature could be named after one man, what used to be called modernism has not been expanded or even changed very much; rather, it lives on, in a mummified state to provide a determinate negation for its successor.[18]

It is my contention in this project that if the "high/low" divide is in fact a convenient fiction, then it might be best ignored in genealogies of modernism. I aim to develop an argument about masculinity in American modernism that does not make strong distinctions between, say, dime novels and experimental novels.

Not only does this study seek to demonstrate the usefulness of ignoring the high/low divide when writing about modernism, it also strives to locate at the core of modernism a dependence on the genre of the Western. While her reading of masculinity relies on masculinity's relationship to femininity rather than masculinity itself, Felski also argues that "we need to take more seriously the distinctive and determining, rather than simply determined, nature of generic forms such as romance and melodrama in shaping the culture of modernity."[19] I seek to follow this claim in two ways. First, I argue that modernism is not separable from "the culture of modernity." This book begins with an analysis of two dime novels first published in 1860 and 1877, historically prior to modernism's generally accepted flourishing from the 1910s through the 1940s. By pointing out the experimental uses of masculinity in both late nineteenth-century popular literature and "high modernist" texts from the twentieth century, I hope to demonstrate that the divide between popular, genteel, or sentimental literature and modernist literature is a false distinction that can be productively set aside. Furthermore, I locate the Western genre at the center of modernism's concern with masculinity. Dime novels and the Western writings of Owen Wister, Theodore Roosevelt, and Nat Love contain emergent traces of modernist literary form. As Douglas Mao and Rebecca Walkowitz argue in their essay on "The New Modernist Studies," modernism as both a historical period and an aesthetic style has been fruitfully expanded "in what we might think of as temporal, spatial, and vertical directions."[20] Following this directive, I expand the concept of modernism, first, by including works that are historically prior to conventional periodizations of modernism; second, by focusing on a region, the American West, distant from the urban centers of traditional modernist literary production; and, third, by arguing that the masculinity emergent in dime-novel Westerns is a formal model for masculine self-fashioning in the twentieth-century United States. If modernism is to be liberated, as a literary category, from its rarefied status in late twentieth-century literary criticism, then it seems necessary to seek out proto-modernist texts and include them in the study of modernism. The cult of literary genius that has proven so central to the study and canonization of modernist texts can, I think, best be complicated by a focus on form and its histories. Modernism, I argue, should be far more synonymous with modernity and does not delimit a cluster of texts but instead a series of literary styles and strategies that exceed the modernist canon.

The spatial modification and revision of modernism that I undertake in this book is conceived to position the American frontier—and particularly the cowboy masculinity associated with it—as a central factor in U.S. modernism. Modernism is most often associated with urban space, yet this book makes a case for the significance of the American West to modernism. In this sense, *Masculine Style* aims to complicate the ways in which we value cosmopolitan urbanity in modernist literature and to demonstrate how a critical focus on cosmopolitanism creates a myopia when it comes to the very important claims of nationalism, regionalism, and rural environments on modernist texts. Since the American West is so often thought to be emblematic of the nation, I argue for the importance of multiple nationalisms within modernism. The nation remains a significant category for modernist writers, especially those who write about the American West, but nationalism is heterogeneous in its aesthetic roles and political valences. Ultimately, all of these complications to modernism—its reliance on the high/low divide, its common periodization from about 1890 to 1940, and its locus in cosmopolitan urban centers—stem from a desire, in Raymond William's words, to "search out and counterpose an alternative [Modernist] tradition taken from the neglected works left in the wide margin of the [twentieth] century, a tradition which may address itself…to a modern *future* in which community may be imagined again."[21]

To illustrate the promise of masculinity to modernism, and the necessity of complicating critical paradigms about masculinity's relationship to power, I will turn to two poems, one by E. E. Cummings, the other by T. S. Eliot. Both poems dwell on and revalue cowboy masculinity. In the 1923 collection *Tulips and Chimneys*, E. E. Cummings' well-known poem about Buffalo Bill both glories in the passing of nineteenth-century spectacle and mourns Buffalo Bill's masculine appeal. The poem casts Buffalo Bill in a state of boyishness infused with homoeroticism. The poem begins by mourning Buffalo Bill and describing his marksmanship, and it concludes with a question, "how do you like your blueeyed boy / Mister Death."[22] "Mister Death" figures here as an older, patriarchal figure who, the narrator sarcastically comments, desires the "boy," Buffalo Bill. The poem evokes a breathtaking awe at Buffalo Bill's handsomeness and marksmanship, contributing to Bill's youthful, sexy cowboy image. Cummings's teasing homoerotic joke at the end of the poem coupled with a pause of genuine, breathless appreciation of Buffalo Bill's shooting skills and good looks generate a curious view of nineteenth-century popular culture and American masculinity, one not often associated with modernism. One of the most common tropes for discussing modernist literature is the emphasis on newness and originality, along with a disdain for mass culture.[23] Yet rather than finding fault in Buffalo Bill's mass culture appeal, Cummings's poem meditates on his beauty, dexterity, and grace. As such, the poem unabashedly revels in the pleasures of mass culture, only to turn Buffalo Bill, ironically, into a "blueeyed boy" at the poem's conclusion, now under the control of the patriarchal, pedophiliac "Mister Death."

Buffalo Bill is one of the hallmarks of American masculinity in the late nineteenth century. A former Pony Express rider turned performer and dime novelist, William "Buffalo Bill" Cody capitalized on the popular fascination with rugged, frontier masculinity in the late nineteenth and early twentieth centuries.[24] As much as Cummings's poem mocks Buffalo Bill's larger-than-life status by imagining him with "Mister Death," the poem nonetheless relies on popular Western masculinity to construct a complex synthesis of irony, loss, and longing. Likewise, the modernist canon is overrun with masculine figures as interested in self-stylization as Buffalo Bill, from Gertrude Stein, Djuna Barnes, Natalie Barney, and other manly women on the Left Bank in Paris to hard-living icons such as William Faulkner, F. Scott Fitzgerald, and Ernest Hemingway. Masculinity provides a bridge from nineteenth-century mass culture to modernism. Nineteenth-century Western masculinity surfaces throughout modernism in the forms of leisure activities, fashion, speech, and an insistence on living outside of social conventions. Moreover, if one takes into account that William Cody died in 1917, the year America entered World War I, one can read into Cummings's mourning of Buffalo Bill an implication that his brand of self-made manhood gives way to a wounded manhood emblematic of masculinist modernist fiction.[25] As Cummings's poem so astutely demonstrates, these two masculinities—the cowboy masculinity of the late nineteenth century and modernist masculinity—are not separated by a radical divide between the lowbrow and the highbrow, the sentimental and the modernist, or the robust and the wounded. Instead, nineteenth-century "cowboy" masculinity carries over into modernism as both a model of awesome embodiment and a gendered position that allows for non-normative intimacies, even with "Mister Death." In cowboy masculinity, American modernism finds a model of gender performance that both produces new ways of thinking about embodiment and manifests a critique of dominant power relations.

For this reason, I look to the Western as a tremendous influence on American modernism's masculine productions. Even T. S. Eliot's 1922 *The Waste Land* borrows from the Western to figure recognition and community amid an alienating landscape. In the first section of the poem, "The Burial of the Dead," the narrator sees a familiar figure among a crowd on London Bridge:

> There I saw one I knew, and stopped him crying: "Stetson!
> "You who were with me in the ships at Mylae!
> "That corpse you planted last year in your garden,
> "Has it begun to sprout? Will it bloom this year?
> "Or has the sudden frost disturbed its bed?
> "Oh keep the Dog far hence, that's friend to men,
> "Or with nails he'll dig it up again!
> "You! hypocrite lecteur!—mon semblable,—mon frere!"[26]

The Stetson hat serves as a synecdoche for the poet's ghostly companion, marking the crucial significance of Western tropes for thinking about modernist masculinity. "Stetson" holds a series of relations to the narrator: a long-lost companion, a brother, a killer, and a mirror-image of the narrator himself.[27] Furthermore, "Stetson" has a close tie to the animalistic, through his proximity to the "Dog…that's friend to men." This bestial intimacy functions throughout modernism as a way of distancing masculinity from social conventions. Eliot's interpellation of "Stetson" as attempting to sprout something from death, just as *The Waste Land* as a whole attempts to do in its concluding prayer and pastiche of fragments, is complemented by the articulation of a homosocial, brotherly bond. Like Buffalo Bill in Cummings's poem, "Stetson" in *The Waste Land* is tinged with a mixture of critique—Stetson is "hypocrite lecteur"—desire, and identification. While Eliot acknowledges the violence enacted by masculinities past, "Stetson" still holds out a promise for an unearthed truth, a renewed brotherhood.

In both poems, "cowboy masculinity" connotes loss, irony, and affection. The figures of repetition in the poems—Eliot's digging dog and Cummings's rapid-fire shooting—serve as reminders of the American West and forms of frontier masculinity, an underlying context for modernist stylization.[28] In *The Great Gatsby*, Fitzgerald's narrator, Nick Carraway, links the West to modernist narrative: "I see now that this has been as story of the West, after all—Tom and Gatsby, Daisy and Jordan and I, were all Westerners, and perhaps we possessed some deficiency in common which made us subtly unadaptable to Eastern life."[29] Michael T. Gilmore finds in the novel's title character, Jay Gatsby, and in the novel's invocations of the West, "the uncivilized energies emanating from the frontier," against and alongside of which the urban, cosmopolitan styles of modernism emerge.[30] The West and the popular narratives that represent the region to readers in the late nineteenth and twentieth centuries intertwine with American modernism as a reference point to a time before modernism and, more importantly, a cluster of generative tropes for twentieth-century American literature.

As in Fitzgerald's use of the West to signal unruly forces, American modernist texts more generally employ popular literary traditions to signal unique orientations toward time and space, undoing the conventional norms that figure time as reproductive futurity and space as personal property. Masculinity is a key site for this revision of space and time, as writers experiment with masculine styles that come from the spatial and temporal logics of manifest destiny and popular fiction. For example, in William Faulkner's *Light in August*, after killing Joanna Burden, Joe Christmas hides in the woods and reads a pulp magazine:

> He had previously read but one story; he began now upon the second one, reading the magazine straight through as though it were a novel…He turned the pages in steady progression, though now and then he would seem to linger upon one page, one line, perhaps one word. He would not look up then. He would not move, apparently arrested and held immobile by a single word which had perhaps not yet impacted, his whole being suspended by a trivial combination of letters in quiet and sunny space, so that hanging motionless and without physical weight he seemed to watch the slow flowing of time beneath him, thinking *All I wanted was peace* thinking, "She ought not to started praying over me."[31]

Christmas's reading blurs time and space, raising him above the "slow flowing of time" and putting him in a "sunny space." This scene of reading both demonstrates the therapeutic effect of mass culture, for it suspends Joe Christmas from his current predicament, and also produces a formal congruence between *Light in August* and popular literature. *Light in August*, like Christmas's magazine, contains multiple stories from different times and places, juxtaposed against one another. When Christmas finishes the magazine, he burns it, "[prodding] it patiently until it was totally consumed."[32] The consumption of the magazine plays with consumption as reading and as destruction. Christmas not only consumes but also is consumed by popular literature.[33]

All of this is to say that masculinity is a site for some modernist writers to experiment with the divide between reality and representation, object and subject, the outside and the inside. As Bill Brown argues in *A Sense of Things*, one of modernism's major aesthetic principles is the refashioning of representation and interiority into exteriority:

> This effort to fathom the concrete, and to imagine the work of art as a different mode of mimesis—not one that serves to represent a thing, but one that seeks to attain the status of a thing—is a fundamental strain of modernism, as characteristic of Stein as it is of Malevich, of Picasso as it is of Zukofsky. The question of things becomes a question about whether the literary object should be understood as the object that literature represents or the object that literature has as its aim, the object that literature is.[34]

I would add that masculinity is a crucial mode of disciplining the body, externalizing the self, and objectifying sentiments within modernism. Willa Cather and Ernest Hemingway, two key proponents of modernist masculinity, both define their prose styles against interior decorating, and this trope also figures their approach to masculine embodiment: Cather expresses disdain for the "over-furnished novel" in "The Novel Démeublé," and Hemingway claims in *Death in the Afternoon* that "prose is architecture, not interior decoration."[35] This aesthetic principle applies not just to prose style but also to the ways in which each author depicts the development of a masculine persona. One becomes masculine not through the interior but through external self-fashioning, through bodily discipline. Cather and Hemingway's critiques of the "interior" link modernism's interest in the object to the treatment of the gendered body itself as an object, an artifact, that can be molded and shaped according to aesthetic principles. Rather than furnishing lavish interiors, modernist writers produce sparse, controlled exteriors. The emphasis on exterior performativity serves as a figure for the self, for the ways in which self-discipline shapes and produces the masculine body. Through this interest in the objectivity of the self, masculinity becomes a way of refashioning not only the individual but also publics and collectives.

While writing this book, I have tried to think of masculinity both synchronically and diachronically, as both a theoretical and an historical object. Theoretically, this book makes a case for the heterogeneity, aesthetic plenitude, and erotic possibility of masculinity when it is imagined as a performative gender rather than an appendage of hegemony. Historically, I trace the emergence of masculine self-fashioning from the late nineteenth-century up to the early years of the Cold War in the United States. The authors and texts that I analyze are part of a larger history, as I hope has been signaled in this introduction with the brief readings of Cummings, Eliot, Faulkner, and Fitzgerald. This study originated with my interest in late nineteenth-century dime-novel Westerns, the books that invented the modern Western hero.[36] In dime novels, I encountered a masculinity very different from the imperialist, misogynist, and racist manhood often thought indicative of late nineteenth-century America. Chapter one offers close readings of two of the most popular, often reprinted, and widely anthologized dime-novel Westerns from the late nineteenth century: Edward S. Ellis's *Seth Jones; or, the Captives of the Frontier* and Edward Wheeler's *Deadwood Dick, the Prince of the Road; or, the Black Rider of the Black Hills.* The masculine heroes—bandits, cowboys, and woodsmen—that recur in dime novels cross class boundaries by taking on multiple names and identities and repeatedly thwart social conventions through their class and gender illegibility. In so doing, late nineteenth-century dime-novel Westerns use masculinity to contest normative gender and marriage conventions. As such, my reading of turn-of-the-century dime novels finds that masculinity is a way of eluding social boundaries by troubling the naturalized, essentialized ontology of gender, though that troubling ultimately relies on a racist construction of white, frontier masculinity.

Nat Love and Theodore Roosevelt are problematic figures in scholarship on the American West and imperialism. Often cast as masculine personifications of American expansionism and its concomitant racism, these two men both wrote memoirs chronicling their experiences in the American West and in war. To complicate the dominant portrayal of Love and Roosevelt, I argue in chapter two that Love's *The Life and Adventures of Nat Love* along with Roosevelt's *The Rough Riders* and *An Autobiography* depict masculinity as egalitarian. For Love and Roosevelt, especially in their accounts of Western adventure and military service, masculinity offers a way of constructing the self outside of birth-, class-, race-, and even sex-based hierarchies. These hierarchies enter their thinking as a way not to reinforce but to curb masculinity.

Chapter three explores Owen Wister's *The Virginian: A Horseman of the Plains.* *The Virginian* is often treated as an exemplary Western, dramatizing many of the national, imperial, and gender hierarchies central to the genre. While Wister's politics were certainly imperialist, *The Virginian* itself constructs a nostalgic Wild West open to intimate relations across sexual, generational, racial, and even species boundaries. In so doing, the novel offers a competing vision of domestic intimacy that does not rely on marriage and reproduction. Instead, masculinity thrives in *The Virginian* because it nurtures individual and collective intimacies with all subjects in a frontier territory, even animals.

Chapter four focuses on how Willa Cather revises treatments of the frontier by featuring masculine heroines in *O Pioneers!* and *My Ántonia*. These novels represent pioneer women who, in Ántonia Shimerda's words, "like to be like a man." On the Nebraskan frontier, Cather finds a site for the exploration of masculinities that flourish in bodies, relations, and publics other than the domestic, familial, and reproductive. While Alexandra Bergson in *O Pioneers!* imagines her masculine body becoming one with the land, Ántonia Shimerda's story is framed as a history of alternative masculinity by *My Ántonia*'s layered narrative form.

I then turn to the writer most famous for his masculinity, Ernest Hemingway. *Death in the Afternoon* stands out as both one of Hemingway's most difficult texts to categorize and the one that contains the most direct discussion of masculinity. Published in 1932, *Death in the Afternoon* was written during the period many critics identify as Hemingway's most misogynist and narcissistic. Yet Hemingway's fixation on the tragedy of the bullfight, the tradition of homosexuality in painting and literature, the dangers of literary celebrity in an age of mass media, and authentic rather than conventional emotion construct an account of masculinity that is very distant from the wounded, oedipalized, and boisterous Hemingway one expects. Chapter five explores how *Death in the Afternoon* envisions masculinity as a way of disciplining and shaping the self. Hemingway values subjects who mold their emotions, bodies, and styles as if they were themselves works of art, and *Death in the Afternoon* is a meditation on how to fashion oneself as a masculine subject.

Chapter six focuses on John Steinbeck's *The Grapes of Wrath*. In this novel, Steinbeck uses both experimentally collectivist and sentimental novelistic techniques. *The Grapes of Wrath* dramatizes modernist masculinity at its most performative, even sentimental, yet in so doing, it also gestures to the impossibility of masculine activism within corporate capitalism. I then turn briefly to two of Steinbeck's works after *The Grapes of Wrath,* the documentary script *The Forgotten Village* and the U.S. military promotional book *Bombs Away*. In these works, I find the beginnings of a shift from modernist masculinity to the professional manhood so emblematic of Cold War America.

Masculine Style concludes with a reading of *Shane*—both Jack Schaefer's novel and George Stevens's film—as indicative of a shift in American culture from a valorization of masculinity as a liberatory mode of self-fashioning to representations of masculinity as primarily hostile to the stability and unity of the family. *Shane* signals a broader change in American literature from a modernist project of creating new modes of masculine embodiment to Cold War narratives that cast masculinity as beset with unsatisfied longing, loss, and melancholy. The nostalgia in *Shane* for masculinity, most famously articulated by little Joey's plea, "Come back, Shane!," functions as a containment strategy that, in the end, defines masculinity as a threat to the stability of the family.

In late nineteenth- and early twentieth-century American literature, masculinity is a site for the production of new social possibilities. While there were certainly genteel and paternalistic masculinities interested in the consolidation of wealth, the creation of insurmountable obstacles in the way of gender and racial equality, and aggressive American expansionism on the global scene from the 1860s to the 1950s, the literary texts of the period feature masculinities that produce new ways of thinking about gender, sexuality, the family, property, and public culture. This project aims to uncover the hidden side of masculinity, a masculinity that is both coextensive with and critical of dominant manhood.

CHAPTER 1

Masculinity for the Million: Gender in Dime-Novel Westerns

The world is a great dodger, and the Americans the greatest.
Because they dodge their own very selves.
    —D. H. Lawrence, *Studies in Classic American Literature*

Published in 1883, Anthony Comstock's *Traps for the Young* catalogs the corruptions awaiting children in the new industrial age. Among Comstock's "traps" are dime novels, which he describes as "the eggs from which all kinds of villainy are hatched."[1] Comstock faults dime novels not for being particularly bloody or for depicting acts of rampant murder and violence but instead for flagrantly disregarding the genteel codes that locate wealth and beauty in stable bodies. The main character

> in many, if not the vast majority of these stories, is some boy or girl who possesses usually extraordinary beauty of countenance, the most superb clothing, abundant wealth, the strength of a giant, the agility of a squirrel, the cunning of a fox, the brazen effrontery of the most daring villain, and who is utterly destitute of any regard for the laws of God or man.[2]

For Comstock, these qualities are fantastical breaches of the social order. Accordingly, Comstock ends this passage by equating these overthrows of "the laws of God and man" with the destabilization and troubling of gender codes; he concludes that dime novels "favor violation of marriage laws and cheapen female virtue."[3] Because of their depictions of unstable, improper characters, dime novels, according to Comstock, subvert a basic operation of power: the gendered valuation of bodies. The dime novel's radical disregard of genteel virtue and gender roles poses a direct threat to what Dana D. Nelson refers to as "the imagined fraternity of white men" that constitutes the American patriarchal order.[4] Even a complimentary review of Beadle and Adams' dime novels in 1864 warns, "a serious responsibility rests on [Beadle and Adams]. They are wielding an instrument of immense power in education and civilization."[5] To the disapproval of moral reformers such as Comstock, though, dime novels use masculine heroes to critique genteel patriarchy's reliance on gender and class hierarchies to secure dominance.[6]

Anthony Comstock's anxiety about the effects of the new mass literature on the youth of America was very common among morally upright citizens in the latter half of nineteenth century. This anxiety was due to dime novels' development of a distinct masculinity that both resists and, in many cases, directly opposes genteel social conventions that code social behavior through gender.[7] For example, the *New York Times* ran brief stories about "students of the dime novel" throughout the late nineteenth century that described the effects of this threatening masculinity. These bits of sensationalist journalism detailed the crimes, secret societies, and schemes planned by juvenile imitators of dime-novel heroes. On October 23, 1888, the *New York Times* reported a dime-novel-inspired incident in Stockton, California. With the headline "She Wants to be a Cowboy," the paragraph-long story concerns Mary Abbott, a sixteen-year-old female who "is the victim of dime novels, and says she wants to be a cowboy." After repeated, failed attempts to leave her family and rough it, Mary went "to her father's barn armed with two pistols. She remained there for several hours, and when discovered, fired a shot, scattering her pursuers. A parson ventured into the barn, hoping to quiet the young girl, but she thrust a pistol into his face and he retired."[8] After fending off the parson, Mary fled the barn, but was stopped when "a constable fired two shots above her head, which startled her, and she sprang into some bushes which stopped her progress and she was captured."[9] This episode demonstrates just how fluid masculinity is in late nineteenth-century America. Mary's desire to become a cowboy temporarily dislodges masculinity from an essential connection to a male body. For Mary Abbott, being a cowboy in no way requires being a man; one simply needs "a pony, . . . a lot of provisions, a camping outfit, and a pistol," along with the resolve to threaten the life of a parson, to become that prototype of American masculinity—the cowboy.[10]

The challenge here is not, as the *New York Times* suggested, Mary's "victimization" by dime novels but rather Mary's active affront to dominant power—her father, the parson, and the police, or patriarchy, religion, and the state. Mary's masculine performance belongs to a neglected history of female masculinity in literature of the American West. In the popular dime novels featuring Deadwood Dick, for example, Calamity Jane is a recurring character who dresses, fights, and curses like a man.[11] Scholars associate nineteenth-century frontier masculinity with jingoism and imperialism, usually figured through the influence of Andrew Jackson and Theodore Roosevelt. Remarkably, though, the masculine heroes in dime novels and their real-life imitators adopt masculinity to produce alternatives to those very institutions of power.[12] Mary Abbott's masculine rebellion and the popular press' hand-wringing response convey the threat masculinity posed to late nineteenth-century genteel norms and institutions, particularly through a proliferation of masculinities that are not bound to a legibly male body.

Comstock's belief and the *New York Times*' anecdotal evidence that this new form of mass culture would corrupt the minds and bodies of the young seems quaint by today's standards. By 1922, dime novels had become objects not of scorn but of wistful nostalgia when Dr. Frank P. O'Brien's dime-novel collection was put on exhibit at the New York Public Library.[13] After World War I and the dime novel's demise in the face of more graphic and seductively illustrated pulp magazines and comic books, critics viewed dime novels as evidence of an innocent past rather than a chronicle of insipid and dangerous mass culture. However, it is important to use historical sources such as Anthony Comstock's *Traps for the Young* and the *New York Times*' "Students of the Dime Novel" column to contextualize the threats to gentility that dime novels posed in the late nineteenth century. Dime-novel narratives routinely question the structures of belonging central to what Dana D. Nelson describes as the "imagined fraternity of white men," namely, the genteel juxtaposition of scientific knowledge, propriety, and moralism with patriarchal control of property, family life, and women's bodies.[14] Furthermore, dime novels have an influence on literary modernism; the unconventional masculinity developed in the dime novel provides a model for modernism's project of remaking both literary form and art's relationship to the social world.

As a body of literature, dime novels are a heteroglot collection of texts; many are expanded versions of sensational crime reports, many reference actual historical events and figures, and many were reprinted in different series, under different author's names, different titles, and even by different publishers, multiple times.[15] Consistent throughout this sprawling mass press is the production of a unique masculinity that critiques normative gender roles and social conventions. I will turn to two popular dime-novel Westerns of the late nineteenth century, Edward S. Ellis's *Seth Jones; or, the Captives of the Frontier* and Edward Wheeler's *Deadwood Dick, the Prince of the Road; or, the Black Rider of the Black Hills,* as representative examples of the dime-novel Western's depiction of masculinity. These dime novels were tremendously popular, and they were reprinted a number of times by their publishers throughout the late nineteenth century. Together, they chart a shift in the dime-novel Western from a more traditional narrative, owing much to James Fenimore Cooper's Leatherstocking Tales, to a more contemporary bandit narrative about the mining industry in the Western territories of the 1870s. I juxtapose Seth Jones, the older frontiersman hero, with Deadwood Dick, the newer bandit hero, to demonstrate how dime novels gradually develop a unique and ultimately modernist narrative form.

The emergence of the dime novel represents a turning point in American publishing. The first dime-novel publisher, Beadle and Adams, founded the first national book distribution company, was the first to copyright its most popular characters as intellectual property, and notably marketed its books to members of the working class. *Seth Jones* and *Deadwood Dick* were both published by Beadle and Adams. The company's advertising slogan, "Books for the Million," emphasizes the dime novel's centrality to mass culture in the late nineteenth century, and this mass cultural appeal was manifest through a "masculinity for the million" that could be performed by both frontier heroes such as Deadwood Dick and sixteen-year-old Mary Abbott from Stockton, California.

Dime novels posed a particular problem for writers and publishers interested in using a recurring popular character. Conventional novelistic form, especially the genteel realism and sentimental romance narratives dominant in the late nineteenth century, demands a stabilizing ending. That is to say, characters must marry or die at the end of the novel in order to produce a sense of closure. However, a hero like Deadwood Dick could not enter into social stability at the end of a dime novel if he was to return as the same heroic, adventuresome bandit figure in subsequent dime novels. To accommodate this need to have the popular trademark character return in each dime novel in the same social context as before—that is, undomesticated, alive, and without children—dime novelists modified conventional narrative form. Instead of ending with a moment of social closure, such as marriage, dime novels adopt open-ended narratives and often provide a critique of genteel and sentimental marriage plots along with their emphasis on heroic masculinity unhinged from the demands of heterosexual coupling and reproduction.[16] *Seth Jones* offers a critique of class-based identity by contrasting gentility with frontier masculinity. Expanding that critique, *Deadwood Dick* avoids traditional narrative closure and features masculine bodies that emphasize the porosity of social hierarchies.[17]

The Doubled Frontiersman in Edward S. Ellis's *Seth Jones; or, the Captives of the Frontier*

Beadle and Adams published Edward S. Ellis's *Seth Jones; or, the Captives of the Frontier* after an unprecedented promotional campaign. On September 29, 1860, the publishers took out advertisements in the *New York Tribune* and pasted up placards asking the question "Who is Seth Jones?," followed by posters bearing an illustration of the fictional frontiersman.[18] *Seth Jones; or, the Captives of the Frontier* would be reprinted in Beadle and Adams' dime-novel series seven times (figure 1.1).[19] *Seth Jones* is a captivity narrative, featuring two heroes—Seth Jones, a Yankee frontiersman, and Haldidge, a New York settler whose family was murdered by Indians. Seth Jones and Haldidge team up to pursue a band of Indians that have kidnapped Mary Haverland, the daughter of another settler. Seth Jones and Haldidge are both single males, both expert trackers and fighters, and both of these heroic figures live outside of the conventional family structure. *Seth Jones* centers on a democratic masculinity that can be convincingly performed without necessary ties to a socially legible male body. In *Seth Jones*'s refusal of gender and class as essential markings on the body, despite its more conventional narrative structure, I find the emergence of a performative masculinity that is unhinged from essential ties to bodies, politics, and social conventions.

Seth Jones claims in the beginning of the novel to be "of the Joneses," a "pretty generally known" family, and therefore a universal Anglo-American with no particular pedigree.[20] While Jones's past is unknown, Haldidge's past is narrated explicitly. Indians murdered his wife and child, and Haldidge found their bodies "tomahawked, side by side, and weltering in each other's blood."[21] Devastated by this loss and driven by the desire for revenge, Haldidge devotes his life to Indian massacre: "his natural aversion to the race…had become so distinguished, that his name was a terror to the savages in that section." *Seth Jones* thus crudely stages the dialectic between the civilized white man and the savage that would later be theorized by Frederick Jackson Turner through its competing visions of masculine

Figure 1.1 *Beadle's Half-Dime Library* 8, November 9, 1877. Robert D. Farber University Archives and Special Collections Department, Brandeis University.

performance, the violent Haldidge and the more taciturn Seth Jones.[22] Haldidge's "Indian-hater" persona relies on mobility, linking him to the very "savages" he wishes to exterminate. In effect, Haldidge embraces the mobility attributed to the nomadic, villainous Indians by Seth Jones when he complains that "they are *going* all the time."[23] Since Haldidge's own family is lost, his sense of familial belonging is expanded into the larger notion of race, which he protects and preserves through his self-appointed mission of Indian massacre. In this broader sense of social belonging, however faulty its racial logic, Haldidge creates a world full of social obligations that revise domestic belonging into the larger network of racial belonging.[24]

While on the one hand, Haldidge is a conventional "Indian-hater" figure, he also has a more romantic appreciation of the natural landscape. His last act in *Seth Jones* is to force the returning war party to stop and "see what a fine view we shall have" outside of the newly constructed New York settlement.[25] While Seth Jones complains that "we've no time for views," Haldidge insists that the party stop to appreciate the "unusually beautiful" view of the village from a hilltop. Haldidge's savagery mixes here with the pastoralism of James Fenimore Cooper's Natty Bumppo, blending romanticism with savagery, calm reflection with violent action. Haldidge's savagery does not rob him of the more abstract faculties of reflection and aesthetic taste. He is able to appreciate a landscape though he may also value mobility over stability. Even the "Indian-hater" in *Seth Jones* embodies a complex masculinity that is not reducible to mere dominance.

While Haldidge remains endlessly vigilant throughout the novel, Seth Jones eventually unburdens himself and gets married. He reveals his true identity in the last chapter, fittingly titled "Denouement." Seth Jones, it turns out, is actually Eugene Morton, a member of the nobility masquerading as a woodsman. He reveals his identity to his future wife Mary Haverland after her rescue. By exposing the narrative structure of the dime novel in the chapter heading, *Seth Jones* implicitly casts the marriage plot as mere artifice, a mechanical necessity rather than the natural culmination of the novel's events.[26] However, this moment is not necessarily a mark of the novel's reliance on narrative convention. As Michael Denning claims, the dime novel does not occupy the same discursive space as the bourgeois novel:

> As a cultural form, dime novels were *not* part of the popular culture of the "middle-class." The magazines were the key literary form in that cultural universe; its metaphoric centers were the "self-made" entrepreneur and the "domestic" household. The dime novels were part

of the popular culture of the "producing classes," a plebian culture whose metaphoric centers of gravity were the "honest mechanic" and the virtuous "working-girl."[27]

Denning views class as foundational to identity in dime novels; however, he does not address the ways in which gender, and particularly masculinity, trouble socially legible bodies. While the gendered positions of the "honest mechanic" and the "working-girl" might provide foundations for social hierarchies, the dime novel uses masculinity as an escape from that social foundation. Seth Jones's frontiersman performance allows him to move in a variety of social circles, to forge different relations to social conventions, and to undo the very stability and legibility Denning finds in class identity. In this light, Seth Jones's eventual unmasking does not endorse class essentialism or the compulsion to marry only class equals. Instead, Seth Jones's shift from one class to the next offers a utopian imagining of class mobility through gender performance.

Seth Jones's transformation into the aristocratic Eugene Morton exhibits the malleability of gender performance in opposition to the stability of class identification. Eugene Morton treats class as an essential attribute, while masculinity allows him the freedom to act and form social connections. After revealing his true identity to his fiancé, Seth Jones/Eugene Morton explains his performance: "Seth Jones is a myth, and to *my* knowledge, no such person ever existed . . . I felt some amusement in the part I was playing, and often enjoyed the speculation I created by giving you, as it were, a glimpse now and then into my real nature. I varied my actions and language on purpose to increase your wonder."[28] While the figure's class identity serves to produce a stable ending to the dime novel through a proper marriage between class equals, Seth Jones and his frontier masculinity cross social hierarchies. Class might provide a stable ground to the dime novel's convoluted plot, but masculinity provides action and variation. Only through the invocation of class as, to borrow Denning's phrase, a "center of gravity" does the dime novel end with a conventional marriage.[29]

The importance of class identity has been central to readings of the dime novel, especially in Denning's *Mechanic Accents* and Richard Slotkin's *Gunfighter Nation*. Slotkin gives a summary of this interpretative tradition: "Although the West still serves as the site of an imaginary future, what the mythic Frontier of the dime novel actually embodies is a world in which the values and practices of the pre-industrial order are given renewed life."[30] While this reading certainly resonates with the importance of class to narratives like *Seth Jones*, the very fact that preindustrial manhood is receding detaches gender from a necessary equivalence with class. Masculinity is no longer bound to artisan labor, and in the face of industrialization, the "producing classes" morph into factory workers, no longer producing a total commodity but instead one fraction of a larger commodity on the assembly line. Rather than reinforcing an older class structure, masculinity allows Seth Jones to cross class boundaries. Out of this dime novel's nostalgia for the preindustrial order, masculinity emerges as a style. Though often bound up in class identifications, gender can still be manipulated while class identity remains foundational to one's social standing.[31] In this extrication of gender from the body, masculinity becomes a democratic enterprise in this dime-novel Western. By focusing on class at the expense of gender, classic interpretations of the dime novel overlook how the social vision of the genre is more than mere nostalgia for an older economic order. In Seth Jones's masculine performance lies a new form of identification unhinged from the social stability associated with the preindustrial economy. This new, stylized mode of self-fashioning spurs on the panic expressed by Anthony Comstock and the *New York Times*' "Students of the Dime Novel" column, for masculinity comes to signify unruly possibilities.

Seth Jones subtly foregrounds the destabilization of normative structures of romance and gentility in another instance. At Eugene Morton and Mary's wedding, the issue of profanity emerges when the fiddler launches into a song entitled "Devil's Dream." "A timid elderly lady" asks the fiddler, "Isn't that a profane tune?"[32] The fiddler responds by saying "No, it's Old Hundred with variations. Don't bother me," while "relieving his mouth of a quantity of tobacco juice at the same time." This entrance of manners is quickly silenced when the minister asks the elderly lady to dance, and "they disappeared in the whirling mass."[33] This elimination of censorship and moral authority through the joy of an indistinctly individuated mass of dancers dramatizes the dime novel's negation of genteel values. The mass market text demands that one withhold old-fashioned ideas of propriety and consume the new—and perhaps "profane"—popular fiction. As Christine Bold has remarked, "the market operates visibly on the dime novel as a product," and this moment is one of those instances.[34] The immanent crowd, which literally swallows up the "timid elderly lady" and the minister, exemplifies the dime novel's vision of society as a series of relations that resist hierarchy. Like Seth Jones, who is of all classes at the same time, the "whirling mass" engulfs the genteel with its penchant for "variations," for repetition of narrative forms that undo the structures that make individuals intelligible within social hierarchies.

The Bandit with No Family Name in Edward L. Wheeler's *Deadwood Dick, The Prince of the Road; or, the Black Rider of the Black Hills*

Deadwood Dick was one of the most renowned of the dime-novel heroes, ranking with "real" characters such as Buffalo Bill, Wild Bill Hickock, and Calamity Jane in American popular culture. Deadwood Dick appeared in 1877 in the first number of *Beadle's Half-Dime Library*, a new and even cheaper publication than the original *Beadle's Dime Novel* series.[35] *Deadwood Dick, Prince of the Road* tells the story of how Deadwood Dick fights off "the old mechanic" and his henchmen and also reveals Deadwood Dick's alternate identity as the young aristocrat Ned Harris. However, this doubling is not resolved as it is in *Seth Jones*. Instead, the bandit ultimately refuses to name a "real" identity. Both Deadwood Dick and Ned Harris are performed masculinities, and neither trumps the other as more foundational. Like Seth Jones, Deadwood Dick has multiple names; unlike Seth Jones, Deadwood Dick does not have one real identity but instead a repertoire of masculinities, strategically enacted. As such, *Deadwood Dick, The Prince of the Road* offers an even more radical masculinity than *Seth Jones*. Rather than capitulate to an essential class identity, Deadwood Dick's bandit narrative frames masculinity as socially legible but without any foundation in a legible social order. As leader of his band of rebels, Deadwood Dick forms a community free of social hierarchy. This "dauntless band" is described as a group of singing males, exquisitely dressed and on sleek horses, yet containing a diverse assemblage of voices:

> There is a chatter of hooves, a chorus of strange and varied voices swelling out in a wild mountain song, and up through the very heart of the diminutive city, where the gold-fever has dropped a few sanguine souls, dash a cavalcade of masked horsemen, attired in the picturesque garb of the mountaineer, and mounted on animals of superior speed and endurance.[36]

Deadwood Dick's band blends the cultivated with the uncultivated. While Seth Jones ultimately gives way to the imperative of the marriage plot, Deadwood Dick persists in using masculinity to produce new forms of social belonging.

Set in the year of its publication, the novel describes the town of Deadwood—in present-day South Dakota—as a burgeoning one, no longer the idyllic frontier but a populated area that has been rigorously segmented into individual properties:

> Deadwood! the scene of the most astonishing bustle and activity, this year (1877.) The place where men are literally made rich and poor in one day and night. Prior to 1877 the Black Hills have been for a greater part undeveloped, but now, what a change! In Deadwood districts, every foot of available ground has been "claimed" and staked out; the population has increased from fifteen to more than twenty-five hundred souls.[37]

Rather than a nostalgic yearning for the open frontier, an escape from the brutal realities of industrialization, *Deadwood Dick* takes place within the very territorializing machinery of capitalism, the mining camp. In fact, the town of Deadwood became part of the United States in 1877, the year in which *Deadwood Dick* takes place, violating the 1868 Fort Laramie Treaty that accorded the land to the Sioux. The land itself is no longer "virgin," to borrow an expression from Henry Nash Smith, but has been claimed as both national and economic territory.[38]

Michael Denning argues that one can read Deadwood Dick and the other dime-novel bandits, such as the James Boys, Diamond Dick, and Sierra Sam, as a response to industrialization:

> The dime novel outlaws also marked this adaptation of social banditry to capitalism, and they are perhaps less sons of Leatherstocking than sons of Molly Maguire, less stories of the Wild West than stories of Labor and Capital. The enemies of the James brothers are the Pinkertons, not Indians. Read in this light, the mining towns in which Deadwood Dick lives, and his "concern with social problems," are not anomalous but are central.[39]

As Denning argues, *Deadwood Dick* narrates the destruction of the wilderness and the implementation of an industrial apparatus. Preoccupied with the class struggle on the quickly industrializing frontier, Deadwood Dick represents the fluid justice called for in a time of political and economic upheaval; the bandit hero has a sense of right and wrong that is not hampered by rules of law or class bias. Instead, Deadwood Dick and his band of outlaws work for the collective interest.

Deadwood Dick's multiple personas provide vantage points for a critique of class hierarchies. In this dime novel, masculinity becomes a way of relating to others, a way of belonging apart from hierarchical structures. Significantly, Deadwood Dick is introduced as entirely surface:

> He was a youth of an age somewhere between sixteen and twenty, trim and compactly built, with a preponderance of muscular development and animal spirits; broad and deep of chest, with square, iron-cast shoulders; limbs small yet like bars of steel, and with a grace of position in the saddle rarely equaled; he made a fine picture for an artist's brush or a poet's pen.[40]

This surface elegance—a perfect male form described as a combination of mercurial "animal spirits" and solid "iron-cast shoulders"—casts Deadwood Dick as a composite and contradictory figure. This confusion of metaphor figures Deadwood Dick's body in multiple, competing registers. He is natural and industrial, small and large, visual and textual. Deadwood Dick's dress also renders him mysterious; he is masked and wears a suspicious amount of black:

> His form was clothed in a tight-fitting habit of buck-skin, which was colored a jetty black, and presented a striking contrast to anything one sees as a garment in the wild far West. And this was not all, either. A broad black hat was slouched down over his eyes; he wore a thick black veil over the upper portion of his face, through the eye-holes of which there gleamed a pair of orbs of piercing intensity, and his hands, large and knotted, were hidden in a pair of kid gloves of a light color.[41]

Deadwood Dick's hands are those of a worker, deformed through labor into their "large and knotted" shape. The bandit stands out not as one from the "wild West," already, by 1877, a mythological place, but instead, through his workers' hands, one who is rooted in material conditions. As a working-class figure, Deadwood Dick poses a direct threat to his enemy, the "old mechanic," an unspecified villain who, by his name alone, seems to mark out the older artisan class, unionized and unwilling to join ranks with unskilled laborers.[42] However, Deadwood Dick's hands are dressed in "kid gloves," in a garment that contrasts with the "large and knotted" hands underneath them. Like the combination and coexistence of the natural and industrial in Deadwood Dick's body, time and age are blurred on this figure, distancing him from any stable identity.

Deadwood Dick's unstable identity is further reinforced in the cover illustration to the novel, which depicts Deadwood Dick, masked and on his black steed, reading a notice that is reprinted in the beginning of the dime novel's second chapter (figure 1.2):

> $500 Reward: For the apprehension and arrest of a notorious young desperado who hails to the name of Deadwood Dick. His present whereabouts are somewhat contiguous to the Black Hills. For further information, and so forth, apply immediately to
>
> Hugh Vansevere
> "At Metropolitan Saloon, Deadwood City."[43]

The notice casts suspicion upon the validity of Deadwood Dick's identity through the interesting use of the clause "who hails to the name of Deadwood Dick." This notice constructs Deadwood Dick as both an individual criminal and a public figure at large. Deadwood Dick's group of bandits and the town of Deadwood, which supports and accepts his existence, give Deadwood Dick his name, but Deadwood Dick continually eludes concrete identity through disguises and myth-making.[44] The novel thus charts Deadwood Dick's flexible identity through performative acts of hailing.

Upon reading the notice, Deadwood Dick remarks, "Hugh Vansevere; let me see—I don't think I've got that registered in my collection of appellatives. Perhaps he is a new tool in the employ of the old mechanic."[45] In contrast to Deadwood Dick, Hugh Vansevere is not hailed but is treated as if his name is a possession. When Deadwood Dick ventures to the Metropolitan Saloon, he asks, "Is there a man among you, gentlemen, who bears the name of Hugh Vansevere?"[46] As opposed to the bandit's identity, which is constituted through hailing, an active procedure that must be repeated over and over again, Hugh Vansevere, the "tool," bears a name, and even responds to Deadwood Dick by exclaiming, "That is my handle, pilgrim!"[47] Vansevere is secure in his name, while Deadwood Dick involves himself in unstable narratives based on collective recognition and reiteration, not private possession. Following Vansevere's response, and right before shooting him, Deadwood Dick offers yet more proof of his unstable identity. He exclaims, "You are advertising for one Deadwood Dick, and he has come to pay you his respects!"[48] Advertising, in this sense, fails to provide a stable consumer but draws out an unstable producer. Deadwood Dick fashions himself through

No. 1

THE ARTHUR WESTBROOK CO.
Cleveland, Ohio

Vol. I

DEADWOOD DICK, THE PRINCE OF THE ROAD:
Or, The Black Rider of the Black Hills.

BY EDWARD L. WHEELER.

"Ha ha ha isn't that rich, now? Ha! ha! ha! arrest Deadwood Dick if you can!"

Figure 1.2 *Deadwood Dick Library* 1, March 15, 1899. Robert D. Farber University Archives and Special Collections Department, Brandeis University.

narrative devices: stylization, call and response, and the embodiment of metaphor and synecdoche. This indeterminate and uncertain naming is also present in a literary precursor to dime-novel Westerns, James Fenimore Cooper's Leatherstocking Tales. As Philip Fisher argues, Cooper's frontier is a place where "overlapping claims and descriptions, and the multiplied names that result, have not yet been simplified into what we call 'Proper Names.' "[49] The major distinction between Cooper's Leatherstocking Tales and the dime novel, though, is the dime novel's departure from what Jane Tompkins describes as Cooper's imperative that "a person must belong to one class, one totem, one tribe."[50] Dime novels avoid resolving identity with name; instead, dime novels proliferate names and identities.

Further emphasizing the fluidity of Deadwood Dick's identity, it is later revealed that the bandit doubles as a young, handsome lad, bearing none of the bodily markings that characterize Deadwood Dick as a member of the working class. Ned Harris is first introduced in the Metropolitan saloon on a crowded Saturday night and looks every bit the dandy:

> He was of medium height, straight as an arrow, and clad in a loose-fitting costume. A broad sombrero was set jauntily upon the left side of his head, the hair of which had been cut close down to the scalp. His face—a pleasant, handsome, youthful face—was devoid of hirsute covering, he having evidently been recently handled by the barber.[51]

The narrator goes on to describe Harris's hands, which seem to mark him as a feminized member of the upper class:

> [Ned Harris] took the revolvers from the table, changed his position so that his face was just in the opposite direction of what it had been, and commenced to pare his finger nails. The fingers were as white and soft as any girl's. In his hand he also held a strangely-angled little box, the sides of which were mirror-glass. Looking at his finger-nails he also looked into the mirror, which gave a complete view of the card-sharp, as he sat at the table.[52]

Harris uses his mirror-box to detect the card-sharp's method of cheating, hiding cards "in Chinaman fashion up his sleeve."[53] The performance of idleness allows Harris access to the sharp's cheating method, and Harris quickly exchanges the role of idle detective with that of violent provocateur. He orders Redburn, the duped card player, to shoot the card-sharp. While Deadwood Dick violently resists instrumentalized labor and commodification, Ned Harris uses aristocratic privilege as a means to expose and punish economic injustice.

In contrast to *Seth Jones*, the narrative form developed to retain the serial character of Deadwood Dick as a recurring masculine hero avoids narrative closure through marriage or the revelation of hidden family heritage. While the narrative cannot end tragically, for Deadwood Dick cannot die if he is to return in the next installment, the narrative must also refuse the conventional happy ending, marriage. Instead, the novel concludes with an open ending, that of the solitary hero riding off into the sunset. In *Seth Jones*, marriage and revealed aristocratic heritage make for a concise denouement. In *Deadwood Dick, the Prince of the Road*, both of these formal closures are disrupted. Deadwood Dick does reveal himself to be Ned Harris, but this revelation is incomplete. Deadwood Dick does not reveal his actual family name: " 'My name is, to you, *Edward Harris!*' and here the road-agent flung aside the black mask, revealing the smiling face of the young card-sharp. 'I have another—my family name—but I do not use it, preferring Harris to it. Anita, yonder, is my sister.' "[54] Despite this revelation, and his avowal of his sister, Harris does not disclose his "family name" but reveals "Harris" to be another mask. After this curious turn of events, Deadwood Dick then asks not one but two women for their hands in marriage and is rejected by both. He asks Alice Terry, referred to as Miss Terry throughout the novel, but she denies him, saying that "I cannot love you, and never can be your wife."[55] Unsatisfied, Deadwood Dick asks Calamity Jane if she will "marry me and become my queen?" Jane's response is immediate and harsh: " 'No!' said the girl, haughtily, sternly. 'I have had all the *man* I care for. We can be friends, Dick; more we can never be!' " Ned Harris, then, keeps his family name secret, and Deadwood Dick remains the "Prince of the Road," never to become the "King."

Masculine Style

Deadwood Dick's inability to marry is both a formal requirement dictated by a publishing industry that wanted to capitalize on a recurring character and evidence of the disjunction between masculinity and social conventions. In later dime novels, Deadwood Dick would marry or make reference to a number of wives, but the multiplicity of these marriages undermines their stability. No marriage actually binds Deadwood Dick to a conventional domestic setting. For example, in Edward L. Wheeler's *Deadwood Dick on Deck*, the bandit hero goes home to his wife "Leone" who never appears in the story but instead serves as a reason for the hero to fade into the background, followed by the narrator's promise of continued masquerades and subterfuges: "occasionally there is some new and odd character created in the mines, under which Deadwood Dick generally manages to keep on Deck."[56] Marriage becomes a strategic device rather than a governing institution, while masculinity is privileged as a way of guaranteeing Deadwood Dick's commitment to struggles for the collective interest.[57]

I have argued that class-based readings of dime novels obscure the powerful thrust of masculinity removed from older class affiliations. Masculinity becomes a style, a mode of self-fashioning, rather than a stable social identity. This masculine style provides a mode of embodiment that produces alternatives to social norms. In this light, dime-novel Westerns are an important part of the history of alternative masculinities, often characterized in the twentieth century by appropriations of working-class bodies and fashions.[58] Deadwood Dick's removal from the conventional marriage economy spins him into an alternate temporality. He exists outside of the normal rhythms of marriage and reproduction.[59]

This masculine style, though, still connotes whiteness. While masculinity can be performed across class and sex in dime novels, the same cannot be said for racial difference. In *American Sensations,* Shelley Streeby reads the dime novel's predecessors in the popular story papers "as discursive weapons in an ongoing battle to subsume incidents of border warfare, which suggest a different North/South axis—that of the Americas—within a linear national narrative." Popular Western stories like those in dime novels are inextricably bound to the racial and national consolidation inherent to manifest destiny. It is not my contention that dime novels are devoid of nationalism or exempt from the racist imagination of late nineteenth-century America. However, I do argue that masculinity is far more than a mere appendage to this monolithic nationalism. There is an upside to frontier masculinity that has been overlooked in research on the links between patriarchy, nationalism, and imperialism. While not free of the prejudices of their time, late nineteenth-century frontier heroes offer a compelling model of masculinity unhinged from class hierarchies among whites, while still operating as a category of privilege in larger national and transnational contexts. Through figures such as Seth Jones and Deadwood Dick, dime novels produce a masculinity that thrives on crossing social boundaries rather than policing them. Through their representation of masculine self-fashioning, dime novels critique patriarchal dominance and industrial oppression. What could be more promising to an alternative history of masculinity than a genre that, in the words of Anthony Comstock, "is utterly destitute of any regard for the laws of God and man"?[61]

Usually, a narrative of decline accompanies treatments of the dime novel. After Beadle and Adams's collapse in 1897, dime novels became entirely devoted to a juvenile readership and were replaced by pulp magazines. As lamented by Robert Peabody Bellows in an essay originally delivered at Harvard's Commencement on June 28, 1899, "the masses that once read such harmless chronicles as 'Red Thunderbolt's Secret,' or 'Denver Doll, the Detective Queen,' now turn to the debasing columns of police crime and scandal in the daily papers."[62] However, the masculinity produced by dime novels as both a subject position and a narrative form continues into the twentieth century. Modernist masculinity emerges from this mass literature. As D. H. Lawrence noted in a 1927 review of *In Our Time*, Ernest Hemingway's recurring character Nick Adams "is the remains of the lone trapper and cowboy," the types of figures disseminated to a mass readership in dime novels.[63] The writers that follow, from Nat Love and Theodore Roosevelt to Willa Cather and John Steinbeck, use masculinity to signal unruly alternatives, elaborating upon the ways in which Seth Jones and Deadwood Dick fashion masculine selves that turn identity into style. In the following chapter, I will chart how "cowboy masculinity" becomes not just a means to imagine malleable subjectivity in popular literature but also a means to refashion more material selves.

CHAPTER 2

Between Anarchy and Hierarchy: Nat Love's and Theodore Roosevelt's Manly Feelings

As I emerged from the water I heard the little Wood boy calling frantically to the General: "Oh! oh! The father of all the children fell into the creek"—which made me feel like an uncommonly moist patriarch.

—Theodore Roosevelt, *An Autobiography*

Nat Love's 1907 memoir, *The Life and Adventures of Nat Love*, contains a well-known and often-reproduced photograph of the author, dressed up as a cowboy with all of the ubiquitous accessories: saddle, lasso, bandana, hat, chaps, revolver, and rifle (figure 2.1). Love claims to be the real-life model for "Deadwood Dick," and while this claim is unsubstantiated, it does give a new meaning to the dime-novel hero's black leather costume since Love, himself, was an African American born into slavery who, after emancipation, eventually made his way West to work as a cowboy. While in dime novels flexible, heroic masculinity remains bound to whiteness, Love demonstrates that cowboy masculinity can cross racial as well as class boundaries. Made in a studio with a decorative screen behind the figure, this photograph evidences the enigmatic power of cowboy masculinity in the turn-of-the-century United States. Love's relaxed posture resonates the calm confidence often associated with the Western hero. Notably, this heroic stature is produced through Love's use of cowboy accessories. His leg rests on his saddle, one thumb hooks into his ammunition belt, and his hand rests atop his rifle. Like T. S. Eliot's "Stetson" or Deadwood Dick's "kid gloves," fashion constructs cowboy masculinity, and this cowboy masculinity connotes strength and mobility.

In My Fighting Clothes

Figure 2.1 "In My Fighting Clothes," Portrait of Nat Love, from *The Life and Adventures of Nat Love*, 1907.

Love's self-fashioning here points to the power of cowboy masculinity to complicate and potentially erode one of the central oppressive
structures of U.S. culture: racial hierarchy. As in dime novels, cowboy
masculinity for Nat Love is a site for the reinvention of the self and for
mobility within seemingly stable social hierarchies. In this chapter, I
will explore how masculine self-fashioning is thought to undo masculinity's traditional ties to racial and class hierarchies in Love's memoir
and in the writing of another figure central to turn-of-the-century
American masculinity, Theodore Roosevelt.

Nat Love and Theodore Roosevelt are, to say the least, problematic figures in Western American Literature. Nat Love's memoir,
though written by an African American cowboy, poses difficulty
for critics because of his lack of attention to race, while Theodore
Roosevelt's autobiographical writings are often read as exemplary
of turn-of-the-century U.S. imperialism.[1] Love and Roosevelt's
cowboy masculinity seems to be evidence of the interpenetration
of manhood, patriarchy, conquest, and imperialism in U.S. culture.
Yet while both Love and Roosevelt write from within and rearticu-
late hierarchies of their historical moments, their constructions of
masculinity do not recapitulate those hierarchies. In fact, Love and
Roosevelt reimagine masculinity as an unruly, democratic performance that must ultimately be contained and curtailed by external
forces. By juxtaposing Love and Roosevelt, this chapter aims to artic-
ulate masculinity's utopian potential as a means of self-fashioning
in turn-of-the-century U.S. culture. For both Love and Roosevelt,
cowboy masculinity promises to unify Americans through democratic, egalitarian feeling.

Theodore Roosevelt's Bellicose Masculinity

One of Theodore Roosevelt's most remarkable achievements was his
own transformation from New York dandy to adventurous outdoors-
man.[2] This masculine makeover took place through both action—
most notably Roosevelt's participation in the Spanish-American
War as a Rough Rider—and writing—Roosevelt's autobiographical
accounts of the Rough Riders, hunting trips, and politics, as well as his
multivolume history *The Winning of the West*. Theodore Roosevelt's
reinvigorated masculinity was initially produced by his 1883 hunting trip to Dakota, bound to imperial adventure through his vocal
advocacy of military engagement with Spain in 1898, and followed
by his subsequent roles as lieutenant colonel and colonel of the First

U.S. Volunteer Cavalry Regiment, popularized as the Rough Riders. This masculine development propelled Roosevelt to the forefront of national politics and played a major role in his election to governor of the state of New York in 1898 on an anticorruption campaign as well as his election to vice president under McKinley in 1900. Less than a year into his term as president, McKinley was assassinated, which left the presidency to Roosevelt. Roosevelt was reelected to another term in 1904, during which he would embrace more radical trust-busting reforms that ultimately resulted in his break with the Republican Party.

Particularly significant for my concerns here are the ways in which Roosevelt's masculinity is a textual production. His autobiographical writings foreground his understanding of selfhood as a composite of environmental factors, social influence, and exposure to the arts. In *An Autobiography*, he advocates for literature as a character-building device, making it clear that his Rough Rider masculinity is just as much a literary as a physical endeavor. Fiction provides both pleasure and instruction:

> Of course any reader ought to cultivate his or her taste so that good books will appeal to it, and that trash won't. But after this point has once been reached, the needs of each reader must be met in a fashion that will appeal to those needs. Personally the books by which I have profited infinitely more than by any others have been those in which profit was a by-product of the pleasure; that is, I read them because I enjoyed them, because I liked reading them, and the profit came in as part of the enjoyment.[3]

Roosevelt goes on to claim that one who reads books "[furnishes] himself with much ammunition which he will find of use in the battle of life."[4] Reading cultivates selfhood, and for Roosevelt, that cultivation involves the development of a masculine style through enjoyment. Earlier in *An Autobiography*, Roosevelt chronicles his own childhood reading—including the guilty pleasures of dime novels and more acceptable Mayne Reid adventure tales. Like Mary Abbott, the dime-novel reader who "wants to be a cowboy," Roosevelt develops through the mobility afforded by literary signifiers of masculinity.

Furthermore, *An Autobiography* chronicles how the democratic enterprise of ranch work shaped his masculine persona, just as it could shape any man's:

> I never became a first-flight man in the hunting field, and never even approached the bronco-busting class in the West. Any man, if

he chooses, can gradually school himself to the requisite nerve, and gradually learn the requisite seat and hands, that will enable him to do respectably across country, or to perform the average work on a ranch.[5]

Roosevelt's emphasis on a combination of fiction, education, and experience as suitable training for anyone evidences the discursive and social nature, as opposed to the hereditary character, of masculine individualism in his thinking.[6] Roosevelt's environment, rather than some innate quality, directs him toward the formulation of his brand of national masculinity.[7]

In dime novels, masculinity provides characters with a means to play with, cross, and even ignore social hierarchies. That is, masculinity can reshape selves and their social relations. The cultural icons of the cowboy, the expatriate, the New Woman, the flapper, and the butch pioneer are products of this cultivation of the self as it moves through modernism, and it is my contention that the Rough Rider president also fits within this tradition. In his efforts to reinvigorate the nation, Theodore Roosevelt repeatedly emphasized the importance of fashion, bodily discipline, and intimacy to the production of masculinity, particularly in his memoirs *Rough Riders* and *An Autobiography*. The central difference between a figure like Roosevelt and later modernist accounts of masculine self-fashioning is that Roosevelt channels masculinity into a narrative of national dominance. However, I want to emphasize that this hierarchical telos is often in tension with Roosevelt's cultivation of masculinity as an individualizing and even egalitarian national force. While Roosevelt's writings are not experimental on the level of literary form, Roosevelt's masculinity is an experimental, provisional mode of self-fashioning.

Roosevelt's writings and public persona reveal a disparity between the genteel man of letters and the rugged frontiersman, which parallels his contradictory emphases on individual flourishing and national homogeneity. Critics have read this duality as evidence of Roosevelt's exemplarity as a man suffering from neurasthenia, the nineteenth-century diagnosis of nervous exhaustion brought on by the repetitiveness and malaise of modern life.[8] The cure for this disorder, as prescribed by S. Weir Mitchell, was outdoor exertion for men and bed rest for women. Neurasthenia's gendered cures are clearly related to the polarizing policies of American imperialism's drives of violent conquest and progressive reform. Because of the beneficial health value attributed to strenuous activities by doctors like Mitchell, reinvigorated masculinity seems to provide a template for the imperialist citizen, and Roosevelt often uses the abundant masculinity of the American citizen as evidence of America's global superiority. What has gone underemphasized, though, are the ways in which masculinity exceeds its associations with imperial politics. Roosevelt's masculine performances often resist the social hierarchies that he seeks to reinforce. For example, as a member of an elite class, Roosevelt's policies often relied upon a genteel progressivism; however, the masculine Rough Rider persona that Roosevelt adopted set the stage for a more cantankerous relationship to the elite class to which he belonged. After all, there is a democratic promise to Roosevelt's notion, in *An Autobiography*, that reading and experience can mold anyone into anything. Roosevelt's nationalism, then, is both jingoistic and egalitarian.

In *Gunfighter Nation*, Richard Slotkin argues that Theodore Roosevelt, along with fellow historian Frederic Jackson Turner, helped to create a mythological frontier. Instead of envisioning the American West as a region with a history, Slotkin argues, it became a narrative form in Turner and Roosevelt's writings, a way of staging the battle of good versus evil, civilization versus savagery:

> In 1893 the Frontier was no longer (as Turner saw it) a geographical place and a set of facts requiring a historical explanation. Through the agency of writers like Turner and Roosevelt, it was becoming a set of symbols that constituted an explanation of history. Its signification as a mythic space began to outweigh its importance as a real place, with its own peculiar geography, politics, and cultures.[9]

This narrative trajectory often privileged white men as the rightful heirs to empire. While Roosevelt's insistence on a "clash of civilizations" model of global politics often used this Western narrative to support imperialism and male dominance, this same narrative also relies on tropes of masculinity, self-determination, and individualism that can just as easily resist as conform to American expansionism. While it is certainly true that the synecdoche between masculinity and the nation is ever-present in Roosevelt's writing, it is also the case that Roosevelt's own conception of masculinity as a product of sentiment, exertion, and literacy exceeds these nationalist narratives. Just as sex, gender, and sexuality can be thought apart despite their interconnectedness, gender and politics must be carefully separated so as to uncover the possibilities offered by gender that are not subject to dominant politics but instead project alternatives to those dominant politics.

Roosevelt's nationalism serves both imperialist and egalitarian purposes. In *The Rough Riders*, Roosevelt frequently identifies masculinity as being the deciding factor in a soldier's worth rather than class, ethnicity, or race:

> [The Rough Riders] understood that I paid no heed to where they came from; no heed to their creed, politics, or social standing; that I would care for them to the utmost of my power, but that I demanded the highest performance of duty; while in return I had seen them tested, and knew I could depend absolutely on their courage, hardihood, obedience, and individual initiative.[10]

Like American identity, this vision of masculine camaraderie offers a sense of inclusiveness. Rather than older divisions of region, class, and race, masculinity unites Roosevelt's soldiers:

> All—Easterners and Westerners, Northerners and Southerners, officers and men, cow-boys and college graduates, wherever they came from, and whatever their social position—possessed in common the traits of hardihood and a thirst for adventure. They were to a man born adventurers, in the old sense of the word.[11]

Roosevelt uses the West as a way of reaching across difference. As Slotkin argues, the West comes to signify a kind of symbolic, democratic masculinity for Roosevelt. In a typical male-bonding scene, the Rough Riders swap stories with one another while traveling back to the United States after the war's end. Roosevelt places extra emphasis on Western-themed stories precisely because of their egalitarian nature:

> Much of the time when there as little to do we simply sat together and talked, each man contributing from the fund of his own experiences. Voyages around Cape Horn, yacht races for the America's cup, experiences on foot-ball teams which are famous in the annals of college sport; more serious feats of desperate prowess in Indian fighting and in breaking up gangs of white outlaws; adventures in hunting big game, in breaking wild horses, in tending great herds of cattle, and in wandering winter and summer among the mountains and across the lonely plains—the men who told the tales could draw upon countless memories such as these of the things they had done and the things they had seen others do.[12]

While it is clear that not all men on the voyage had Western experiences, Roosevelt weights stories about the West more heavily than tales of South American travel, yacht racing, and college football. The list of stories itself makes clear just how elite many of the Rough Riders were, yet Roosevelt places more frivolous activities that connote class privilege, like yacht racing, at the beginning of his list, subordinating them to the "more serious" activities of the "lonely plains."

Yet while Roosevelt capitalizes on the popular appeal of Western stories, he views the frontier as a vanished environment. In its place, Roosevelt substitutes militarization. The Rough Riders already knew how to ride horses and use firearms upon volunteering, so most of the men's training revolved around military etiquette and the erasure of the very regional difference that Roosevelt prizes in his Western friends:

> It was astonishing how soon the men got over these little peculiarities. They speedily grew to recognize the fact that the observance of certain forms was essential to the maintenance of proper discipline. They became scrupulously careful in touching their hats, and always came to attention when spoken to. They saw that we did not insist upon the observance of these forms to humiliate them; that we were as anxious to learn our own duties as we were to have them learn theirs, and as scrupulous in paying respect to our superiors as we were in exacting the acknowledgement due our rank from those below us; moreover, what was very important, they saw that we were careful to look after their interests in every way, and were doing all that was possible to hurry up the equipment and drill of the regiment, so as to get into war.[13]

This passage clearly prioritizes the nation over the individual and the region. War with Spain subordinates all individuals to military hierarchy. Roosevelt's own accounts of masculine individualism and messy egalitarianism stand in contrast to this vision of a national telos. While masculinity provides a way to refashion the self, nationalism allows for that refashioned self to be reassimilated into a culture governed by hierarchies. The very "anarchy of empire" that Amy Kaplan finds central to U.S. imperialism is here signified by masculinity.[14] Moreover, participation in war is a site for the exercise of individualism that nonetheless demands the yielding of individualism to the military chain of command. The military is paradoxically both rigidly hierarchical and utterly individualistic.

In recent scholarship on the turn-of-the-century United States, Roosevelt's unification of individual exertion with national hierarchies registers as the underlying logic of American imperialism. For example, the influential anthology *Cultures of United States Imperialism*, edited by Amy Kaplan and Donald Pease, casts Roosevelt as an icon of American expansionism. The first two sections of the anthology, "Nation-Building as Empire-Building" and "Borderline Negotiations of Race, Gender, and Nation," detail the ways in which U.S. imperialism shapes national identity and defines those outside of the nation's borders. These two sections provide a kind of historical background for the remaining two sections—on resistance to U.S. imperialism and the First Gulf War. In both of these early sections, Theodore Roosevelt has a starring role. Moreover, Bill Brown, Donna Haraway, Amy Kaplan, and Richard Slotkin all see Roosevelt as a key figure in the cluster of discourses around late nineteenth- and twentieth-century American imperial involvements in Cuba, the Philippines, and Panama.[15]

While this scholarship has done much to uncover how U.S. imperialism thrived in turn-of-the-century America, its reliance on imperialism as a hegemonic—even dominant—discourse entails an all-too-easy jump from Roosevelt's masculine persona to American foreign policy. Donna Haraway's "Teddy Bear Patriarchy," for example, links Roosevelt's masculinity to imperialism through his interests in hunting and the display of taxidermic animals at the American Museum of Natural History in New York City:

> This is the effective truth of manhood, the state conferred on the visitor who successfully passes through the trial of the museum. The body can be transcended…In the upside down world of Teddy Bear Patriarchy, it is in the craft of killing that life is constructed, not in the accident of personal, material birth. Roosevelt is clearly the locus genii and patron saint for the museum and its task of regeneration of a miscellaneous, incoherent urban public threatened with genetic and social decadence, threatened with the prolific bodies of the new immigrants, threatened with the failure of manhood.[16]

Haraway's article offers a rich account of the connections between Roosevelt's interests in the natural world, the public trust, and manhood. In her account, late nineteenth-century imperial culture can be summarized in this way: while civilized life exposes natural, robust manhood to the feminizing forces of consumerism, managerial labor, and ennui, exposure to nature renews manly virtue. In a similar vein, Gail Bederman's study of manhood and American culture at the turn of the century offers a concise explanation of how masculinity gets equated with imperialist politics: "For Roosevelt, the purpose of American expansionism and national greatness was always the millennial purpose behind human evolution—human racial advancement toward a higher civilization. And the race that could best achieve this perfected civilization was, by definition, the one with the most superior manhood."[17] While Haraway and Bederman's readings do resonate with some of Roosevelt's political statements, it is also the case that masculinity is not reducible to its function as a motor of civilization or some kind of natural truth. While these critics have brought a crucial part of American cultural history to light, they often rush to conflate American imperialism with masculinity.[18]

As Amy Kaplan argues, Roosevelt endowed the Rough Riders with a strong sense of national purpose rooted in egalitarian social relations, and that national sentiment has remained very powerful: "The Rough Riders have been understood as a unifying cultural symbol—between North and South, West and East, working class and patrician, cowboy and Indian, and this unity is grounded in the notion of manliness, in the physicality of the male body that transcends or underlies social difference."[19] Kaplan's model here does not account for the possibility that "physicality" might neither transcend nor underlie but instead offer an alternative set of social signifiers that aim to flatten out "social difference." That is, the egalitarianism that Kaplan locates in Roosevelt's Rough Riders might be enacted by Roosevelt's Rough Rider masculinity rather than hindered by it. Masculinity is not different in kind from other signifiers; instead, it is a set of signifiers that can usurp, trouble, or complicate others.

The military is central to the leveling out of class and racial hierarchies emphasized in *The Rough Riders*. In the memoir, Roosevelt makes much of the democratic possibilities offered by military service. *The Rough Riders* not only reconciles the split between North and South, as Amy Kaplan argues, but it also strives to level out distinctions based on class and race.[20] Roosevelt makes this leveling out of class and racial difference explicit in his description of the burial of the dead following the battle at Las Guasimas:

> Vast numbers of vultures were wheeling round and round in great circles through the blue sky overhead. There could be no more honorable burial than that of these men in a common grave—Indian and cow-boy, miner, packer, and college athlete—the man of unknown ancestry from the lonely Western plains and the man who carried on his watch the crests of the Stuyvesants and the Fishes, one in the way they had met death, just as during life they had been one in their daring and their loyalty.[21]

Roosevelt juxtaposes the wealthy soldiers' family crests with the "unknown ancestry" of the Western soldier as a way of stressing the egalitarianism of military involvement. The heirloom watches bearing the names of wealthy, elite families stand in contrast to Roosevelt's own use of symbolic objects in both *The Rough Riders* and *An Autobiography* as symbols of national rather than class-based identity. During the charge at San Juan Hill, for example, Roosevelt kills a Spanish soldier with a revolver from the *Maine*, the battleship that was allegedly destroyed by the Spanish Army and provided a rationale for war. In *An Autobiography*, Roosevelt notes that, during his presidential inauguration, he wore a ring "containing the hair of Abraham Lincoln."[22] Roosevelt's ring bearing a lock of Abraham Lincoln's hair, similar to the grave containing "Indian and cow-boy," "Stutvesants and Fishes," symbolizes racial equality under the banner of national belonging. Roosevelt adorns his body and his texts with these national images, a gun and a ring, thereby linking his "cowboy masculinity" to both military exertion and democratic national bonds. While Roosevelt gestures to national unity, he grounds that belonging in heterogeneous, yet national, symbols.

Roosevelt's emphasis on the democratic bonds of military service, however, does not preclude individualism. Indeed, one of the consistent points that Roosevelt makes throughout *The Rough Riders* is the importance of individualism to the formation of a collective. This might seem contradictory. Roosevelt puts forth a theory of militaristic individualism that seems to endorse a Social Darwinist viewpoint—that the strongest individuals will rise to the top through competition. Yet, this militaristic individualism also foregrounds egalitarian competition, facilitated through the state. In a lengthy passage, Roosevelt writes of the value of individual initiative in a military slow to accomplish simple tasks, elaborating upon both his advocacy of individual initiative and his distrust of hierarchy. Roosevelt remarks that he has been reading Edmond Demolins' *A Quoi Tient La Supériorité des Anglo-Saxons?*, published in 1897 and translated into English in 1898 as *Anglo-Saxon Superiority: To What It Is Due*. Differentiating Americans from Anglo-Saxons, Roosevelt claims that the American military prizes individualism rather than blind obedience:

> I can assure the excellent French publicist that American "militarism," at least of the volunteer sort, has points of difference from the militarism of Continental Europe. The battalion chief of a newly raised American regiment, when striving to get into a war which the American people have undertaken with buoyant and light-hearted

indifference to detail, has positively unlimited opportunity of the display of "individual initiative," and is in no danger whatever either of suffering from unhealthy suppression of personal will, or of finding his faculties of self-help numbed by becoming a cog in a gigantic and smooth-running machine.[23]

Roosevelt's defense of individualism relies on the American public's whimsical "light-heartedness" in declaring war on Spain, and while this might at first glance seem to be a slight, it is in fact precisely the relation to the war that Roosevelt endorsed. Aware of military unpreparedness, Roosevelt advocated for war nonetheless as a way of cultivating the very "inventiveness" he values in American culture. The naïve buoyancy of American volunteers merely adds to the possibility for individual initiative, remaking the military into a federation of battalion chiefs and soldiers and moving away from the monolithic "machine" emblematic of "Anglo-Saxons." As he does throughout his written work, Roosevelt here differentiates Americans from Anglo-Saxons, claiming that Americans are a distinct race. While Anglo-Saxons work within homogenizing machines, Roosevelt argues that Americanness emerges within a loose set of collectives made up of distinct individuals.[24] Homogeneity and sovereignty create stagnation, while heterogeneity and collectivity allow individual inventiveness, a quality defined here as distinctly American, to flourish. This individual exertion results, in Roosevelt's own assessment, in the cultivation of masculinity as a way of facilitating creativity and heterogeneity rather than consolidating power in a monolithic, patriarchal structure.

The Rough Riders' conclusion offers another example of the open-endedness of Roosevelt's masculine ideal. Roosevelt reproduces a letter from a teacher on an Indian Reservation. This letter juxtaposes the militarist masculinity that Roosevelt is often associated with and the more learned, sentimental masculinity that Roosevelt also values. Again, these two poles of Roosevelt's masculinity seem to contradict one another. However, the teacher's letter and its placement at the very end of The Rough Riders serves as evidence for the role of sentimentality within masculinity. Indeed, sentimentality and the cultivation of sympathy are key to, rather than stays against, masculine self-fashioning. After his involvement in war, Roosevelt can be sentimental and sympathetic, in keeping with the collectivist ties of military individualism. The letter occurs at the end of the memoir, when, while tracking down members of his disbanded regiment, Roosevelt contacts Alice M. Robertson, "a teacher in an academy in the Indian Territory" "to ask if she could not use a little money among the Rough Riders, white, Indian, and half-breed, that she might personally know."[25] The teacher responds:

> My Dear Colonel Roosevelt: I did not at once reply to your letter…because I waited for a time to see if there should be need among any of our Rough Riders, of the money you so kindly offered. Some of the boys are poor, and in one or two cases they seemed to me really needy, but they all said no. More than once I saw the tears come to their eyes, at thought of your care for them, as I told them of your letter. Did you hear any echoes of our Indian war-whoops at your election? They were pretty loud.[26]

The teacher speaks for the Native American Rough Riders, complimenting their unique combination of sentimentality—the tears in their eyes when they think of Roosevelt's offer—and self-sufficiency— their stoic refusal of charity. Following this letter, Roosevelt concludes the memoir with the rhetorical question, "is it any wonder that I loved my regiment?"[27] This final flourish absorbs the sentimentality of the schoolteacher's letter into Roosevelt's own love of his fellow men. Masculinity, then, seems not to be opposed to sentimentality but instead blends sympathy with independence, love with action. Sentimentality provides a series of intimate connections, from the Rough Riders to the schoolteacher to the president, that constitute the nation as a collective, bound by intimacy and individualism, sentimentality and self-reliance. This sentimentality, though, is voiced through the schoolteacher, and the Native American veterans are not given voice in the text. Their "war-whoops" are only reported secondhand; Roosevelt's democratic bonds do not, in fact, distribute signifiers evenly.

    In Theodore Roosevelt's writing, then, masculinity provides a way for individuals to flourish, though the ways in which masculine subjects are then unified under the figure of the nation is clearly uneven in practice. It is certainly true that Roosevelt was part of an elite class that fetishized sports, hunting, and military involvement precisely because they were so distant from, and offered a romantic alternative to, brutal social and economic realities. It is also clear, however, that many of Roosevelt's policies as governor of New York, president, and Bull-Moose presidential candidate were directed against the dominance of the wealthy elite. Roosevelt's foreign policy might have been arcane, misguided, and exploitative, and he certainly leveraged masculinity to support those causes.[28] However, he also found in that masculinity a way of resisting Tammany Hall in New York, the oil and coal trusts as president, and Nativist-inflected isolationism in U.S. foreign policy.

In both Gail Bederman and Amy Kaplan's work, Roosevelt's thoughts on marriage and children are seen as further elaborations of his hierarchical understanding of national activity rather than examples of the sentimental egalitarianism that binds citizens into a nation. However, just as masculinity is too often viewed as an appendage of imperialism, femininity is too often treated as if it is coextensive with domesticity. For Roosevelt, domestic space is not necessarily feminine. Instead, Roosevelt's emphasis on maternity is a curious way of reforming gender roles. Indeed, Roosevelt consistently casts himself as maternal. In *An Autobiography*, he describes himself as a "vice-mother" and even "an uncommonly moist patriarch."[29] These associations with shared parenting duties and with moisture resonate with the sentimental side of Roosevelt's masculinity. Emotion, intimacy, attachment, even weeping are all facets of the masculine self. Roosevelt's manufactured masculinity crosses binaries (public/private, active/passive, imperial/domestic, stoic/sentimental, unity/multiplicity) rather than maintaining their separation.

In a letter to G. Stanley Hall, the psychologist who endorsed unleashing the "little savage" in young boys, Roosevelt expresses just how malleable masculinity is. Roosevelt heartily agrees with Hall that violence helps young boys develop into rugged men. Kenneth Kidd describes this turn-of-the-century emphasis on primitive violence in boys as the "feral tale," and in this school of thought, the savagery of little boys was thought to be not only necessary to their development as men but also part of Lamarckian evolution, played out in the phenotype as well as the genotype.[30] That is to say, each individual boy developed from a state of primitive savagery to civilized self-discipline, just as the human race developed over millennia from primitive man to the modern national subject. This condensation of time from the species to the individual makes each child into a living, breathing, evolutionary narrative. There is a curious temporality in this evolutionary model of childhood development. Within each man resides the history of life on this planet, and the development of each child offers the possibility of changing that evolution. This account offers a phenomenal open-endedness to the trajectory of the human and the possibility for social change. While Roosevelt finds in Hall's psychology a rationale for the development of a militaristic national manhood, he also sees the possibility for new developments that do not rely on violence. As he states in the letter to Hall:

> Oversentimentality, oversoftness, in fact, washiness and mushiness are the great dangers of this age and of this people. Unless we keep the barbarian virtues, gaining the civilized ones will be of little avail. I am particularly glad that you emphasize the probable selfishness of a milk-sop. My experience has been that weak and effeminate men are not quite as apt to have undesirable qualities as strong and vigorous men. I thoroughly believe in cleanliness and decency, and I utterly disbelieve in brutality and cruelty, but I feel we cannot too strongly insist upon the need of the rough, manly virtues.[31]

Violence and dominance are, then, not constitutive of masculinity but instead are in a dialectical relationship with that other masculine quality that he prides in himself and in men and women alike, a collective, affective bond to others. Even more striking in this passage, Roosevelt associates "selfishness" with effeminacy, implicitly linking altruism to "undesirable" masculine qualities. While Roosevelt seems to have viewed masculinity as a way of strengthening the United States' position in world affairs, he also contributed to the development of masculinity as a mode of self-fashioning, as a way of producing egalitarian intimacies and emotional ties that traverse the traditional division of feminine and masculine affect. For Roosevelt, cowboy masculinity is a discipline of the self that allows for the elaboration of heterogeneous individualities, though Roosevelt was careful to limit the forms that this heterogeneity could take.

NAT LOVE AND DEMOCRATIC AFFECT

Published in 1907, *The Life and Adventures of Nat Love, Better Known in the Cattle Country as "Deadwood Dick," A True History of Slavery Days, Life on the Great Cattle Ranges and on the Plains of the "Wild and Woolly" West, Based on Facts, and Personal Experiences of the Author* traces a life from slavery through cowpunching to, finally, employment as a Pullman Porter. Nat Love casts himself as evidence of American meritocracy and takes on the role of national booster, especially in the memoir's section titled "See America, Then Your Chest Will Swell With Pride That You Are An American," which documents the wonders one encounters while travelling the nation in a Pullman car.[32] As in Roosevelt's autobiographical writings, Love's memoir both prizes individual ingenuity and relishes in the egalitarian collectives provided by masculine exertion. By juxtaposing Love with Roosevelt, I hope to point to masculinity's utopian potential as a means of self-fashioning in turn-of-the-century U.S. culture, particularly since, in Love's memoir, masculinity seems to undo race as a marker of social inequality, at least temporarily. Both Love and Roosevelt emphasize the egalitarian promise of masculinity at the turn of the century, and for both of them, masculinity erodes race as an identity category in a way that is both utopian and myopic.

The reduction of Western history and literature to mere nationalism is one of the reasons Blake Allmendinger gives in *Ten Most Wanted* for the subordination of Western literary studies to other regional and thematic frames in American literary studies. One should attempt, according to Allmendinger, to negotiate between regional and national frames when interpreting Western American literature:

> Anyone working in western literature faces the challenge of reconciling two conflicting imperatives: the desire to claim importance for the work that he does by relating it to larger theoretical constructs, national literary movements, outside historical or political forces, and external trends; and the need not to lose sight of what makes a work distinctive, "western," unique.[33]

However, Allmendinger does not follow his own methodology of balancing the national with the regional in his reading of Nat Love's memoir. In the first chapter of *Ten Most Wanted*, "The White Open Spaces," Allmendinger argues that *The Life and Adventures of Nat Love* "invokes white traditions—not black ones—and masters them, assimilating its protagonist within a conventional framework of power."[34] This argument, that the Western genre is an inherently "white" narrative that unproblematically supports "a conventional framework of power," seems to be precisely what Allmendinger warns against in the introduction to *Ten Most Wanted*. It is imperative to complicate the conflation of the American West with dominant whiteness, and Nat Love's text provides a site for the reconfiguration of national belonging as constituted not by racial hierarchy but by masculine merit.[35]

In the memoir's second chapter, Nat Love briefly entertains military involvement. Love details childhood fantasies of fighting in the Civil War:

> The Union was "IT," and we were all Yankees. Not being able to go to war as our masters did, we concluded to play war, accordingly I gathered all the boys of the neighborhood together, into a regiment,

which it was my intention to divide into two parties of Rebels and Yankees, but in this I met an insurmountable obstacle. Not one of the boys wanted to be a Rebel, consequently we had to look elsewhere for an enemy to give us battle, and serve as a vent for our growing enthusiasm.[36]

The slave children go on to identify nests of yellow jackets and hornets as "Rebels" and declare war on them, ultimately triumphant if occasionally stung. Critical works on Nat Love's memoir do not dwell on this passage, but it seems to color the supposed "white tradition" in which Nat Love partakes. This passage suggests that Love imagines a nation that values heterogeneity more than he capitulates to a nationalism saturated with racial hierarchy. It is significant to note here, too, that contemporary critics like Allmendinger might too quickly assume that whiteness registers as the absence of race in turn-of-the-century texts. Love's disavowal of race signifies differently in an era where whiteness itself was in the process of consolidation and was by no means the seemingly homogeneous, hollow category it would become later in twentieth-century American culture. However problematically, Love's text erases race to envision a type of national belonging that values masculinity as a marker of merit.

After emancipation, Love works in the South for a number of years until one day, by chance, he wins a raffle twice and earns enough money to venture west and "[start] out for the first time alone in a world I knew very little about."[37] Love becomes a cowpuncher, renowned for his ability to tame wild horses and read cattle brands. As Susan Scheckel argues in her reading of Nat Love's memoir, Love adopts the dress and habits of the cowboy self-consciously; this overt performativity—and the benefits that ensue—are apparent in the many passages of self-description and photographs in the book. Furthermore, Scheckel argues that Love's cowboy masculinity "[forms] the basis of a new identity that transcends the limiting categories of race and class."[38] The aforementioned photograph, in particular, displays Love's typical Western garb—a wide-brimmed hat, bandana, chaps, lasso, saddle, and rifle. Race, in Love's description of the West, does not dissociate him from the cowboy culture he enjoys:

On our own ranch, among my own companions, my position was as a high as a king, enjoying the trust and confidence of my employers and the homage of the men many of whom were indebted to me on many occasions when my long rope or ever ready forty-five colt pistol had saved them from serious injury or death…Mounted on my favorite horse, my long horsehide lariat near my hand, and my trusty guns in my belt and the broad plains stretching away for miles and miles, every foot of which I was familiar with, I felt I could defy the world.[39]

While Love is a wage laborer, he feels as if he is "a king" working in the West, in part because of the meritocracy in which he gains recognition. As a cowboy, he is renamed three times—once as "Red River Dick," again as "Deadwood Dick," and by Indians as "Buffalo Papoose"—in evidence of his skill as a bronco buster and fighter. As with Roosevelt, masculine exertion proves worth and entails, even more so for Love, a reinvention of self. Nat Love is emblematic of masculinity's power in the turn of the century, particularly in the American West, to mobilize signifiers of social hierarchy even against racial hierarchies. As evident in the passage's nostalgia, Love's memoir is a narrative of vanished possibility, of multiplicity stabilized by modernity.

In his memoir, Love speaks from a position of corporate comfort; he has given up life on the range and "is at the present time connected with the General Securities Company in Los Angeles."[40] Writing from this secure position, Love foregrounds novelty and mobility in his account of cowboy masculinity. Once in the West, he immediately likes cowboy labor because

it was free and wild and contained the elements of danger which my nature craved and which began to manifest itself when I was a pugnacious youngster on the old plantation in our rock battles and the breaking of wild horses. I gloried in the danger, and the wild and free life of the plains, the new country I was continually traversing, and the many new scenes and incidents continually arising in the life of a rough rider.[41]

Love emphasizes the flux and novelty of cowboy life, and his pursuit of freedom is also, importantly, a pursuit of new experiences and places couched in a phrase, "rough rider," borrowed from Roosevelt. This emphasis on novelty links Love's text to modernism. At the level of content, Love's text contains a modernist ideology: novelty, experimentation, and alienation produce beneficial results. Love himself changes so radically that his material form is also rendered unrecognizable. He addresses his reader and makes explicit the radical changes he undergoes: "To see me now you would not recognize the bronze hardened dare devil cow boy, the slave boy who a few years ago hunted rabbits in his shirt tail on the old plantation in Tennessee, or the tenderfoot who shrank shaking all over at the sight of a band of painted Indians."[42] As mentioned earlier, Love claims in his memoir to be the real-life "Deadwood Dick" and his description of his chameleon material form provide a palpable link to the bandit hero. Love's masculinity entails radical changes not only in style, fashion, speech, and labor, but also in materiality itself.[43] Like the dime-novel hero Deadwood Dick, Love's masculinity entails multiple performative identities.

As with Roosevelt's memoir, which fails to give voice to the Native American and African American Rough Riders so central to his vision of masculine meritocracy, Love's memoir also uses race to limit those who qualify as worthy of meritocratic consideration. The sheer number of references to Indian killing in the memoir points to the "legacy of conquest" in the text, even in one that so actively dissociates itself from the divide between black and white Americans. Love chronicles his killing, but is also quick to justify his violence: "It is a terrible thing to kill a man no matter what the cause. But as I am writing a true history of my life, I cannot leave these facts out. But every man who died at my hands was either seeking my life or died in open warfare, when it was a case of killing or being killed."[44] Love's apologetic yet not fully convincing justification of violence is markedly different from an undying and unquestioning nationalism that endorses the redemptive function of legitimate violence. Instead, violence is deployed in particular conditions, not for its own purposes but in order to protect a collective, be it a herd of cattle or a group of cowboys. This mode of being can be thought of as, to use Michael Warner's phrase, "a discipline of subjectivity."[45] Rather than the abstract violence produced by the liberal state in the interest of a Christian eschatology, Nat Love's violence serves a secular group of individuals who are bound together and rendered intelligible by various practices, including, among others, cattle herding, brand reading, and bronco busting. In this sense, Love's sense of collective entanglement privileges the same type of belonging as Roosevelt's vision of haphazard military engagement; both find meritocratic value in masculine exertion. The limit of Love's masculine meritocracy, though, seems to be racial and national difference, like Roosevelt's. Conceiving of Native Americans as a collective formation, Love designates them as other and therefore dangerous to American individualism. Masculine meritocracy, then, undoes certain social and racial hierarchies yet remains uneven in its egalitarian impulse.

Love's meritocratic vision of the erosion of social hierarchies in the wake of masculine self-fashioning has obvious limitations. Georgina Dodge remarks that Love imagines "universal manhood" from "within the texual realm," and even within the memoir itself, masculinity is limited by social hierarchy.[46] As Michael K. Johnson argues, Love's "racelessness" emerges through his labor as a cowboy, which is organized around the protection of private property: "By enacting violence that is unlike the savagery of white outlaws and American Indians, Love represents the law itself—the protection of property in opposition to the savages who attempt to ignore property rights, the cornerstone of civilization."[47] This fixation on property rights serves as a dramatic marker of the difference between Love's memoir and dime-novel Westerns. Love's masculinity is primarily a personal project rather than a collective engagement. In this sense, masculinity becomes an individual aesthetic in Love's memoir, a matter of personal style. This is both where masculinity becomes utopian and malleable and also the limit of Love's masculine self-fashioning. Masculine style transforms Love but does not transform the economic order that facilitates, prioritizes, and rewards cowboy masculinity in social hierarchies.

MERITOCRACY AND MODERNISM

The discourse of Western expansion certainly served the exploitative interests of imperialism, racism, and patriarchy, but it also produced the possibility for participating in a social world that was free from the social hierarchies dominant in the East, though that possibility is only unevenly articulated by Love and Roosevelt's texts. While Love's text is certainly nationalist, it produces a form of national belonging that promises to do away with racism toward African Americans. Love engages in frontier mythology not to support national interest but to endorse democratic mobility. Love captures a community that, while certainly a part of capitalist development and imperial expansion, envisions the role of the nation not as a protector or redeemer but as a democratic bond held together by ritual practice. Indeed, both Nat Love and Theodore Roosevelt locate in masculinity a means of feeling equal, albeit an equality facilitated through violence and exclusion.

It is significant that these texts are memoirs; they are more about how masculinity feels and the social promises of those feelings than about social structures abstracted from individual affect. While this utopian set of "masculine feelings" does not explain the social working of imperialist America, it does, I think, complicate our common assumption that masculinity supports imperialism in the United States wholesale at the turn of the century. If it does, it does so unevenly, for masculinity in the turn-of-century U.S. privileges mobility above all else, with all of its potential for the reconfiguration of social life. These autobiographical writings, then, represent masculine self-fashioning as a way to remake social belonging. Embedded within the content of Roosevelt and Nat Love's memoirs, then, is experimentation, though at the level of personal representation rather than prose style or literary form. In *The Virginian*, Owen Wister adapts this model of masculinity to literary aesthetics.

CHAPTER 3

Marrying Men: Intimacy in Owen Wister's *The Virginian*

Why wasn't some Kipling saving the sage-brush for American literature, before the sage-brush and all that it signified went the way of the California forty-niner, went the way of the Mississippi steamboat, went the way of everything?...But what was fiction doing, fiction, the only thing that has always outlived fact? Must it be perpetual tea-cups?

—Owen Wister, *Roosevelt: The Story of a Friendship*

Owen Wister's *The Virginian: A Horseman of the Plains* is often described as the first "literary" Western, owing in part to Wister's own pretensions in the novel's introduction. Throughout the late nineteenth century, Western literature enjoyed marketplace success in both popular and literary forms. However, Wister's novel stands out not simply because of its immense popularity as fiction and a successful stage play, spawning multiple film adaptations in the first half of the twentieth century, but also, in Wister's own words, as an authentic "historical novel" that depicts "a vanished world."[1] Arguing against the novel's publicity, that it is a "colonial romance," Wister claims that his work is as historical as William Dean Howells's *The Rise of Silas Lapham*, Nathaniel Hawthorne's *The Scarlet Letter*, or Harriet Beecher Stowe's *Uncle Tom's Cabin*, a curious catalog of "historical" texts that seeks to implant realism as the dominant form of classic American literature. Wister's realist aesthetic values novels that "[present] faithfully a day and a generation."[2] *The Virginian*, then, is written with high literary pretensions and synthesizes, precisely because of its realist aspirations, the two dominant genres of late nineteenth-century Western literature: romantic adventure tales such as those found in dime novels, and memoirs such as Nat Love's and Theodore Roosevelt's accounts of frontier exertion and wartime heroics. Thus, *The Virginian* synthesizes the unruly masculinities of the dime novel and the Western memoir. In this mixture of imaginative and historical writing, Wister paves the way for further experiments in literary form that seek to reimagine subjectivity and social life through masculinity.

The Virginian's marriage plot—and the ideological purposes it serves—figures prominently in the scholarship on the novel. The novel concludes with the marriage of the Virginian, a heroic cowboy, to Molly, who traveled to Wyoming from her native Vermont to teach grade school. Many critics agree with Henry James's criticism, written in a letter to Wister in 1902 shortly after the novel was published, that "nothing would have induced me to unite him [the Virginian] to the little Vermont person [Molly]...I wouldn't have let him live & be happy; I should have made him perish in his flower & in some splendid way."[3] Modifying James's claim, Forrest Robinson argues that "it is the very key to the success of *The Virginian* that it enables the reader to have the Virginian both ways, as the ruggedly individualistic American Adam and as the natural Western gentleman and paterfamilias, even as it insists that the two roles are incompatible."[4] Lee Clark Mitchell unifies these disparate tendencies by acknowledging that "the achievement of *The Virginian* resides...in its capacity to satisfy contradictory expectations: the desire for nostalgic escapism into an exclusively masculine West and yet the need for a resolution to the more immediately vexing national question of gender relations."[5] These readings figure the marriage that concludes *The Virginian* as primarily aimed at resolving cultural contradictions derived from women's suffrage debates and the general sense of emasculation commonly associated with Gilded-Age manhood. *The Virginian*'s final marriage plot certainly serves the overt purpose of unifying the North and South—Vermont and Virginia—in a consolidated whiteness, particularly when read in conjunction with Wister's political essay on the frontier, "The Evolution of the Cow-Puncher."[6] In total, these readings treat the novel's ending as contradictory to the rest of the novel, as a forced political ending that supports Wister's own convictions about eugenics and nationalism.

Broadening the analysis of marriage in *The Virginian*, William Handley's scholarship on marriage, violence, and nationalism in the Western emphasizes the ways in which the Virginian's marriage encapsulates forms of patriarchal and national violence in terms of legitimate power:

> What is remarkable about the world of *The Virginian* is that so much violence serves as the prelude to marriage and hence that so many other codes of morality feeling—including not only Molly's against lynchings and shoot-outs, but also the Virginian's "inward tide of feeling" for Steve—should be subordinated before the altar of marriage for the sake of nation's racial future out West.[7]

Rather than providing a mere surface resolution to cultural contradiction, Handley's reading locates marriage as a central ideological formation that naturalizes gender and racial hierarchies and legitimates violence. This reading treats the novel as an ideological whole, leveling out disparate narrative trajectories in the service of a nationalist ideology that supports white, patriarchal privilege. Handley's emphasis on the Western's complicity with national hierarchies assumes outright that *The Virginian* ultimately endorses a particular form of hierarchical, racist, and patriarchal nationalism.

In what follows, I seek to reconcile these two dominant claims about *The Virginian*: on the one hand, that it contains contradictory models of national belonging, as argued by Forrest Robinson and Lee Clark Mitchell, and on the other, that one dominant vision of nationalism subordinates all others, as argued by William Handley. To do this, I will argue that the novel articulates alternative models of public formation that exceed dominant nationalism because of Wister's nostalgia for cowboy masculinity and its heterogeneity. Both the contestations over marriage as an institution in the nineteenth century and the proliferation of sentimentality and intimacy in Wister's Wyoming allow masculinity to flourish in the frontier as an unruly mode of embodiment, as quick to nurture intimacies as to act violently. The Virginian and his "cow-puncher" friends cultivate a masculinity that exceeds the normalcy often entailed by the marriage plot.

OWEN WISTER'S REALISM

In the note "To the Reader" that prefaces *The Virginian*, Wister states that his novel is both historically accurate and universal. The Virginian, Wister writes, "has been among us always, since the beginning: a young man with his temptations, a hero without wings."[8] This claim that the Western hero transcends a particular historical moment is complicated by Wister's insistence on verisimilitude. The novel takes place in "Wyoming between 1874 and 1890." For Wister, historical specificity and aesthetic universality intertwine because of the exemplarity of the frontier hero, especially compared to the incoherent present of 1902:

> He and his brief epoch make a complete picture, for in themselves they were as complete as the pioneers of the land or the explorers of the sea. A transition followed the horseman of the plains; a shapeless state, a condition of men and manners unlovely as that bald moment in the year when winter is gone and spring not come, and the face of Nature is ugly.[9]

Wister's historical continuum in the note "To the Reader" complicates the common reading of *The Virginian* as an imperialist romance, consolidating a violent-yet-noble white masculinity with a morally upright domestic femininity through marriage. *The Virginian* nostalgically celebrates the fluidity of the "vanished" in the face of the "ugly" present of imperial conquest, racial purity, and heteronormative reproductivity. In so doing, Wister's nostalgia for the frontier resuscitates intimacies under the guise of the coherent work of art.

Along with Frederic Remington and Theodore Roosevelt, Wister belonged to a coterie of privileged men fascinated by the vanishing—or vanished—frontier at the end of the nineteenth century.[10] Wister was convinced that the frontier would bring out the displaced Anglo-Saxon heritage of the white American while whittling down populations of immigrants, Hispanics, and African Americans. In keeping with this theory of racial progress, Wister's "democratic" vision privileges, to use the distinction forwarded by the Virginian, "quality" over "equality."[11] As Barbara Will argues, the Virginian "offers himself up as both the model of balanced modern masculinity and the auspicious symbol of a strenuous expansionist ideology at the turn of the century."[12] This expansionist ideology hinges on the ability of a new aristocracy to emerge through strenuous activities such as hunting, sports, and combat. Marriage also occupies a central role in Wister's commitment to an imperial white masculinity as the mechanism through which "quality" is consolidated and reproduced. However, despite this compulsion toward heteronormative reproductivity, Wister's masculine romances often short-circuit their own nationalist imperatives by repeatedly undoing marriage as a natural, permanent bond and instead depicting marriage as a provisional coupling with no particular species, gender, age, or sex restrictions. These heterogeneous intimacies set Wister's novel apart from James Fenimore Cooper's Leatherstocking Tales, which is nonetheless a clear influence on Wister. As David Greven notes, both *The Pathfinder* and *The Deerslayer* develop "the great *anti*-marriage plot in American literature," barring Natty from both heterosexual and homoerotic intimacies, all the while representing him as a force who "prevails, vanquished yet forever intransigently, unyieldingly present."[13] While Cooper's Natty Bumppo remains inviolate, Wister's Virginian is swamped by the messiness of desire, intimacy, and loss. Wister pushes his Western hero into, rather than away from, intimate relationships. Wister's Western writings mask the possibility for relations beyond heteronormative white marriage in genteel language, but his preoccupation with realistic representation allows for a proliferation of relations and alliances illegible within the conventions of literary realism.

Wister's pretensions toward literary realism are further explicated in his journals. In an entry from June 20, 1891, for example, during a trip through Wyoming, Wister articulates his desire to rank among prominent European realists by depicting the richness of the West:

> Did I believe in the efficacy of prayer, I should petition to be the hand that once and for all chronicled and laid bare the virtues and the vices of this extraordinary phase of American social progress. Nobody has done it. Nobody has touched anywhere near it. A few have described external sights and incidents but the grand total thing—its rise, its hysterical unreal prosperity, and its disenchanting downfall. All this and its influence on the various sorts of human character that has been subjected to it has not been hinted at by a single writer that I, at least, have heard of. The fact is, it is quite worthy of Tolstoi or George Eliot or Dickens. Thackeray wouldn't do.[14]

In her study of American literary realism, Amy Kaplan argues that realism, as practiced by William Dean Howells, equated "true life—reality…with work, which is viewed not simply as an occupation but more importantly as a system of value which privileges industriousness and self-discipline as the basis of communal life."[15] Realism here occupies a tension between genteel society and the upside-down world of industrial capitalism, and Wister's journal entry certainly emphasizes both economics and individuality. In an entry from June 26, 1891, Wister alludes to this engagement with manners and values when describing Smith, a man he meets in Wyoming:

> He is not a half way man. Not the Bret Harte villain with the heart of a woman. Not the mixed dish of Cambric tea so dear to modern

novelists. He is just bad through and through without a scruple and without an affection…When I come to my Castle in Spain, my book about Wyoming, I shall strain my muscles to catch Smith. I'm getting to believe that mixed characters are not the only ones in the world.[16]

Wister's rejection of "the Bret Harte villain" speaks to his realist affinities, yet his need to depict Smith honestly, as an "unmixed character," also forces a moral judgment about Smith as "bad through and through." Wister engages directly the tension between the graphically real and the properly mannered. He is careful to maintain a genteel manner when writing about a part of the country not famous for its propriety. That is, Smith's "badness," his lack of a "woman's heart," evidences the ways in which Wister's realism is a careful demarcation of genteel sentiment and a romanticized West that purports to be somehow more real than realism itself can accommodate in its privileging of complex, "mixed characters." In his pursuit of realism, Wister undermines one of the major precepts of Anglophone realism, namely, the notion that characters are not types but complex.[17]

In an effort, perhaps, to bolster his claim to realism, Wister carried a camera on many of his trips to Wyoming and Texas. In his journal from 1891, Wister gives a reason for taking photographs during his trip after noticing a beautiful hidden stream he was led to:

But thank the Lord [the stream] is nameless and unknown save to Indians, cowboys, and horse thieves; and it flows down through its pine forests and cliffs entirely at peace. Some day, no doubt, when civilization crawls here, this poor creek with its cañon and natural bridges will echo with the howling of the summer mob who will have easy paths made for them, and stair cases, and elevators perhaps too. There will be sign posts directing you to Minerva Terrace, Calypso Garden, Siren Grotto, for every unfortunate ledge and point will be saddled with a hateful name rotten with inappropriateness. And gentlemen from all over great cities will deposit their cards on every shelf and carve their names on every tree with that fetid vulgarity that is innate in our American race and appears on the surface as soon as they rise to prosperity and begin to travel. I hope at least some of the photographs I took will succeed.[18]

Wister's opposition to mass culture, and the regional tourism he predicts in Yellowstone, leads him to chronicle the vanishing West in writing and to document the Western landscape through photography before it is given a "name rotten with inappropriateness."

The mythological names Wister predicts have high art pretensions, yet would appeal to a mass culture audience rather than a cultural elite. Wister desires to depict the frontier without pretentious ornamentation. His realism is an attempt to produce a literary account of the West and to distance the West from neoclassicism, which he clearly identifies with middlebrow taste. Wister's work must be realistic while not falling into the category of popular fiction; however, by taking photographs of his Western journey, Wister participates in a prominent mass cultural practice of the late nineteenth century: photographing the West.

As Martha A. Sandweiss has chronicled, photographs of the West were sold widely as postcards, in albums, and as stereographs in the late nineteenth century. Landscape photographs dominated Western photography, and Sandweiss argues that photographs of the West as a vacant landscape serve an ideological purpose:

> [The West's] meaning and importance lay in the future, in its potential as a site of natural wealth and spiritual renewal for the expanding American nation. Such a transcendent, forward-looking narrative depended on the imaginative erasure of the land's native inhabitants whose very presence challenged the notion of the West as an empty and available landscape.[19]

Figure 3.1 Owen Wister on horseback, by F. J. Haynes & Brothers, St. Paul, Minnesota, undated. Owen Wister Collection, American Heritage Center, University of Wyoming.

Figure 3.2 "That's All," Owen Wister carrying camera, undated. Owen Wister Collection, American Heritage Center, University of Wyoming.

Two photographs of Wister—an image of Wister on a horse (figure 3.1) and "That's All" (figure 3.2), a photograph of Wister with his camera—depict the writer as a solitary figure in the vacant Western landscape. These photographs play into the construction of the West as a virgin land, awaiting civilization. In particular, "That's All" depicts a scene that connotes Wister's realism. The photograph contains an image of an unshaven Wister, carrying a large camera. The caption both belittles and aggrandizes Wister and his pursuit of authentic Western scenes by implying that Wister is nothing more than a scraggly man with a camera and, at the same time, that this one lone person, and this person only, will represent the West with a single camera. While the photos of Wister on horseback portray a West that is a blank landscape only to be traveled through, "That's All" depicts Wister as a kind of masculine settler. Photography was notably bound up in discourse about the role of the artist in the late nineteenth century. For example, Peter Henry Emerson, the proponent of naturalist photography, describes photography as a primarily artistic, rather than technological, endeavor. After instructing the photographer to "avoid prettiness" in his essay "Hints on Art," Emerson goes on to claim that "it is not the apparatus that chooses the picture, but the *man* who wields it."[20] This stress on "*man*" aligns photography, and particularly Western landscape photography, with the regenerative promise that brought Wister and Theodore Roosevelt out West in the late nineteenth century. Through the photographic gaze, by capturing nature and by producing images of the West, Wister lays claim to the natural world as an artist. In so doing, he regains a "natural" self that is not subject to the crippling effects of modern, urban life.

Not all of Wister's photographs play into the cultural fantasy of the vacant Western wilderness. As Sandweiss notes, other common subjects of Western photography were Native Americans. While Western landscapes and pictures of lone men on the frontier produce a vision of the vacant West, waiting to be settled, photographs of Native Americans were often captioned with claims about the "vanishing race" populating the frontier:

> The Indians existed as a foil and backdrop for the inevitable Americanization of the West. Though a single photograph, alone, might not be able to convey this message, photographs juxtaposed in pairs, arranged in series, or explicated with words could convey to the buying public the evolving story of the vanishing race. The story was not a static one. As the Indians ceased to be a military threat by the end of the nineteenth century, the pictorial and emotional quality of the story began to change.[21]

This shift in representation, from depictions of warlike savages to a romanticized portrait of the vanishing Native American, precedes Wister's trips to the West. In her analysis of Wister's Native American photographs, Jennifer S. Tuttle finds that Native Americans pose a problem for Wister: "His photographs suggest an increasing realization of his inability to represent abstract Indianness without the intrusion of living, breathing Indians, whose lives on the reservation disrupt the narrative that he would like to tell."[22] In contrast to the work of a photographer like Edward Curtis, Wister is unable to capture the romanticized vanishing Native American; Wister's photographs instead place Native Americans within the discourse of gentility. For example, "Shoshone Ladies Lunching" is one of a series of photos Wister took of the Shoshone tribe (figure 3.3). This photograph depicts a cluster of Shoshone women, some sitting, some standing, along with a horse and two dogs. Like his short stories, in particular "Little Big Horn Medicine," which mock Native Americans, Wister's handwritten caption translates the scene into a parody of genteel femininity. The Shoshone women lose their particularity as Native Americans with cultural practices that might differ from the ladies to which Wister compares them, and they become legible only through the genteel discourse of white, middle-class culture. Interestingly, the photograph betrays Wister's familiar language. The women's backs are turned to the camera, their bodies covered in blankets. The photo testifies to the photographer's inability to witness these subjects. The

Figure 3.3 "Shoshone Ladies Lunching," 1891. Owen Wister Collection, American Heritage Center, University of Wyoming.

fence directly behind the ladies also resonates with Wister's inability to depict a romantic Native subject. Instead, the Shoshone women exist within the settled, fenced-in West. Rather than inhabiting an imaginary landscape, "Shoshone Ladies Lunching" reveals the social relations already in place in the West.

Furthermore, Wister's photos of his guides, horses, and supplies speak to a different form of social belonging than the fraternity of white men consolidated through the common tropes of the virgin land and the vanishing American. For example, "Buffalo Forks, Wyoming Territory" (figure 3.4) undermines the images of the lone horseman and photographer. Instead of existing in a landscape pregnant with futurity or documenting a vanishing indigenous culture, Wister's group photograph offers an account of social relations present in the West that does not necessarily fit into the nostalgic or forward-looking narratives of manifest destiny. This photograph emphasizes the communal life common to frontier living as well as the sheer amount of people and possessions that accompanied Wister on his Western trips.[23] Furthermore, as in many of his photographs of his trips to the West, animals are consistent companions. These photographs contain remarkable and heterogeneous implications about social belonging and intimacy. "Buffalo Forks, Wyoming Territory"

Figure 3.4 "Buffalo Forks, Wyoming Territory," undated. Owen Wister Collection, American Heritage Center, University of Wyoming.

depicts a space of belonging from within a set of tropes, institutions, and actions that typically privilege the individual white male. While Wister does not ultimately endorse this heterogeneous collectivity, his work does rely on it to represent the aesthetic and historical value of the American West.

Wister's photographs and his distaste for mass culture engage tensions common to realism. He both emphasizes his own genteel propriety in contrast to Wyoming's ruffians and Native Americans and insists on accurate and truthful representation that does not romanticize a landscape already vanished. This struggle to remain genteel yet engage in realist representation creates a problem for Wister: how does one accurately and disinterestedly represent a population that does not adhere to genteel codes, while retaining a genteel voice? This paradox arises in part because of Wister's distaste for aestheticized and romantic accounts of the frontier. However, Wister's own prose and photography take part in the commodification of the West as a romantic, even mythological, place. John Dorst argues that Wister's desire to photograph the West "is the quintessential gesture of precisely that modern mass tourism he anticipates so pessimistically. He is already part of the spectacle that he imagines as yet to come. One might say he is both the observer of its emergence and simultaneously one of its harbingers."[24] While Wister is certainly part of the "spectacle" of the West, it is my contention that Wister's depictions of the West vary widely from the mass cultural West he vehemently and anticipatorily criticizes. Wister's prose, journal entries, and tourist photography do not seamlessly blend into popular representations of the frontier but instead, because of Wister's own interest in realism, provide remarkably uneven accounts of Wyoming society. The nonnormative relations that abound in Wister's photographs—groups of men of mixed class and ethnicity, Shoshone women who become "ladies lunching"—also recur in his texts. The genteel values Wister forces onto his narratives obscure a set of relations that deny classification in that very style, opening up his representation of the West, momentarily, not to a popularized and vulgar mass culture but to alternative social relations.

On "Queer" Marriage

Owen Wister's *The Virginian* contains many disparate plot lines, only some of which are contained by the central romance, thus representing Wyoming as a heterogeneous social field. A storyteller figure who relates stories about the locals, the narrator is often thought to be a stand-in for Wister himself; he visits Wyoming from the East and over the course of the novel develops a friendship with the Virginian, a noble cowboy who originally hails from Virginia, hence his name. The Virginian is a prototypical Western hero; he is strong, quiet, contemplative, yet violent when called upon to act. The narrator chronicles the Virginian's confrontations with rustlers and witnesses his romance with Molly Wood, a schoolteacher from Vermont. Along with this central story arc, the narrator also relates occasional incidents that read more like short stories and tall tales about the Virginian and other Wyoming characters. Yet while stories multiply, marriage stands out as a recurring theme that preoccupies all characters in the novel.

In the opening chapter of *The Virginian*, the narrator arrives from the East for a stay with Judge Henry, a family friend and cattle rancher, and is immediately fixated by a discussion of marriage. Overhearing the Virginian's imploration, "Off to get married *again*? Oh, don't!," the narrator has "no desire but for more of this conversation."[25] The Virginian is speaking with "Uncle Hughey," not an actual uncle but an older man in town noted for his multiple marriages. The Virginian's interrogation of Uncle Hughey lights upon the older man's clothes, for "they are speakin' mighty loud o' nuptials." This devaluation of marriage to merely a matter of dress serves as prelude to the narrator's marriage fantasy: "Had I been the bride, I should have taken the giant, dust and all."[26] In the opening scene, homosocial discourse gives way to a stronger intimacy that takes the form of the narrator's homoerotic hypothetical. This moment inaugurates the mobile, multiple, and unconventional intimacies that constitute Wister's nostalgic West.

In this opening scene, the Virginian tries to dissuade Uncle Hughey from marriage, all the while acknowledging that his attitude toward matrimony will change over time: "Course I expect to think different when my age is different. I'm havin' the thoughts proper to twenty-four."[27] This episode comments and plays on marriage as an unstable cluster of affects and relationships as well as the ease with which marriages could be sealed and dissolved.[28] While marriage is a common trope in the novel, it is not a stable institution. As Uncle Hughey's dress makes clear, marriage is just as much a matter of fashion as it is a private, romantic relationship broadcast through the legitimizing powers of the state. Furthermore, the central romance of *The Virginian*, the courtship and marriage of the Virginian and Molly Wood, is known publicly before it is manifest privately. As Lin McLean tells the Virginian after his engagement to Molly is finally announced, "Lord! Everybody has knowed it right along...Mrs. McLean will be glad. She told me to give yu' her congratulations quite awhile ago. I was to have 'em ready just as soon as ever yu' asked for 'em yourself."[29] Within the context of the novel, private feelings of love and commitment are apparent to others before they are to the lovers themselves. Marriage, then, becomes another mode of self-fashioning for the Virginian and his frontier comrades, blending individual desire with outward performance, interiority with the perception of the body as an object in space, intimacy with social norms.

In *The Virginian*, letter-writing figures romance as a mixture of the private with the public, interiority with objectivity. The narrator describes the Virginian's attempt to write a letter to Molly:

> But his first message to his lady was scarcely written with ease. It must be classed, I think, among those productions which are styled literary *efforts*. It was completed in pencil before it was copied in ink; and that first draft of it in pencil was well-nigh illegible with erasures and amendments.[30]

The Virginian's writing is fractured and tentative. Unlike the communications he often writes to his rancher boss Judge Henry, in writing this letter he is "a little anxious lest any sustained production from his pen might contain blunders that would too staringly remind her of his scant learning."[31] His romantic gesture is tentative because it is not a mode of performance with which the Virginian feels comfortable. The narrator becomes omniscient in this scene of writing, freely circulating with the letter and through characters' interiors, and this intrusion into the Virginian's interiority allows for not only his cowboy body but also his own interiority to be the product of stylization. The Virginian must learn how to perform in heterosexual romance, and the novel will dedicate many pages to the narration of his acquisition of romantic savvy. In this sense, romance, and its culmination with the Virginian's marriage to Molly, is in no way natural but is instead a matter of self-fashioning that requires an intensive overhaul of the Virginian's emotional life. In particular, he undergoes a transformation in how his emotions are produced by and for others. This transformation sets *The Virginian* apart from the early frontiersman hero, as depicted in James Fenimore Cooper's Leatherstocking Tales. Instead of sticking to his principles with religious, stoic conviction, as Natty Bumppo does, for example, at the conclusion of *The Deerslayer*, the Virginian is an heir to dime-novel figures such as Seth Jones and Deadwood Dick in his willingness to change according to the demands of the moment.

Public sentiment occurs in the feminine and domestic spaces of the novel as well. Mrs. Taylor, Molly's landlady, claims knowledge of Molly's feelings well before Molly acknowledges them. When asking Mrs. Taylor if she should marry for love, Mrs. Taylor asserts full awareness of Molly's feelings: "Child, you are talking cross to-day because you're at outs with yourself. You've been at outs ever since you took this idea of leaving the school and us and everything this needless way. You have not treated [the Virginian] right."[32] Emotions in *The Virginian* are legible in public but often opaque in private. Only after an emotion has been noted by another can the feeling subject recognize the emotion, as with Molly's emotional "outs."[33] This seems to be the crux not only of romance in the novel but also of the masculine verbal play that, for example, the Virginian takes part in with Uncle Hughey.[34] By eliciting a response in a listener, the speaker can best the listener by retroactively positing deep-seated emotion as the precondition of one's public utterance. But, this externalization of emotion—as something caused in public and later acknowledged privately—does not so much naturalize as publicize marriage.

The obvious implication of the marriage plot, that marriage is a natural and inevitable relation between a man and a woman, turns out to be not at all the case in *The Virginian*. Speaking with Scipio le Moyne, one of his closest friends, the Virginian remarks, "Nothing's queer...except marriage and lightning. Them two occurrences can still give me a sensation of surprise."[35] Lightning would be surprising to a cowboy, for it is often followed by thunder, which can cause a stampede. What also seems surprising about lightning is the fact that it occurs without sound. Only after it has struck does its aural counterpart follow. In the novel, romantic love and marriage function in a similar fashion. Romance is seen before it is felt, or is recognized by others before consciously experienced by the enamored. This disjuncture, between exteriority and interiority, or between the witnessed and the experienced, constitutes the "queerness" of marriage. Ideologically, proper marriages occur through spoken consent, but couplings in the novel occur without spoken consent and simply through public acknowledgment. Marriage relations in *The Virginian* seem unhinged even from performative utterance. As Nancy Cott charts in her history of marriage in America, monogamous marriage in which both partners consent became a hallmark of national belonging in the late nineteenth and early twentieth centuries in response to perceived threats posed by polygamy and divorce: "The choice and consent embodied in approved marital union, its legality, its monogamous (Christian) morality—all these could be corrupted, compromising civic participation and governance, as Mormons had shown. If marriage produced the polity, then wrongfully joined marriage could be fatal."[36] The precariousness of marriage—as a product of public recognition that also bears an overdetermined national meaning—makes the institution itself a provocative site for remaking social relations. Since it is a function of public discourse, marriage can describe and delimit a far broader array of intimacies than national legislation allows.

One of the most striking examples of non-normative coupling in *The Virginian* is the story of Shorty and his horse, Pedro. This story is one of the occasional, local color pieces that pepper the novel. Shorty, a cowboy who the narrator refers to as "a lost dog," has a loving relationship with his horse. Shorty rides Pedro onto a ranch owned by the notoriously cruel Balaam and is eventually convinced to sell the horse. Balaam persuades Shorty by claiming that Pedro is "quite a lady's little pet!... Pity this isn't New York, now, where there's a big market for harmless horses. Gee-gees, the children call them."[37] Balaam insults Shorty's horse by feminizing the owner. By casting Pedro as a "lady's pet," Shorty becomes the lady that has feminized his otherwise manly horse. Frontier masculinity is then threatened and corrupted by civilizing femininity and domesticity. Changing course, Balaam then goes on to insinuate that Pedro's leg is sprung, "that's always to be expected when they're worked too young."[38] This comment colors Shorty as a cruel taskmaster and Pedro as the victim of Shorty's tyranny. In the logic of marriage relations, Shorty is the cruel husband, Pedro the abused wife who is "worked too young." Balaam is eventually successful in separating Shorty from his horse, having negotiated two tropes about marriage. As Shorty leaves Pedro on Balaam's ranch, the narrative uses melodramatic language to emphasize the heartbreak of separation, focusing on the gazes of both man and horse:

> After breakfast [Shorty] and his belongings departed to Drybone, and Pedro from his field calmly watched this departure; for horses must recognize even less than men the black corners that their destinies turn. The pony stopped feeding to look at the mail-wagon pass by; but the master sitting in the wagon forebore to turn his head.[39]

Shorty's refusal to look at Pedro evidences the immorality of selling the horse to Balaam, a rancher noted for his cruel treatment of animals. Balaam uses the language of marriage to successfully separate

Shorty from Pedro, by playing on the disdain for marriage inherent to a masculinity that longs for escape. However, the narrative goes on to punish both Balaam and Shorty for severing the cowboy from his partner, Pedro the horse.[40]

Immediately following this episode, the chapter "Balaam and Pedro" depicts Balaam's cruelty toward the horse and the horse's eventual death. Balaam's disposition becomes apparent in his screed against horses:

> They're all the same. Not a bastard one but's laying for his chance to do for you. Some'll buck you off, and some'll roll with you, and some'll fight you with their forefeet. They may play good for a year, but the Western pony's man's enemy, and when he judges he's got his chance, he's going to do his best. And if you come out alive it won't be his fault.[41]

Balaam's logic, that horses "play good for a year" and then reveal their true nefarious intentions, both humanizes and demonizes the animals. Following this dialogue, Balaam proceeds to beat Pedro and, in a scene that Wister edited because of Theodore Roosevelt's advice, pulls out Pedro's eye.[42] The Virginian, witnessing "the monstrosity," in turn beats Balaam into "a blurred, dingy, wet pulp."[43] Then, Balaam accidentally shoots and kills Pedro. When Shorty has earned enough to buy Pedro back and returns to the ranch, Balaam tells him that the horse was shot by Indians. As he leaves Balaam's ranch, Shorty's relationship to his horse is again described as a relationship between people: "Shorty rode away in mournful spirits. For he had made sure of once more riding and talking with Pedro, his friend whom he had taught to shake hands."[44] Shorty and Pedro are intimate partners, a couple marked by the horse's ability to "shake hands," a form of contractual assent similar to the performative utterance "I do." Shorty sells Pedro out of shame, fearing that he is either feminizing the horse or abusing him. Instead, Shorty and Pedro are a couple severed by narrative conceits about conventional marriage.

The discourse of marriage, particularly the ways in which marriage is criticized as either feminizing or a form of slavery, results in Shorty and Pedro's separation. By casting marriage as both patriarchal dominance and subjection to domesticity, Balaam destroys the unruly intimacy that unites Shorty and Pedro. The normalization of marriage in the late nineteenth century does not allow for non-normative coupling. In the novel's prefatory note to the reader, Wister explicitly bemoans the fact that "time has flowed faster than my ink" and that the life he depicts is no longer available.[45] In this sense, Wister himself mourns the lost intimacy between Shorty and Pedro. Readings of *The Virginian* tend to overlook the utopian component of Wister's nostalgia; he does not celebrate the new, married West but instead chronicles the possibilities left behind on the frontier. The Virginian, the rugged main character himself, also experiences heartbreak when he is forced to order the lynching of his friend Steve, a cow-puncher turned rustler. After hanging Steve, the Virginian bursts forth with regret and mourning:

> [The Virginian] was lost in a fog of sentiment. He knew, knew passionately, that he had done right; but the silence of his old friend to him through those last hours left a sting that no reasoning could assuage. "He told good-bye to the rest of the boys; but not to me." And nothing I could point out in common sense turned him from the thread of his own argument. He worked round the circle again to self-justification: "Was it him I was deserting? Was not the deserting done by him the day I spoke my mind about stealing calves? I have kept my ways the same. He is the one that took to new ones. The man I used to travel with is not the man back there. Same name, to be sure. And same body. But different in—and yet he had the memory! You can't never change your memory!"[46]

The Virginian depicts his relationship with Steve as a marriage—Steve deserts him, and therefore the marriage ends. Desertion was one of the rationales for divorce on the frontier territories, and Wister himself depicts a marriage ended by desertion in his 1897 novel *Lin McLean*. The Virginian comforts himself by claiming that Steve, his partner, "is not the man back there," in an attempt to convince himself that a change in company and behavior results in a change of identity. The Virginian's mourning is marked by the fact that, as he exclaims to the narrator, he "knew Steve awful well!"[47] The Virginian's emotions express the uncertainty and instability of coupling. He is unable to control the actions of his partner, who can take on "new ways." But this painful uncertainty is filtered through the narrator's genteel discourse, never directly stating the Virginian's emotional state or the significance of the relationship. As the Virginian talks about his youthful experiences with Steve, the narrator glosses over much of the monologue: "And he fell into elemental talk of sex, such talk as would be an elk's or a tiger's; and spoken so by him, simply and naturally, as we speak of the seasons,

or of death, or of any actuality, it was without offence. But it would
be offence should I repeat it."[48] The narrator's gentility masks the
relationship that the narrator and the Virginian both mourn, the
coupling of men.

After the lynching and his initial outburst, the Virginian describes
himself as fractured:

> I expect in many growed-up men you'd call sensible there's a little boy
> sleepin'—the little kid they once was—that still keeps his fear of the
> dark. You mentioned the dark yourself yesterday. Well, this experience
> has woken up that little kid in me, and blamed if I can coax the little
> cuss to go to sleep again! I keep a-telling him daylight will come, but
> he keeps a-crying and holding on to me.[49]

Rather than attributing emotion to interiority, he externalizes
and others emotion from himself through the figure of the inner
child. The novel again figures sentiment as public, a relation of
one to another. Emotions demand a relation to something outside of the self, such that even the narrator figures the Virginian's
most private moments as public relations with other bodies. The
novel's representation of public feeling is in keeping with the aesthetic, affective, and political trajectory of sentimental literature, as
charted by Lauren Berlant: "the very emphasis on feeling that radi-
calizes the sentimental critique also muffles the solutions it often
imagines or distorts and displaces them from the places toward
which they ought to be directed."[50] The Virginian's emphasis on
another—here the "little boy"—as a supplemental embodiment of
the authentic emotions that remain unspeakable within the novel
functions as a way of containing the rampant and unruly intimacies invoked and mourned by Wister's nostalgic representation of
the West.

National Romance and Masculine Fashions

The central romance in *The Virginian*, between the Southern cowboy
and the Vermont schoolmarm Molly Stark Wood, is variously metaphorized, and in this novel, even heterosexual, normative marriage
is unorthodox. A chapter titled "The Spinster Meets the Unknown"
introduces Molly. The "Unknown" of the chapter title refers not just
to the Wyoming territory but also to the Virginian. The novel spends a
great deal of space describing their slow courtship. The two first meet
when the Virginian rescues Molly from a stagecoach accident, and

Molly subsequently treats the Virginian "saucily."[51] The Virginian, tired of the conversational games, describes Molly and himself as children:

> Don't you think pretendin' yu' don't know a man,—his name's nothin', but him—a man whom you were glad enough to let assist yu' when somebody was needed,—don't you think that's mighty close to hide-and-seek them children plays? I ain't so sure but what there's a pair of us children in this hyeh room.[52]

This is the first of many moments that cast the Virginian and Molly's romance in curious terms. After Molly agrees to "come a-ridin'" with him, the Virginian exclaims, "You're a gentleman!"[53] The Virginian also claims that he intends "to be your best scholar" to Molly.[54] The novel's central heterosexual couple, then, have a playful, childish relationship, but that relationship is multiply modeled as both a fraternal and pedagogical bond. The various gender and social positions here, along with the repeated description of Molly as having a "fortress within her," complicate the power structure governing the couple.

Although the narrator remarks that Molly, "in her day, was not a New Woman," the narrative repeatedly describes Molly as in a position of power, as a "gentleman" and as the Virginian's teacher.[55] In contrast, the Virginian has an unstable body, more vibrant to Molly than her previous suitor, Sam Bannett:

> Her woman's fortress was shaken by a force unknown to her before. Sam Bannett did not have it in him to look as this man could look, when the cold luster of his eyes grew hot with internal fire. What color they were baffled her still. "Can it possibly change?" she wondered.[56]

Once again, masculinity is linked to an unruly body. Like Deadwood Dick and Seth Jones, the Virginian's body eludes social hierarchies not through transcendence but through shape-shifting. The Virginian is both hot and cold, passionate and reserved.

This distinction between Molly and the Virginian comes to a climax at the end of the novel when the Virginian is faced with a conflict, one taken up in countless subsequent Westerns. After being insulted by Trampas, the novel's chief cattle rustler and villain, the Virginian is forced to confront him in a gunfight to regain his honor. Opposed to vigilante justice, Molly threatens to leave the Virginian if he goes through with the gunfight. Though he is reluctant to tell

Molly about Trampas, the Virginian ultimately decides to tell her because of their intimate bond:

> Having read his sweetheart's mind very plainly, the lover now broke his dearest custom. It was his code never to speak ill of any man to any woman. Men's quarrels were not for women's ears. In his scheme, good women were to know only a fragment of men's lives. He had lived many outlaw years, and his wide knowledge of evil made innocence doubly precious to him. But to-day he must depart from his code, having read her mind well. He would speak evil of one man to one woman, because his reticence had hurt her—and was she not far from her mother, and very lonely, do what he could? She should know the story of his quarrel in language as light and casual as he could veil it with.[57]

The reader soon learns, however, that Molly already knows about the bad blood between the Virginian and Trampas because Molly's friend and confidante, Mrs. Taylor, relays gossip from her husband to the schoolteacher. The Virginian responds by claiming that "husbands are a special kind of man," bound to share "men's quarrels" with women. This egalitarianism achieved through marriage collapses hierarchies and inequalities between the couple. Just as Shorty misses shaking hands with his horse and the Virginian reminisces about his openness with Steve, the Taylors' intimacy erodes hierarchy.

The Virginian and Molly then argue about the gunfight and its necessity. Molly, arguing that the public is insignificant to true self worth, claims that "there is a higher courage than fear of outside opinion."[58] The Virginian, countering her, claims "cert'nly there is. That's what I'm showing in going against yours." The Virginian goes on to externalize his emotions once again:

> If any man happened to say I was a thief and I heard about it, would I let him go on spreadin' such a thing of me? Don't I owe my own honesty something better than that? Would I sit down in a corner rubbin' my honesty and whisperin' to it, "There! there! I know you ain't a thief"? No, seh; not a little bit! What men say about my nature is not just merely an outside thing.[59]

The argument relies on competing conceptions of the self and the public. While Molly asserts that public sentiment is merely a matter of "outside opinion," the Virginian argues that public sentiment produces subjects. His masculinity is performed as "an outside thing" that then becomes something more than "merely an outside thing," and thus he must go through with the gunfight.

In keeping with this emphasis on externality, the gunfight scene is narrated as a disembodied activity, one not consciously willed but instead a response to another force: "A wind seemed to blow his sleeve off his arm, and he replied to it, and saw Trampas pitch forward...A little smoke was rising from the pistol on the ground, and he looked at his own, and saw the smoke flowing upward out of it."[60] This distant activity, unwilled and unconscious, emphasizes the entrenchment of gender performativity; it is less a conscious production than a set of behaviors familiar through repetition.

After the shoot-out, the Virginian and Molly are married and settle down into a life of industry and profit:

> But the railroad came, and built a branch to that land of the Virginian's where the coal was. By that time he was an important man with a strong grip on many various enterprises, and able to give his wife all and more than she asked or desired. Sometimes she missed the Bear Creek days, when she and he had ridden together, and sometimes she declared that his work would kill him. But it does not seem to have done so. Their eldest boy rides the horse Monte; and, strictly between ourselves, I think his father is going to live a long while.[61]

This happy ending is often brought up in criticism as evidence of the novel's commitment to a national allegory that supports racial consolidation. Alexander Saxton argues that

> instead of pursuing the vanishing American wilderness, [the Virginian] will settle down under the auspices of his employer and patron on a homestead that contains not only an upper-class wife but coal deposits for the coming railroad. All this suggests a harmonious community in which the Virginian, having left lower-class origins behind him, may become one of ours.[62]

Moreover, Amy Kaplan argues that the Virginian, along with many other masculine heroes of the period, "is delineated by [his] rejection of feminization and racial otherness, but...is mobile and flexible enough to make itself at home anywhere in the world."[63] Following this line of criticism, Jane Kuenz finds that "*The Virginian* thus participates in a larger national project of reunification and reconciliation after the Civil War that in many ways forged 'unity' by simply ignoring anyone who might complicate that picture."[64]

These views of imperial white masculinity are valid interpretations, but they ignore the other possibilities in the text, namely, the utopian mobility implied in Kaplan's reading. Indeed, the novel's final marriage undermines its own allegory of national reconciliation. The Virginian and Molly are married, but "Monte the horse" is also involved in the relationship. Monte stands as a remainder that is not contained in institutional marriage but nonetheless proves central to the romance. The Virginian's relationship with Molly is mediated through riding, and Monte the horse functions as a crucial component to the composition of the couple. While the marriage does seem to function in part as a national allegory of class and racial consolidation, it may also involve a more expansive view of social belonging than the overt national allegory acknowledges. As the Virginian and Molly marry and produce offspring, in keeping with American imperialist ideology, their "eldest son" embraces Monte the horse, engaging in the same intimate relations that exceed marriage conventions as his father once did in the nostalgia-laden West.[65] As Cary Wolfe suggests, human relations with animals "link us to a larger repertoire and history of signification not specifically human and yet intimately so."[66] The Virginian's "eldest son" engages in intimate relationships with animals, just as his father and Western companions did, and just as Wister documents in his photographs of men and women accompanied by the ubiquitous horse or dog. These animals resonate as bearers of alternative intimacies and relations that exceed normative gender and sexual roles, though in the novel's closing this interspecies intimacy is contained by the marriage plot.

Expansive Kinship

A self-contained chapter toward the beginning of *The Virginian*, "Em'ly," illustrates the expansive network of social belonging so central to the novel's construction of the West. The story is about a hen who "came near being a rooster" and instead of laying eggs claims other eggs and animal young as her own, regardless of species.[67] Jane Tompkins reads this story as evidence of the novel's denigration of women: "Some hatred of the female puts forth its features in this episode, a hatred that seems directly related to feelings of solidarity and intimacy among men. It suggests that the paradise of heterosexual love the novel is headed toward is more of a dream than a reality."[68] The "paradise of heterosexual love" is indeed "a dream," secured by relations external to institutional marriage, exemplified by the presence of Monte the horse as mediator and companion to the happy couple. Rather than exposing "hatred of the female," though, the Em'ly story is a striking example of the expansive intimate relations that the novel repeatedly invokes.

In the chapter, Em'ly raises a litter of puppies and attempts to raise turkeys and bantams. After witnessing her child-rearing abilities, the Virginian begins to grow fond of the hen: "I'm regular getting stuck on Em'ly…Yu' needn't to laugh. Don't yu' see she's got sort o' human feelin's and desires? I always knowed hawses was like people, and my collie, of course."[69] The Virginian identifies with Em'ly's apparent humanity, and, in an attempt to please her, he gives her a real egg. When it hatches, Em'ly becomes frantic and dies. By wanting merely to raise young creatures, Em'ly ignores species distinctions and only perishes when natural reproduction seems to take place. The narrator characterizes the hen as "demented," "so civilized and so perverted."[70] However, this account differs substantially from the Virginian's own feelings. The Virginian buries her, claiming that "I have buried some citizens here and there…that I have respected less."[71] Closing the chapter, the Virginian comments that "she is just one o' them parables"; the hen's relationships across species lines resonate with a nostalgic view of the frontier, where non-normative relationships flourish.

While Owen Wister certainly advocated Social Darwinism and eugenics, his nostalgia for the frontier in *The Virginian* eulogizes the demise of alternate public forms—different concepts of gender roles, coupling, and maternity—that his politics would not otherwise have accommodated. In a September 15, 1893, journal entry concluding a trip West that allowed Wister to stop over at the World's Fair in Chicago, he remarks, "So our Western trip…began and ended at the same place, just like a work of Art."[72] This emphasis on aesthetic unity occurs as well in *The Virginian* through the genteel voice of the narrator, who filters non-normative relations through his own language or simply refuses to explicate conversations and gestures. Wister's fixation on producing a literary work about the frontier forces an adherence to certain genteel conventions. At the same time, however, the desire to depict a vanished world realistically entails the inclusion of expansive possibilities into Wister's prose. Guided by Wister's interest in formal unity and verisimilitude, *The Virginian* contains characters that are fashioned as aesthetic objects, and cowboy masculinity exceeds Wister's own genteel propriety. In Willa Cather's Nebraska novels, masculinity continues to exceed what seems proper to more conventional subjects.

CHAPTER 4

"I Like to Be Like a Man": Female Masculinity in Willa Cather's *O Pioneers!* and *My Ántonia*

As everyone knows, Nebraska is distinctly déclassé as a literary background; its very name throws the delicately tuned critic into a clammy shiver of embarrassment. Kansas is almost as unpromising. Colorado, on the contrary, is considered quite possible. Wyoming really has some class, of its own kind, like well-cut riding breeches. But a New York critic voiced a very general opinion when he said, "I simply don't care a damn what happens in Nebraska, no matter who writes about it."

—Willa Cather, *"My First Novels (There Were Two)"*

In her essay "My First Novels (There Were Two)," Willa Cather claims that *O Pioneers!* contains none of the usual trappings of the Western; it is "a slow-moving story, without 'action,' without 'humor,' without a 'hero.' "[1] The novel's "déclassé" Nebraskan setting is a space remarkably devoid of the romantic vision cast over the West by American writers. For Cather, Nebraska functions as an open literary frontier, one that is not "over-furnished," to borrow her phrase from "The Novel Démeublé."[2] Cather's novels, then, might seem to be the opposite of action-packed dime-novel Westerns, but Cather's "unfurnished" style as well as Deadwood Dick's construction around infinitely repeatable narrative conceits both use masculinity to simplify narrative form. That is, masculinity in dime novels and Cather's Nebraska novels facilitates the imagination of subjects and bodies removed from limiting narrative conventions. While Owen Wister's *The Virginian* positions masculine intimacy against social norms despite Wister's own emphasis on imperialist and domestic conventions, Willa Cather's

Nebraska novels employ their sparse setting to explicitly challenge the links between conventional manhood, social norms, and masculinity. Cather's open literary form revises both popular and literary treatments of the frontier, particularly by featuring masculine heroines in *O Pioneers!* and *My Ántonia*. The novels give pioneer women the freedom to "like to be like a man," in Ántonia Shimerda's words.[3]

Both *O Pioneers!* and *My Ántonia* depict Nebraska as a space where female masculinity prospers. In this frontier territory, the novels make a case for female masculinity as not merely a doomed imitation of the naturally masculine but as an authentic subject position. This dislocation of masculinity from the male body disrupts patriarchal entitlements to property and women and reworks marriage conventions and family relations. Masculinity, then, is a strategic performance in Cather's novels, one that requires a peculiar relation to time and space. The Nebraska novels offer an alternate history of masculinity on the frontier at once nostalgic for an idyllic past and pregnant with future promise. That promise of futurity, though, is complicated in the novels by the seeming stability of male dominance in heteronormative reproduction and the difficulty of imagining a future outside of those norms.

My reading of female masculinity in Cather's texts owes much to Judith Halberstam's theory of masculinity as a "multiplicity" in her books *Female Masculinity* and *In a Queer Time and Place*. According to Halberstam, masculinity should be read as a historical mode of performance in female as well as male bodies. Halberstam's insight is vital because gender theory has given masculinity too little attention; it has ignored the ways in which multiple masculinities might complicate the notion that masculinity is merely an extension of heteronormativity and patriarchy. For instance, in Cather studies, the quick equation between lesbianism and female masculinity fails to recognize masculinity as a broader historical construction that might not simply be a screen for an emergent women's community. As Halberstam writes, "by making female masculinity equivalent to lesbianism . . . or reading it as proto-lesbianism awaiting a coming community, we continue to hold female masculinity apart from the making of modern masculinity itself."[4] This subordination of female masculinity to lesbianism, and of gender to sexuality, distinguishes female masculinity from other forms of masculinity, particularly those embodied by males.

As Gayle Rubin argues in "Thinking Sex," it is crucial to think of gender and sexuality as bound together but also operating on different axes from one another. As Rubin claims, feminist analyses that focus on gender often oversimplify the shifting historical relations between gender and sexuality: "feminist thought simply lacks angles of vision which can fully encompass the social organization of sexuality."[5] This perspective offers important insight into how and why Cather scholarship misses out on female masculinity. Without an understanding of how gender and sexuality are disjoined from one another, it is all too easy to make the quick assumption that female masculinity equals a lesbian identification with the feminine. Yet, I will argue that, as Cather's work demonstrates, female masculinity seems to entail an identification with the masculine.

Owing much to Sharon O'Brien's biography, *Willa Cather: The Emerging Voice*, the critical debate surrounding Cather's life and work for over two decades has focused on gender and sexuality.[6] An oft-cited article by Blanche Gelfant that predates Sharon O'Brien's 1987 biography encapsulates the critical tradition in which Cather's masculine identifications are taken as evidence of an unspeakable femininity:

> Clearly, [Cather] identified writing with masculinity, though which of the two constituted her fundamental drive is a matter of psychological dynamics we can never really decide. Like Ántonia, she displayed strong masculine traits, though she loved also feminine frilleries and the art of cuisine. All accounts of her refer to her "masculine personality"— her mannish dress, her deep voice, her energetic stride; and even as a child she affected boyish clothes and cropped hair. Too numerous to document, such references are a running motif throughout the accounts of Mildred Bennett, Elizabeth Sargeant, and E.K. Brown. Their significance is complex and perhaps inescapable, but whatever else they mean, they surely demonstrate Cather's self-assertion: she would create her own role in life, and if being a woman meant sacrificing her art, then she would lead a private and inviolate life in defiance of convention.[7]

What stands out in this passage is not only its exemplarity in posing Cather's masculinity as a sacrifice of an already existing femininity but also the refusal to even entertain the idea that Cather's masculinity is anything but an impoverished—"private and inviolate"—opposite to femininity. In Gelfant's own account, Cather's masculinity manifests itself in ways that are not private but public, not inviolate but "energetic." Gelfant assumes in her article that "being a woman" is a necessarily vibrant position that Cather wishes to inhabit, and one that the writer who preferred to be called "Will" as an adolescent only detaches herself from because of its limitations for someone with literary ambitions.

The key problem with such analyses is the fact that masculinity is never taken seriously as a mode of identification or performance. Instead of positing femininity and womanhood as originary for Cather and her texts, and therefore casting masculinity as a socially necessary façade, Cather's texts feature masculine heroines that do not reject the feminine but instead engage in the production of masculinity apart from, rather than in opposition to, femininity. Only by acknowledging the importance of masculinity to Cather's work can one begin to place her within a history of masculinity that includes all subjects regardless of chromosomal sex. Cather's work, in turn, takes on new relevance as a modernist experiment in gendered self-fashioning that engages with and revises the heterogeneous cowboy masculinity central to modern American literature and culture.

In *Willa Cather: The Emerging Voice*, O'Brien describes the author's life narrative as a development from adolescent tomboy to a mature and essential "female experience," comprising femaleness, womanhood, and femininity.[8] Similarly, for O'Brien, the central character of *O Pioneers!*, Alexandra Bergson, "defies traditional conventions of womanhood, to be sure, but she is a woman nonetheless—not an imitation man, not a grown-up William Cather."[9] O'Brien alludes here to Cather's namesake, her grandfather William Cather, and also Cather's adopted tomboy name, "Will." This characterization of Cather's development bars treatment of female masculinity as anything but a developmental stage on the way to a proper femininity, a stage characterized by mimicry of patriarchs or naïve tomboyism. Rather than reading Alexandra Bergson as defying conventions of womanhood, yet "a woman nonetheless," then, we might more fruitfully read her as adopting conventions of masculinity to become masculine.[10] For Cather, gendered experience was shot through with social conventions that could be reworked and reformed to produce alternative structures of becoming and belonging.

Taking a nuanced approach to the problem of gender and sexuality, Eve Kosofsky Sedgwick strives to locate more complex lesbian identifications in Cather's texts and reads Cather's masculine and male characters in works such as the 1905 short story "Paul's Case" and the 1925 novel *The Professor's House* as interlocutors through which Cather articulates lesbian desire. As Sedgwick argues about "Paul's Case," "the mannish lesbian author's coming together with the effeminate boy on the ground of a certain distinctive position of gender liminality is also a move toward a minority gay identity whose more effectual cleavage, whose more determining separatism, would be that of homo/hetero*sexual* choice rather than that of male/female *gender*."[11] Sedgwick's insightful reading traces the connections and intersections between sexuality and gender as identity categories that are not conjoined but fluid, allowing Cather to voice lesbian desire through an effeminate boy. However, as Judith Butler and Christopher Nealon have argued, the attempt to locate lesbian desire within Cather's novels both oversimplifies the work that Cather's novels perform against social structures of kinship and patriarchal privilege and relies too heavily on anachronistic constructions of lesbian identity. As Butler claims in *Bodies That Matter*, "the postulation of an original 'truth' of lesbian sexuality which awaits its adequate historical representation presumes an ahistorical sexuality constituted and intact prior to the discourses by which it is represented."[12] Christopher Nealon builds on Butler's claim and reads Cather's uses of gender inversion and their relation to sexuality as "out of step with modernity," as resistant to modern forms of identity.[13]

In what follows, I will push Butler and Nealon's arguments further by claiming that Cather's use of masculinity does not mask an "unspeakable" yet authentic lesbian desire but instead constitutes a desiring subject in itself. Rather than an imitation of masculinity that must be read as a closeted version of some other authentic voice, Cather's heroines fashion themselves as masculine subjects and, as a consequence, seek to revise masculinity's role within culture. Masculinity provides a way for Cather to reimagine social relations and belonging; Cather's masculine productions create modes of social belonging that stand in stark contrast to patriarchal systems of property ownership and kinship and, in so doing, constitute a kind of immanent critique of dominant social structures. Furthermore, as Nealon remarks, "Cather is an interesting writer partly because of the acrobatics by which she avoids or dismisses what she does not want to write about."[14] By refusing dominance in a particularly masculine gesture of disavowal and separation, Cather's masculine heroines build their own social orders and subjectivities through reworkings of gender, the family, property, and temporality. For Cather's masculine heroines, reproductive futurity and its connections to traditional gender roles limits this reworking yet also lends self-fashioning an aesthetic dimension precisely because of its curious temporality.[15]

Bodies, Land, and Motion in *O Pioneers!*

In *O Pioneers!*, the first gesture toward a new concept of the subject occurs in the epigraph: the poem "Prairie Spring." The poem begins with a calm and dour description of the Nebraska landscape as "flat land / Rich and somber and always silent."[16] The landscape is further evoked through concrete objects coupled with simple adjectives, lending the scene a lucid materiality: "The growing wheat, the growing weeds, / The toiling horses, the tired men." This description of the "somber" prairie lasts nine lines, and then the poem abruptly shifts its focus with the line, "Against all this, Youth." Unlike the poem's first half, which locates activity in concrete and discrete objects such as "horses," "men," "roads," and "sky," the "Youth" of the poem's second half remains unhinged from a concrete object. "Youth" is abstract, but it nonetheless emerges "Against all this." Yet "Against," in this poem, does not signify oppositionality; "Youth" emerges "against" the backdrop of the somber prairie. "Youth" is immanent in the prairie. It comes into being from the "sullen" landscape yet, in its becoming, manifests qualities unlike those of its surroundings. This immanent "Youth" has an "insupportable sweetness," containing an ephemeral quality in "its fierce necessity / Its sharp desire." The poem closes with: "Out of the lips of silence, / Out of the earthly dusk." Here again, the repeated "Out of," like "Against," is ambivalent. "Youth" emerges in its "insupportable sweetness" from "the lips of silence" and "the earthy dusk" but is also expelled from the land. Like the "Prairie Spring" of the title, "Youth" is a process, a becoming rather than a being, and is therefore not stable but emerging "out of" and fading "out of" the prairie.

The curious movement of an abstract "Youth" produces a relation to time that contrasts with the stasis of the material objects in the first half of the poem. "Youth" is nostalgia and futurity, emerging immanently from a landscape that cannot support its "sharp desire" yet must give in to its "fierce necessity." This reorientation of time as a process of becoming is central to the workings of masculinity in *O Pioneers!*[17] In the stoic and disciplined Alexandra and in the fiery and romantic Emil, this distinct construction of time, as an erosive force against "supportable" or static life, structures masculinity as a process rather than an anchor for property and family. Inhabiting time, both Alexandra and Emil engage in processes of masculine self-fashioning that thrive on the fluctuation and contestation of stabilizing social conventions.

The novel's emphasis on instability and process contrasts with one of the dominant critical readings of American modernism, stemming from Walter Benn Michaels's *Our America*. Marilee Lindemann, for example, reads the novel as foregrounding "queer" bodies to ultimately endorse the normalization of the American citizen, placing *O Pioneers!* in line with the Nativist political project Michaels argues is constitutive of American modernism.[18] Lindemann's reading relies on a linkage between commerce and the body that gives meaning to the heroine Alexandra's masculinity within American culture: "Far from showing Cather's rejection of putatively 'masculine' values and cultural activities, Alexandra's triumph is the apotheosis of Progressive Era values of systemization and efficiency in matters of business and the body."[19] In contrast, I will argue that Alexandra does not recognize the connection between economic success and disciplinary codings of the body. By reformulating property relations, *O Pioneers!* refuses to entertain complicity with patriarchal property relations, the transformation of the body into another object in the marketplace, and the patriarchal and heteronormative logics that ideologically underwrite ownership.

Jonathan Goldberg has pointed out that *O Pioneers!* frequently foregrounds the "instability of gender identity" since "gender, in a word, is crossed from the start; desire even between those of different genders may be following a path that the term 'heterosexual' seems too limited to describe."[20] While Goldberg's supposition that the "heterosexual" does not even begin to describe what appear to be heterosexual relations in Cather's text is compelling, he, like Sedgwick, is too quick to dismiss masculinity and moves too easily from evidence of gender inversion to suppositions about sexual identity and desire. Goldberg's argument, which draws heavily on Sedgwick's reading of "Paul's Case," emphasizes the instability of sexuality and gender categories and their propensity to spin on separate axes in the novel. While this is true, this focus on the slippage in gender and sexual categories forces misrecognition of the strong masculine identifications in the novel. While any gender identification is unstable because it is produced through repetitive performance, the heroine Alexandra Bergson and her brother, the romantic Emil, develop a particular gendered understanding of time that reworks property and familial relations, a relation that does not so much "cross" already existing gender and sexuality nexuses as much as it produces an embodiment that stands against and apart from patriarchal property and family structures. More than just representing play between the poles of gender and sex, Cather's novels produce a mode of embodiment that is resolutely masculine.

O Pioneers! opens by highlighting the unstable bodies of its central characters, a trope common to the dime-novel Westerns discussed earlier. In the first chapter, siblings Alexandra and Emil Bergson are introduced as what Lindemann describes "disorderly" bodies.[21] The narrator begins with Emil, weeping over his cat that has scampered up a tree:

> On the sidewalk in front of one of the stores sat a little Swede boy, crying bitterly. He was about five years old. His black cloth coat was much too big for him and made him look like a little old man. His shrunken brown flannel dress had been washed many times and left a long stretch of stocking between the hem of his skirt and the tops of his clumsy, copper-toed shoes.[22]

Emil's dress crosses both gender and age identifications. He appears to be both an old man because of his coat and also a child in a dress. Moreover, the shrunken flannel dress and the narrator's attention to Emil's visible stockings lend him a hint of feminine coyness, as if he is a failed seductress in "clumsy shoes."[23] This coupling of youth and old age, fading masculinity and blossoming femininity, resists simple identification with either one gender or one age. Emil is both old and young, feminine and masculine.

Emil's cries are interrupted by his sister, Alexandra Bergson:

> His sister was a tall, strong girl, and she walked rapidly and resolutely, as if she knew exactly where she was going and what she was going to do next. She wore a man's long ulster (not as if it were an affliction, but as if it were very comfortable and belonged to her; carried it like a young soldier), and a round plush cap, tied down with a thick veil.[24]

Like Emil, Alexandra contains seemingly contradictory identifications in her dress and physical demeanor. She is masculine in her physical appearance and gait, as well as in her soldierly dress. However, this is contrasted with the "thick veil" that ties down her "plush cap." The veil, a sign of femininity and particularly of mourning or marriage, contrasts sharply with Alexandra's appearance as a "young soldier." Once again, as with Emil, the body signifies both youth and old age along with masculinity and femininity. Alexandra and Emil are figures in motion, figures that are in flux within narrative rather than securely watching events pass by.

The Nebraskan town that Alexandra and Emil live in is just as unstable as the young characters. The narrator goes on to remark upon Emil's usual timidity when in town: "He always felt shy and awkward here, and wanted to hide behind things for fear that someone might laugh at him. Just now, he was too unhappy to care who laughed."[25] The "town" here is a disciplinary structure, yet the members of the town, even the town's architecture, undermine the genteel stability implied by Emil's typical shyness. In the opening paragraph of the novel, even the domestic spaces encircling the small town of Hanover, Nebraska, are described as unstable and impermanent:

> The dwelling-houses were set about haphazardly on the tough prairie sod; some of them looked as if they had been moved in overnight, and others as if they were straying off by themselves, headed straight for the open plain. None of them had any appearance of permanence, and the howling wind blew under them as well as over them.[26]

Contrary to Owen Wister's depiction of settler domesticity as at least momentarily stabilizing the frontier, Cather's prairie is in flux. The domestic spaces surrounding the town are nomadic themselves while the town of Hanover is cowering, hoping to last, "huddled on the gray prairie."

Alexandra and Emil pull the narrative in different directions. *O Pioneers!* contains two romances, one passionate and youthful, one calm and weathered, in keeping with the novel's interest in folding the past and the future together, the aforementioned somber prairie and the passionate youth that emerges from it. The novel treats Alexandra's masculinity as an unproblematic position, and one that is quickly understood by those around her. After being introduced in her manly dress, Alexandra takes off her veil and places it on Emil's head, exposing her hair to the wandering gaze of "a shabby little traveling man" in town: "'My God, girl, what a head of hair!' he exclaimed, quite innocently and foolishly. She stabbed him with a glance of Amazonian fierceness and drew in her lower lip—most unnecessary severity."[27] Alexandra's severe look symbolically castrates the man, who "let his cigar fall to the sidewalk and went off weakly in the teeth of the wind to the saloon." He proceeds to the bar, where the narrator offers one final remark about him: "When a drummer had been knocking about in little drab towns and crawling across the wintry country in dirty smoking-cars, was he to be blamed if, when he chanced upon a fine human creature, he suddenly wished himself more of a man?" The narrator refers to Alexandra as a "human creature," avoiding a gendered noun, and the drummer's frustration at not being "more of a man" stems from his shock that Alexandra has an Amazonian strength about her.

Alexandra refuses to participate in the economy of the gaze typical of consumer culture, and this is emphasized in the next paragraph by Carl Linstrum, Alexandra's friend and future husband, who is in the drug store "turning over a portfolio of chromo 'studies' which the druggist sold to the Hanover women who did china-painting."[28] In contrast to the Amazonian Alexandra, Carl has a "delicate pallor" and a "mouth too sensitive for a boy's." While Carl looks at photographs marketed to women, Alexandra actively resists interpellation within that visual circuit by aggressively looking back at the shocked "shabby little traveling man." Alexandra's stoicism further distances her from the conventional vision of the emotional, domestic female. As the narrator remarks, "there was about Alexandra something of the impervious calm of the fatalist, always disconcerting to very young people, who cannot feel that the heart lives at all unless it is still at the mercy of storms; unless its strings can scream to the touch of pain."[29] This "impervious calm" is linked to Alexandra's refusal of a traditionally domestic role. After becoming a successful farmer, Alexandra still keeps an "uneven" home: "If you go up the hill and enter Alexandra's big house, you will find that it is curiously unfinished and uneven in comfort. One room is papered, carpeted, over-furnished; the next is almost bare."[30] The lack of consistent decoration hints, as the narrator goes on to claim, that "Alexandra's house is the big out-of-doors, and that it is in the soil that she expresses herself best."[31] In Alexandra's resistance to consumerism lies the key to her more general refusal to identify as a female.

Returning to Cather's aesthetic statement in "The Novel Démeublé," domesticity and consumerism are linked to popular entertainment, which Cather distinguishes from art:

> The novel manufactured to entertain great multitudes of people must be considered exactly like a cheap soap or a cheap perfume, or cheap furniture. Fine quality is a distinct disadvantage in articles made for great numbers of people who do not want quality but quantity, who do not want a thing that "wears," but who want change,—a succession of new things that are quickly threadbare and lightly thrown away.[32]

Resisting this proliferation of the "new," Cather suggests that art stands out because of "the inexplicable presence of the thing not named," a phrase that has been read, most persuasively by Judith Butler and Christopher Nealon, as an articulation of Cather's sexuality.[33] The "thing not named" emerges from art as a quality unhinged from what Cather paints as a feminine consumer culture, signified in the essay by mass-produced "Kewpie brides."[34] Alexandra's masculinity is then characterized and bolstered by her negative relation to consumer culture.[35] This negative relation is described by Christopher Nealon as directly related to sexuality:

> Cather's lesbianism, as it shapes her fiction, is to be understood as a resistance to certain modern pressures, such as the pressures of mass culture, which she uses, further, to outmaneuver another imperative placed on novelists, to create a heterosexually binding narrative by writing marriages and childbirth and inheritance into novels, no matter what their subject.[36]

Moreover, Alexandra's masculinity entails a productive vision of the future unbound by heteronormativity. This resistance to heteronormativity is not necessarily a lesbian viewpoint but one that, as Scott Herring argues, "releases [characters] from the imperatives of having a discernible—hence, controllable—middle-class sexual identity."[37] *O Pioneers!* uses masculinity as a way of critiquing heteronormativity, but female masculinity is not synonymous with lesbianism in the text. Neither gender and sexuality, nor desire and identification are yoked together in the novel, and this disconnect creates space for Cather's masculine heroines.

Later in the novel, the narrator again emphasizes Alexandra's disinterest in domestic furnishings:

> Alexandra had put herself in the hands of the Hanover furniture dealer, who had conscientiously done his best to make her dining-room look like his display window. She said frankly that she knew nothing about such things, and she was willing to be governed by the general conviction that the more useless and utterly unusable objects were, the greater their virtue as ornament.[38]

Alexandra refuses to acknowledge the usefulness of any domestic finery, and her stance on the "utterly unusable" décor is placed in stark opposition to the "furniture dealer," an analogue to the popular novelist who writes "over-furnished" novels.

While clearly not a domestic figure, Alexandra's temporal orientation further suggests that she is fashioned as an unstable, contingent subject. In the first section of the novel, Alexandra's dying father leaves the family farm under her control, for she has a remarkable acumen for business: "It was Alexandra who read the papers and followed the markets, and who learned by the mistakes of their neighbors. It was Alexandra who could always tell about what it had cost to fatten each steer, and who could guess the weight of a hog before it went on the scales."³⁹ Alexandra's financial savvy is the product of her ability to understand change over time. Her realist conception of how money accumulates differs significantly from her grandfather's, who, late in life, married "a Stockholm woman of questionable character" and "speculated, lost his own fortune and funds entrusted to him by poor seafaring men, and died disgraced, leaving his children nothing."⁴⁰ While her stoicism seems to distance Alexandra from her passionate, impulsive grandfather, "Alexandra, her father often said to himself, was like her grandfather, which was his way of saying she was intelligent."⁴¹ The dying father sees in Alexandra shades of the older Bergson "who had proved himself to be a man."⁴² Once again, temporal registers are muddied when the narrator describes Alexandra. She is "like her grandfather," yet the comparison with an older generation is also a relation to a speculative future. Her farming innovations embarrass her more conservative brothers. The first section of the novel concludes by casting Alexandra's ability to innovate and speculate as an affective relation to temporal flows: "Under the long shaggy ridges, she felt the future stirring."⁴³ But, like her grandfather, Alexandra's future does not entail leaving money behind for children. She resists her brother's patriarchal desire to place her property within the bounds of kinship and familial inheritance. By taking control of the family farm, Alexandra is able to create a new system of inheritance that bypasses patriarchy.

Over the course of the novel, there are two central moments that involve discussions of property and familial inheritance. On his deathbed, Alexandra's father John Bergson beckons her to him and explains that he wants her to run the family farm. In this dialogue, Alexandra's father separates his daughter out from her brothers, not because she is a woman but because her hands are "strong ones."⁴⁴ In the ensuing discussion, Alexandra imagines a collective "we" out of her father's emphasis on the divide between Alexandra, "you," and her brothers, "them":

> "Alexandra, you will have to do the best you can for your brothers. Everything will come on you."
> "I will do all I can, father."
> "Don't let them get discouraged and go off like Uncle Otto. I want them to keep the land."
> "We will, father. We will never lose the land."⁴⁵

This dialogue foregrounds the patriarchal structure that underpins John Bergson's understanding of property. While Alexandra will take on the burden of running the farm, John nonetheless "[wants] them to keep the land." Alexandra's shift, from "I will do all I can" to "We will," makes room for a collective grouping that falls outside the bounds of the patriarchal "them." Once the brothers arrive, John goes on to explain that "so long as there is one house there must be one head," once again giving authority to Alexandra. This demand is later undercut, however, when John appeals to his children's sense of familial belonging. After the brothers assent to their father's plan, the father questions them, "And you will be guided by your sister, boys, and be good brothers to her, and good sons to your mother?"[46] This reinstallation of kinship relations, casting Alexandra as a "sister" who must be protected by the "good" behavior of the men in the family, rests uneasily against Alexandra's new position as "head" of the family farm. The collective "we" that Alexandra speaks in conversation with her father is repeatedly undone by the reiteration of traditional family structures, which subordinate Alexandra to "them," her brothers.

The tension between Alexandra's masculine independence in economic matters and her subordination as "sister" in the family structure reaches its height years later, when her brothers, Lou and Oscar, approach her demanding that she relinquish control of the farm. The brothers approach her under the cover of public sentiment. Alexandra's fondness for Carl Linstrum, who has recently returned to Nebraska, raises suspicions among the townspeople. Many assume that the destitute Carl is merely after Alexandra's money. Oscar tells Alexandra, "people think you're getting taken in."[47] Lou and Oscar continue to appeal to public sentiment by claiming that Alexandra is making the family "look ridiculous" by engaging in a romance at such an old age. These claims of public sentiment stage a consolidation of the Bergson family, with Lou and Oscar as the patriarchal heads, against some phantom, moralistic public. Lou and Oscar then quickly shift the terms of their argument from what "people" might think to what Alexandra plans to do with "our property."[48]

The language of the family employed by Lou and Oscar leaves no room for Alexandra's alternative "we," that imagined collective outside of patriarchal familial bonds. Lou and Oscar's claims against Alexandra's ownership of her own farm shift into a general misogyny about women and business: "That's the woman of it; she tells you to put in a crop, she thinks she's put it in. It makes women conceited to meddle in business. I shouldn't think you'd want to remind us how hard you were on us, Alexandra, after the way you baby Emil."[49] This claim exposes the contradiction in the brothers'

understanding of the "family" as the basic unit of social organization. For Lou, the family is not a collective but a hierarchical structure. This ambivalence between the family as collective, as "we,"
and the family as a hierarchical structure wherein property "really
belongs to the men," underwrites patriarchal kinship relations and
property structures.[50] Within this context, the family is then both
a collective and a hierarchy, both a way of belonging and a way of
establishing dominance.

Alexandra's vision of family and its claims to land exceed patriarchal kinship. Indeed, she consistently expands her family throughout
the novel by employing Swedish immigrants as maids, taking in Ivar,
a local religious zealot, and, ultimately, marrying Carl Linstrum.
This is not to say that Alexandra is a maternal figure. Susan Rosowski
has argued that Cather's frontier novels "give women's fantasies to
the West and cast their domestic materials on an epic scale."[51] Mary
Paniccia Carden gives a similar reading, arguing that O Pioneers! is a
narrative of "female creativity."[52] But this reading overlooks masculinity as a governing mode of gender performance for the "female"
Alexandra. In conversation with Lou and Oscar, during their property dispute, for example, Alexandra figures herself as anything but
feminine: "Maybe I would never have been very soft, anyhow; but
I certainly didn't choose to be the kind of girl I was. If you take
even a vine and cut it back again and again, it grows hard, like a
tree."[53] Alexandra's "hardness" evokes the patriarchal hierarchical family tree, but is instead a vine, a growth without hierarchical
connotation.

While Alexandra's metaphorical "vine" differs from the patriarchal
family "tree," the "White Mulberry Tree," the novel's fourth part, is
an important moment for the critique of conventional romance. If
conventional gender roles conform to the temporal model of "reproductive futurity," a temporality that locates the future as the telos
of human exertion insofar as the natural product of heteronormative social relations is the production of children, then this section's
"tree"—like Alexandra's "vine"—also signifies a series of affective
relations that fall outside of the bounds of conventional heterosexual romance.[54] "The White Mulberry Tree" tells the story of Emil
Bergson and Marie Shabata's romance and its brutal ending when
Marie's husband, Frank, murders the two lovers as they lie underneath the chapter's eponymous tree. Emil and Marie's romance relies
on a blending of the human with the land as a way of associating
human relations with longer temporal rhythms.

Early in "The White Mulberry Tree" section, Marie serves as a fortuneteller at a village festival, playing with conventions of futurity:

> Marie was clever at fortune-telling, indulging in a light irony that amused the crowd. She told old Brunot, the miser, that he would lose all his money, marry a girl of sixteen, and live happily on a crust. Sholte, the fat Russian boy, who lived for his stomach, was to be disappointed in love, grow thin, and shoot himself from despondency. Amedee was to have twenty children, and nineteen of them were to be girls.[55]

Marie's fortune-telling undoes the life trajectories envisioned by all of the men whose fortunes she tells. While this provides amusement to the crowd at the festival, it also emphasizes the alternatives embedded in the novel's central characters. The fortune-telling produces multiple narrative possibilities for the characters in the text, including Emil and Marie's romance. At the festival, Emil offers one of his turquoise shirt studs for auction. After her husband refuses to bid on it, Marie tells Emil she regrets not having won the token. Emil's response is to produce multiple gifts: "Emil laughed shortly. 'People who want such little things ought surely to have them,' he said dryly. He thrust his hand into the pocket of his velvet trousers and brought out a handful of uncut turquoises, as big as marbles. Leaning over the table, he dropped them into her lap."[56] This multiplication of desire carries a potential for new and exciting imaginings of the future, signified by Emil's supposition after giving them to Marie, "you want me to go away and let you play with them?" Immediately after this moment of playful flirtation, Emil and Marie kiss for the first time. The kiss doubles both Emil and Marie:

> Before she knew what she was doing, she had committed herself to that kiss that was at once a boy's and a man's, as timid as it was tender; so like Emil and so unlike any one else in the world. Not until it was over did she realize what it meant. And Emil, who so often imagined the shock of this first kiss, was surprised at its gentleness and naturalness. It was like a sigh which they had breathed together; almost sorrowful, as if each were afraid of wakening something in the other.[57]

The kiss triggers multiple responses: timidity, imagination, pleasure, fear, and relief. This multiplicity, like the handful of turquoise in the earlier passage, plays on future possibilities, just as Marie's fortune-telling envisions ironic, but nonetheless possible, futures for men who have planned otherwise.

Emil and Marie's youthful affair stands in stark contrast to Alexandra's "impervious calm of the fatalist."[58] While Alexandra combines nostalgia and speculation, Emil's performative masculinity—emphasized by his velvet Mexican costume—and Marie's doll-like body promise an alternative possibility for the young that exists only as a prism, projecting multiple trajectories. This prismatic possibility is figured by two static images in the text. The first is Emil and Alexandra's imaginary duck, which they both imagine "swimming and diving all by herself in the sunlight, a kind of enchanted bird that did not know age or change."[59] A parallel image is articulated through Marie, who, the narrator claims,

> wanted to live and dream—a hundred years, forever! As long as this sweetness welled up in her heart, as long as her breast could hold this treasure of pain! She felt as the pond must feel when it held the moon like that; when it encircled and swelled with that image of gold.[60]

Emil's duck and Marie's moon-imprinted pond both define a mode of being that crystallizes a multiplicity of activities into a dream-like vision. The very mobility of the images—the duck's "swimming and diving" and the pond's "encircling and swelling"—emphasizes their impermanence and instability. Emil and Marie's romance functions in the same way. Emil and Marie have a moment of happiness together, and that moment results in their deaths. Even after Frank has shot them, the scene underneath the Mulberry tree projects the desire for possibility and liberation from the constraints of marriage, which render Emil and Marie's romance untenable and disastrous. After describing the lovers' bodies, embracing one another in death, the narrator goes on:

> But the stained, slippery grass, the darkened mulberries, told only half the story. Above Marie and Emil, two white butterflies from Frank's alfalfa-field were fluttering in and out among the interlacing shadows; diving and soaring, now close together, now far apart; and in the long grass by the fence the last wild roses of the year opened their pink hearts to die.[61]

This flourish resonates with the imagery of "Prairie Spring," the novel's epigraph. Animals and flowers that grow on Frank's farm, the farm owned by the very man that destroys Emil and Marie's romance, symbolize the unruliness of the natural world and, by extension, the young lovers who identify with its wildness. While the novel projects the possibilities of romance that moves outside marriage, the ultimately tragic end of "Youth" foreshadows Emil and Marie's fate. Passion and youthful romance give way to the calm masculinity embodied in Alexandra.

Alexandra does have a recurrent dream that connects her otherwise stoic life to Emil's passionate endeavors. The first description of the dream follows from a discussion of how "most of Alexandra's happy memories were...impersonal...She had never been in love, and she had never indulged in sentimental reveries. Even as a girl she had looked upon men as work-fellows."[62] This claim, that "even as a girl" Alexandra had had no erotic relation to men, reiterates, once again, her distance from heteronormativity. The dream arrives in times of relaxation, in rare moments of leisure:

> Sometimes, as she lay thus luxuriously idle, her eyes closed, she used to have an illusion of being lifted up bodily and carried lightly by someone very strong. It was a man, certainly, who carried her, but he was like no man she knew; he was much larger and stronger and swifter, and he carried her as easily as if she were a sheaf of wheat. She never saw him, but, with eyes closed, she could feel that he was yellow like the sunlight, and there was the smell of ripe cornfields about him.[63]

The man in her dream is "like no man she knew," a mysterious personage who is marked by strength, elegance, and speed, traits not yoked here to a visible body. Alexandra's dream is of qualities without a man instead of a man without qualities. The figure in the dream is ideally masculine, just as Alexandra is masculine, without being completely "like a man." The dream figure's actions alone convince Alexandra that he is "certainly" masculine, without recourse to that most basic function of gender identification, seeing the body. Alexandra knows the figure is masculine without opening her eyes, casting gender as a matter of performance rather than possession. This ideal masculine figure has far more in common with a disciplined dancer than a domineering husband.

Melissa Ryan argues that the dream can be read as an appearance of "the symbolic Indian."[64] The dream figure certainly resonates with tropes and images associated with Native American cultures, notably the smell of corn and his proximity to nature. Alexandra's dream also recalls a long-standing tradition of homosocial escape narratives that center on the white man's renewal through exposure to the primitive.[65] In this sense, the dream of the "golden man" places Alexandra within a long tradition of homosocial desire for the primitive as a means of masculine development. As a marker of maturation, then, Alexandra has a final dream of the primitive homosocial before she marries:

> As she lay with her eyes closed, she had again, more vividly than for many years, the old illusion of her girlhood, of being carried lightly by some one very strong. He was with her a long while this time, and carried her very far, and in his arms she felt free from pain. When he laid her down on her bed again, she opened her eyes and, for the first time in her life, she saw him, saw him clearly, though the room was dark, and his face was covered. He was standing in the doorway of her room. His white cloak was thrown over his face, and his head was bent a little forward. His shoulders seemed as strong as the foundations of the world. His right arm, bared from the elbow, was dark and gleaming, like bronze, and she knew at once that it was the arm of the mightiest of all lovers. She knew at last for whom it was she had waited, and where he would carry her. That, she told herself, was very well. Then she went to sleep.[66]

This premonition of where the "mightiest of all lovers" "would carry her" is entertained and then refused. As her homosocial fantasy of escape blurs into domination by a stronger force, Alexandra chooses rugged independence. When Carl returns to Alexandra, she admits the dream and her rejection of it. Instead of submission to a dominant male, Alexandra chooses to marry a friend. As she explains to Carl, "I think we shall be very happy. I think when friends marry, they are safe. We don't suffer like—those young ones."[67] By marrying Carl, Alexandra undoes the patriarchal demands that marriage be reproductive and require the submission of the female to male dominance.

One of Alexandra's characteristically masculine features is that she does not submit to conventional gender roles, and by doing so places herself within her own trajectory of the past and the future. Her marriage to Carl reinforces this creative reworking of gender and time. In fact, Alexandra refuses one of the basic tents of kinship relations, the inheritance of property:

> "Suppose I do will my land to [my brothers'] children, what difference will that make? The land belongs to the future, Carl; that's the way it seems to me. How many of the names on the country clerk's plat will be there in fifty years? I might as well try to will the sunset over there

to my brothers' children. We come and go, but the land is always here. And the people who love it and understand it are the people who own it—for a little while."[68]

It is hard not to read this passage as mystificatory; Alexandra refuses to acknowledge the role of property and exchanges property for an egalitarian "love" of the land. But, her recognition that those who love the land might only "own it—for a little while" underscores the mobility inherent in Alexandra's understanding of property. She does not view property as a stable object, something that can be handed down. Through this vision of a prehistoric and future commons, she resists the demand her brothers make upon her, to treat property as an object to be inherited through kinship relations.

Moreover, the seeming contradiction between land that is "always here" yet "belongs to the future" sits well with Alexandra's own character, both simultaneously "like her grandfather" and also "like a child." The conjunction of the young and the old undoes gendered constructions of time that emphasize preservation, stability, and legible bloodlines. Through masculinity, Alexandra creates her own public, her own space, and her own time. The novel ends with this very creation and hints at the way in which it will be realized in the future: "Fortunate country, that is one day to receive hearts like Alexandra's into its bosom, to give them out again in the yellow wheat, in the rustling corn, in the shining eyes of youth!"[69] Alexandra's vision of the future contains multiple possibilities. Ultimately, she becomes the "golden man" in her dream, a promise of escape from both domesticity and patriarchy.

Fraternity in *My Ántonia*

While *O Pioneers!* is often treated as Cather's emergence as an artist, the moment in which she found her voice and her region, *My Ántonia* is treated as a masterpiece, as the pinnacle of Cather's Nebraskan imagination. Interestingly, this text often proves even more problematic for feminist readings than *O Pioneers!* because of its narrative form. The novel begins with a complex introduction that prefaces the main text of the novel as written by a narrator, Jim Burden, distinct from the female narrator of the introduction. The narrator of the introduction— a writer who identifies herself as a woman in the 1918 edition and is often considered an autobiographical character —runs into Jim Burden, an old friend from Nebraska. They strike up a conversation based on a shared affiliation: "We agreed that no one who had not grown up in a little prairie town could know anything about it. It was a kind of freemasonry, we said."[70] This claim, that the narrator and Jim are members of the same fraternity, casts them as masculine equals. As Michael Kimmel charts in *Manhood in America,* at the turn of the century "fraternal orders boasted a membership of 5.5 million American men out of a total adult male population of about nineteen million."[71] Throughout the first decades of the twentieth century, fraternal orders provided "a domestic sanctuary outside of the home" along with an "unfeminized church, devoid of clucking mother hens and effete ministers."[72] The fraternity of which the narrator and Jim Burden find themselves a part serves these functions as well, establishing this "freemasonry" as a disciplined grouping of masculine members united by a secret understanding of life on the prairie.

Jim has a youthfulness about him that belies his age: "Jim is still able to lose himself in those big Western dreams. Though he is over forty now, he meets new people and new enterprises with the impulsiveness by which his boyhood friends remember him."[73] This youthfulness and indulgence in dreams make Jim a sympathetic figure and complicate his place as a masculine narrator who imposes narrative possession—the "My" of the title—on a female body. This imposition of ownership on the text creates unease for critic Sharon O'Brien, who wonders "to what extent might his urge to tell Ántonia's story betray a need to control the feminine wealth and power."[74] Instead of reading the "My" as a patriarchal imposition, I argue that the introduction represents Jim's story about Ántonia as the construction of an alternative history of masculinity. The narrator asks Jim to write about Ántonia, and Jim defers, saying, "Of course . . . I should have to do it in a direct way, and say a great deal about myself. It's through myself that I knew and felt her, and I've had no practice in any other forms of presentation."[75] To Jim's trepidation, the narrator replies, "I told him that how he knew her and felt her was exactly what I most wanted to know about Ántonia. He had had opportunities that I, as a little girl who watched her come and go, did not."[76] The narrator's desire for Jim's narrative signifies a desire for an historical account of female masculinity on the frontier, filtered through the eyes of the youthful-minded Jim Burden, who still holds onto his childish sense of Western adventure. Because of this youthfulness, Jim's narrative promises to give the narrator "what I most wanted to know about Ántonia," how she came to signify for both Jim and the narrator the qualities that constitutes the fraternity, "a kind of freemasonry," of masculinity in the West. The novel's introduction seems to set up a triangulation of Ántonia through Jim's text and the narrator's readership. However, this triangulation, which entails an exchange of Ántonia as text between members of a fraternity, is undone by Jim's narrative and the consistent characterization of Ántonia as masculine. Rather than being an object of exchange, Ántonia is a member of the "freemasonry" envisioned and longed for by Jim Burden and the narrator.

In her treatment of Cather's use of "masculine names," Judith Butler provides a compelling reading of *My Ántonia*'s introduction. Butler focuses on Cather's strategy for voicing the narrative through Jim Burden:

> Jim's title [*My Ántonia*] thus converges with Cather's, and the repetition displaces the act by which Jim appeared to have supplanted the narrator in the text. We know that this is, after all, Cather's text, which implies that she is perhaps the anonymous one who dictates what Jim narrates. Figured as an "impressionable" reader, an impressionability which recalls an idealized feminine reader, the one who receives and dictates the text written by a man, Cather first dissimulates through this feminine convention, then disappears in order to finally "possess" the text that she appears to give away.[77]

Butler's reading is ingenious in describing how disavowal produces a stronger mode of avowal and "possession," but it defers too quickly to equating the binary of writer/reader with masculine/feminine. While it is common to think of the reader, in the abstract, as feminine, applying this conceit to *My Ántonia* ignores the claim made early on in the introduction that the narrator and Jim are both members of a fraternal order, effectively subverting this feminine identification. Jim's narrative creates a masculine discursive space. As such, *My Ántonia* claims both reading and writing as masculine practices.

Significantly, the fraternal public envisioned by the text does not rely on the exchange of Ántonia as an object. In fact, Ántonia is repeatedly and consistently figured in the novel as masculine, as constitutive of, as well as a member of, the introduction's fraternal order. As she states in the first section of the text, "I like to be like a man."[78] This phrasing blends two psychoanalytic operations that constitute "normal" gender and sexual identity: desire and identification. One desires what one does not identify with in heteronormative culture. That is, one desires the gender different from one's own, while identifying with the gender that one does not desire. As Judith Butler argues in "Melancholy Gender/Refused Identification," this structure inscribes prohibitions of both identification and desire at the core of the subject in heteronormative culture.[79] However, Ántonia both desires, "I like," and identifies with, "to be like," masculinity, casting masculinity as a gender that is not possessed by an essentially gendered body but an external and ideal mode of performance that one nonetheless identifies with. For Ántonia, masculinity is an accomplishment. Masculinity is constantly renewed as both desire and identification, and Ántonia's claim, "I like to be like a man," emphasizes not the aberrance of her masculinity but the way in which her masculinity is more truthful, because she is more aware of masculinity as a gender, than an identification that is constituted by a barred desire.

Along with Ántonia, Jim Burden's narrative features other masculine figures. The hired hands Jake and Otto figure in the novel as masculine templates, yet their masculinity, like Alexandra's in *O Pioneers!*, relies not on patriarchal standards of private property and familial hierarchy but instead on imagination and fantasy. As Jim notices,

> As I remember them, what unprotected faces they were; their very roughness and violence made them defenseless. These boys had no practiced manner behind which they could retreat and hold people at a distance. They had only their hard fists to batter at the world with. Otto was already one of those drifting, case-hardened laborers who never marry or have children of their own. Yet he was so fond of children!"[80]

The hired hands' masculinity relies on a set of contradictory features, violence and defenselessness. Jake and Otto's masculinity is the product of improvisation, just as, ultimately, Ántonia's own masculinity fuses together remembrance, reproduction, and narration.

As it details Jim and Ántonia's coming of age, *My Ántonia* fittingly concludes with the real production of subjects, unlike Alexandra's vision of the persistence of the land in *O Pioneers!* If *O Pioneers!* focuses on the solace that the land gives to Alexandra and her community in an increasingly patriarchal and rigorously hierarchical public, then *My Ántonia* deals with the possibilities of producing an alternative lineage in the West that allows anyone, male or female, to "be like a man" without entering into patriarchy. *My Ántonia* shifts the vision of an alternative to the normative order from the abstract to a social bond grounded in everyday life. Indeed, even Jim Burden himself has trouble articulating Ántonia's social position without relying on standard kinship relations. When he meets her upon his return to Nebraska, Jim asserts,

> Do you know, Ántonia, since I've been away, I think of you more often than of anyone else in this part of the world. I'd have liked to have you for a sweetheart, or a wife, or my mother or my sister—anything that a woman can be to a man. The idea of you is part of my mind; you influence my likes and dislikes, all my tastes, hundreds of times when I don't realize it. You really are a part of me.[81]

Jim struggles with his desire for Ántonia to become intelligible as a woman, any kind of woman, in a kinship relation of some sort. Rather than grant him this intelligibility, though, Ántonia responds by speaking of "old times" and the future, when her child is "old enough" to be told about their unique childhood in Nebraska. While Jim wants to place Ántonia in a kinship economy, to put her firmly in some relation to him, Ántonia thinks only of narratives that fold time onto itself, depicting relations not in stable connections but in fluid stories. However, departing from the static and nonreproductive social world this meshing of time entails in *O Pioneers!*, Ántonia has children. The novel contains a vision of the future that is not a repetition of the past or a replication of the present but a continuation of a social order that, as becomes clear in the novel's final section, values fluidity over stability.

In the final section of the novel, entitled "Cuzak's Boys," Jim reevaluates his earlier desire to be in some kinship relation to Ántonia by realizing that kinship itself is unstable on Ántonia's family farm. When Jim finds Ántonia, he discovers that she still has a masculine figure: "Ántonia came in and stood before me; a stalwart, brown woman, flat-chested, her curly brown hair a little grizzled."[82] Despite her age, Jim observes that "the changes grew less apparent to me, her identity stronger. She was there, in this full vigor of her personality, battered but not diminished, looking at me, speaking to me in the husky, breathy voice I remembered so well."[83] Her children look to her "for stories and entertainment as we used to do," her husband provides the domestic "corrective" to her masculine "impulse," and, moreover, Cuzak, her husband, is "the instrument of Ántonia's special mission" to remake the prairies and their population.[84] This repeated figuration of Ántonia as masculine is complicated by the metaphor used to describe her: "She was a rich mine of life, like the founders of early races."[85] While the "mine" certainly has feminine connotations, "founders" does not.

Ántonia's body is metaphorized here not as feminine, but as productive. These two modes of describing Ántonia, as a "mine of life" and a "founder," cast her as a multiply gendered figure. Opposed to the conventional notion of the "founder" as, for example, the base upon which descendents build, Ántonia is a foundation that is also a mine, a construction that offers an entry point for further exploration and elaboration.

The expansive family surrounding Ántonia is not limited to children. She also maintains a strong connection to the land, just like Alexandra in *O Pioneers!*. As she remarks to Jim about her trees, "'I love them as if they were people,' she said, rubbing her hand over the bark. 'There wasn't a tree here when we first came. We planted every one, and used to carry water for them, too—after we'd been working in the fields all day…They were on my mind like children.'"[86] Caring for trees as if they were children, as if they were subjects, once again challenges the stable "family tree" of heteronormative kinship. Ántonia is not interested in building one "family tree" but instead grows trees that she includes in her family. This inversion of "tree" into a member of a larger family rather than a consolidated picture of a family's hierarchical structure further signifies the ways in which Ántonia's understanding of affective relations disregards, even playfully, conventional systems of belonging.

Ántonia's family then actively builds its own history and expands outside of the nuclear family. After having dinner with Ántonia and her family, they sit down to look over Ántonia's photographs:

> As Ántonia turned over the pictures, the young Cuzaks stood behind her chair, looking over her shoulder with interested faces. Nina and Jan, after trying to see round the taller ones, quietly brought a chair, climbed upon it, and stood close together, looking. The little boy forgot his shyness and grinned delightedly when familiar faces came into view. In the group about Ántonia I was conscious of a kind of physical harmony. They leaned this way and that, and were not afraid to touch each other. They contemplated the photographs with pleased recognition; looked at some admiringly, as if these characters in their mother's girlhood had been remarkable people. The little children, who could not speak English, murmured comments to each other in their rich old language.[87]

This moment of exhibition fuses Ántonia's family together through expansive relations to others. The children even speak a different language, ripe with "rich" descriptions for these novel personal relations.

This type of history making, creating a collective "physical harmony," is what Cather's vision of masculinity aims to produce. This unorthodox family can be juxtaposed to Carl Linstrum's dissatisfaction in *O Pioneers!* with his career as an engraver. As he remarks to Alexandra after returning to Nebraska, "I've been away engraving other men's pictures, and you've stayed at home and made your own."[88] The photographs in *My Ántonia* have a more democratic possibility for producing modes of social belonging than, for example, the engravings that Carl Linstrum is fascinated by in *O Pioneers!* Ántonia's family history figures her as the centerpiece of the family, the head of the family, for she narrates her own history through connections to photographs, building a family through heterogeneous intimate relations.

The very title of this final section, "Cuzak's Boys," defers to the patronym in a way that undermines Ántonia's centrality. *My Ántonia* does not stage a reimagination of the patriarchal family as much as it places that conventional family within a different context. *O Pioneers!*, too, struggles to imagine a future outside of patriarchal entitlement, ultimately dissolving Alexandra Bergson into the land itself. The novels struggle with the problem of imagining a future outside of heteronormativity and patriarchal kinship relations, yet in *My Ántonia*'s conclusion, the photographic archive itself emerges as a possible device for the continuation of modernist masculinity, a brand of masculinity entrapped by and uneasy within gender conventions.

The novel's closing emphasizes the way in which Ántonia provides a model of masculinity for Jim Burden. During his visit to Ántonia, Jim

> had the sense of coming home to myself, and of having found out what little circle man's experience is. For Ántonia and for me, this had been the road of Destiny; had taken us to those early accidents of fortune which predetermine for us all that we can ever be. Now I understood that the same road was to bring us together again. Whatever we had missed, we possessed together the precious, the incommunicable past.[89]

My Ántonia documents this "incommunicable past," and the novel stands as a record of an unruly fraternity. While *O Pioneers!* ends with the promising persistence of Alexandra's masculinity through "Youth," *My Ántonia* is a history of female masculinity on the frontier, a record—like Ántonia's box of photographs—of human relations that exceed normative gender roles. In her frontier novels,

Willa Cather communicates an "incommunicable past" by blurring time, gender, property, and family in ways that create a masculinity unhinged from the constraints of the normal. While Cather associates masculinity with the natural world in her Nebraska novels, Hemingway casts masculinity as an artifice, one that disciplines the modernist body.

CHAPTER 5

A Discipline of Sentiments: Masculinity in Ernest Hemingway's *Death in the Afternoon*

Style, the utopia of those with almost no place to go.

—D. A. Miller, *Jane Austen, or the Secret of Style*

In the epigraph, D. A. Miller elegantly posits style as a refuge for "the unheterosexual" and "the spinster" within Jane Austen's novels.[1] For Miller, style is a way of articulating difference while remaining beyond the logic of normativity. This seems like an unlikely epigraph to a chapter on Ernest Hemingway's masculinity, which appears at first glance to be anything but the style of someone "with almost no place to go." Yet, it will be my contention here that Hemingway's masculine style does in fact push masculinity beyond socially recognizable embodiment, particularly by casting ideal masculinity as the end result of fashioning the self into an aesthetic object. Hemingway's stylized masculinity strives to turn subjectivity into a pure surface, giving the disruptive masculine bodies in dime-novel Westerns a central position within modernist aesthetics. While Cather's masculine heroines ultimately dissolve into nature or submerge within patriarchal norms, Hemingway's prose attempts to transform masculinity into a style that foregoes social norms entirely by becoming an aesthetic object.[2]

Hemingway's stylized voice became the high literary style of a robust masculinity, in no small part due to the hefty marketing apparatus that popularized his persona.[3] Hemingway has often been accused of being too masculine. To borrow Cary Wolfe's succinct gloss, Hemingway exhibited "a self-commodifying and often desperate chest thumping," for which he became exceptionally well known.[4] Hemingway's celebrity persona still holds a great deal of sway over how he is read. The vast majority of scholarly volumes that deal with Hemingway use his literary works as evidence of the author's psychological hang-ups, repressions, and sublimations, and since the 1950s, scholars have sought to diagnose Hemingway's masculinism as latent homosexuality, fetishism, masochism, or evidence of an unresolved oedipal complex.[5] Hemingway's literary ambitions are often conceived of as at odds with the celebrity persona developed in tandem with them, and this purported disconnect provides an underlying schism readymade for psychoanalytic interpretations of Hemingway's work. What this view often misses is the centrality of the marketplace to modernist literature and the ways in which the perceived disconnect between popular success and literary prestige was manufactured as a way of endowing modernist literature with cultural capital. In fact, modernist aesthetics rely on the workings of celebrity to produce the very effect of artistic autonomy required of the modernist literary work. The celebrity writer exists in a rarefied space, distinct from everyday life, and by extension, the literary productions of that celebrity figure also deserve consumption as unique, autonomous works of art. In this sense, the celebrity persona of a modernist writer is just as much an aesthetic work as his or her novels, poems, or plays. By folding self into aesthetics, Hemingway's prose positions the subject in the "no place to go" that, for Miller, allows for the production of style. That is to say, celebrity might be less of a mask or burden under which the "real" Hemingway struggled but a corollary to his aesthetic project.

Nowhere is Hemingway's project of masculine self-fashioning more evident than in his long, multigenre work *Death in the Afternoon.* On the surface a book about bullfighting, *Death in the Afternoon* contains a blueprint for the transformation of masculinity into style and vice versa. Unlike the texts discussed in previous chapters, *Death in the Afternoon* is not set in the American West but in Europe, yet despite this different locale, Hemingway's masculinity is bound to the traditions of the American West.[6] Like "Stetson" in T. S. Eliot's *The Waste Land*, Hemingway transposes the self-fashioning that emerges in late nineteenth- and twentieth-century representations of the American West onto Europe, especially Spain. Like Alexandra in Willa Cather's *O Pioneers!*, living in the vast plains of Nebraska, Hemingway's "lost generation" figures struggle to fashion masculinities that produce possibilities in, on the one hand, a society built on "old-world" patriarchal principles, and, on the other, a world homogenized by industrialization. Thus in keeping with my analysis of Western masculinity, instead of reading Hemingway's works as evidence of the writer's conflicted psychology, I attempt to uncover how the unruly masculinity developed in writing about the American West provided Hemingway with a distinctly modernist way of fashioning the self.[7]

HEMINGWAY'S MASCULINE FASHIONS

In Malcolm Cowley's *Exile's Return,* his memoir about life as an expatriate in 1920s Paris, Hemingway becomes a shorthand for the fashion, behaviors, and passions of the period. Cowley's first paragraph emphasizes the influence Hemingway had on a generation of young Americans:

> This book is the story to 1930 of what used to be called the lost generation of American writers. It was Gertrude Stein who first applied the phrase to them. "You are all a lost generation," she said to Ernest Hemingway, and Hemingway used the remark as an inscription for his first novel. It was a good novel and became a craze—young men tried to get as imperturbably drunk as the hero, young women of good families took a succession of lovers in the same heartbroken fashion as the heroine, they all talked like Hemingway characters and the name was fixed.[8]

This passage synthesizes two different understandings of culture—that of consumer culture, the Hemingway style as a "craze" along the lines of the Hula Hoop, the Pet Rock, and the Tickle-Me-Elmo, and that of literary, high culture, stemming from Hemingway's mentor, the avant-garde writer Gertrude Stein, and the use of the "Lost Generation" quote as the epigraph to *The Sun Also Rises.* The cultural impact of Hemingway's first novel then blurs the often assumed distance between high art, which values history, tradition, and posterity, and mass culture, which cycles through fads quickly and masks the fact that the latest "craze" is merely one more entry in a long, often uninspired tradition. As Cowley correctly suggests, Hemingway's style offers both high literary status—he wrote difficult texts that merit heavy-duty analysis—and celebrity allure—Hemingway and his characters can be and were imitated in dress, speech, and appetite. This borrowing of the "Hemingway style" parallels Hemingway's own borrowing of Gertrude Stein's style, and this cycle of borrowed, cribbed fashions begins to gesture to the ways in which "authenticity," so often used to discuss Hemingway's style in psychoanalytic and biographical criticism, fails to account for the circulation of style as an impersonal object.

Gertrude Stein also casts Hemingway's style as something that is less authentic than borrowed, and therefore less personal than impersonally aesthetic. In *The Autobiography of Alice B. Toklas*, Gertrude Stein spends a good number of pages describing her relationship with Hemingway. Stein's recurring comment, in her fashion phrased as both a friendly, hopeful suggestion and barbed criticism, is that Hemingway should, but probably never will, write about himself. In this passage, writing from the perspective of Alice B. Toklas, Stein summarizes a conversation with novelist Sherwood Anderson about Hemingway:

> And then they both agreed that they have a weakness for Hemingway because he is such a good pupil…it is so flattering to have a pupil who does it without understanding it, in other words he takes training and anybody who takes training is a favorite pupil…And that is Hemingway, he looks like a modern and he smells of museums. But what a story of the real Hem, and one he should tell himself but alas he never will. After all, as he himself once murmured, there is the career, the career.[9]

For Stein, the master of impersonal modernist prose, an authentic memoir is an unusual genre to hope for. Even her own *Autobiography* is written through the eyes of another, an act of both appropriation and tremendous intimacy. Along with poking fun at the writer's obvious use of his own biography in his fiction, Stein's wish for a confession points to Hemingway's own imitative style, his borrowed masculinity, his cribbed fashions, and the impossibility of ever disclosing some "real Hem."[10] The mixture of modern appearance and the "smells of museums" casts Hemingway as less a modernist innovator than a writer who imitates what he sees. Stein's characterization, while certainly critical, does indeed accurately portray the way in which Hemingway synthesizes literary forms, combining journalistic brevity and Stein's avant-garde prose with melodrama and the operatic bullfight, to construct a masculine literary style. This pastiche of style produces a masculinity that avoids psychology and instead constitutes itself through repetition and corporeality.

Masculinity is key to Hemingway's writings. However, masculinity is neither a natural way of acting in the world, nor is it the outgrowth of anatomical maleness. This is often made explicit in Hemingway's texts, which frequently feature wounded, incomplete heroes who

struggle to cobble together their own masculine style.[11] The disconnect between masculinity and male anatomy is perhaps most blatantly
demonstrated in *The Sun Also Rises*. The novel's narrator, Jake Barnes,
has suffered an injury to the groin in World War I. According to an
Italian officer, he has "given more than his life," a statement that
values sex—as both anatomy and act—over life itself, as if not having
genitals robs life of its own liveliness, its style, its pleasures.[12] In a
passage where Jake describes his apartment in Paris, one realizes that
visual confirmation of his wound frames his everyday life:

> Undressing, I looked at myself in the mirror of the big armoire beside
> the bed. That was a typically French way to furnish a room. Practical,
> too, I suppose. Of all the ways to be wounded. I suppose it was funny.
> I put on my pajamas and got into bed.[13]

The "practical" mirror beside the bed confirms Jake's lack of maleness, yet this reflective moment does not rob Jake of his masculinity.
Instead, this removal of the anatomical signifier, the "funny" disjuncture of sex—male/female—from gender—masculine/feminine—
makes the reader even more aware of Jake's masculinity. The central
figure in *The Sun Also Rises* embodies the mixture of hard-boiled
terseness with romantic longing so emblematic of Hemingway's
narrative style, and he does so through performance, by acting and
narrating in a certain style rather than having a certain anatomical
feature.

In *Death in the Afternoon*, Ernest Hemingway offers an extended
meditation on masculine self-fashioning that not only offers a kind
of guide for emotional discipline but also links masculine style to
modernist aesthetics. For Hemingway, masculinity is a style of acting
in the world that connects art to everyday life. *Death in the Afternoon*
is an exposition of masculinity as a discipline, as a way of controlling
and constructing the self. Moreover, this brand of masculine construction is in stark contrast to the naturalized machismo often associated with "Papa" Hemingway by literary critics and mass culture
alike. Instead of locating masculinity in psychological functions like
the Oedipus complex, Hemingway consistently writes about masculinity as a behavioral discipline that not only requires practice and
concentration but also overcomes crippling psychological impulses
such as jealousy, sentimentality, and rage.[14]

The often-cited Hemingway paper dolls featured in *Vanity
Fair* further illustrates the performative nature of masculinity for
Hemingway, as well as the ways in which his celebrity masculinity

was subject to parody. Published in 1934 as part of a series of celebrity paper dolls, *Vanity Fair*'s Hemingway paper dolls emphasize the "chest-thumping" maschismo associated with the writer in the 1930s.[15] The paper dolls feature a central caricature of Hemingway as "Neanderthal Man," surrounded by four costumes depicting well-known roles in his life and prose: expatriate in a Parisian café, deep sea fisherman, wounded World War I veteran, and bullfighter. However, as the Hemingway paper dolls themselves demonstrate, the writer overtly constructs masculinity as a series of styles. The central image of Hemingway is even a performed role. While paper dolls usually begin with a subject in some state of undress, Hemingway is instead presented as the "Neanderthal Man," dressed in animal skin and holding a dead rabbit and a club. This image shows that even the originary manhood that Hemingway embodies is very much the product of performance, construction, and stylization and links that stylization to the primitivism so central to modernism. By parodying Hemingway's performative masculinity, the caption below the paper dolls casts masculinist modernism as fringed by effeminacy. It claims that Hemingway is "hard-drinking, hard-fighting, hard-loving—all for art's sake," repeating "hard" but also evoking the "art for art's sake" movement and its decadent effeteness. Through association with this dandyish aestheticism, *Vanity Fair*'s emphasis on Hemingway's "hardness" pokes fun at the writer's macho persona. This parody is one example of how complex Hemingway's performance of high modernist masculinity actually is. Even in this mocking magazine feature, Hemingway's masculinity is more than reactionary bravado. The "Ernie as the Lost Generation" and "Ernie as the Unknown Soldier" costumes both cast Hemingway as more than an individual, as a synecdoche for the broader cultural categories—the expatriate writer and the wounded veteran of modern warfare—that the writer helped to concretize. The paper dolls suggest that Hemingway takes on different roles and, further, that it is his assiduous performativity that makes him such a notable artist. By making Hemingway a literal cut-out that can assume different roles by merely changing his dress, this magazine feature serves as an example of how modernist masculinity emerges in the stylized reconfiguration of signifiers, not the articulation of depth.

THE MASCULINE SELF AS MODERNIST OBJECT

Published in 1932, *Death in the Afternoon* was written during the period many critics identify as Hemingway's most misogynist and narcissistic.[16] This long and rambling work of nonfiction details not only how to appreciate bullfighting but also a theory of prose style, a meditation on homosexuality in art and literature, and a series of aesthetic debates between Hemingway and an "Old Lady" interlocutor.[17] These disparate threads are often thought to be unrelated, or only related insofar as they provide Hemingway with a series of tropes and discourses through which he can claim his own dominance. However, all of the threads in *Death in the Afternoon* share a unique vision of masculinity as a production of repetition and discipline. In so doing, the book envisions a model of masculinity as fluid style. That is, in this text, masculine identity is founded on impermanence, openness to change, and a readiness to accept loss. Masculine plasticity, though, comes with the corollary stylistic imperative to undo conventional psychic depth. In this sense, Hemingway's masculine self-fashionings entail, in their attempts to flatten the subject into surface and style, that psychological depth is itself a mark of conventionality, and hence, of weakness.

One of Ernest Hemingway's pithiest aesthetic statements lies buried in a two-page paragraph in *Death in the Afternoon*: "Prose is architecture, not interior decoration, and the Baroque is over."[18] This statement positions Hemingway's aesthetic against genteel fiction of the type associated with realists such as Henry James and Edith Wharton. The slogan favors modernism's emphasis on the external, on "things" and "words" in themselves, what Hugh Kenner called the "homemade world" of language.[19] The emphasis on externality, on "architecture" over "interior decoration," not only suggests a shift in representation but also a shift in the gendering of prose. By moving away from "interior decoration," Hemingway advocates a shift away from literary forms that are culturally coded as feminine. The focus on externality, on the signifier itself, is how masculinity is figured from dime novels through "high" modernism, and this metamorphosis of identity into style entails flexibility and multiplicity.

Hemingway's aesthetic claim resonates with Willa Cather's claim in "The Novel Démeublé" that one must move away from the "over-furnished novel." Both authors resist a genteel "interior," and both worked to develop a sparse prose style that resonates as a masculine voice. Through a focus on externality—Hemingway's "architecture"—this masculine style casts the social world as a series of performances, as outward actions rather than interior deliberations. Both Cather and Hemingway advocate exteriority as a stylistic technique, and this technique produces venues for the production of gender apart from rigid interior limitations.[20] Cather and Hemingway then share not only a critique of genteel fiction but also an interest in the usefulness of a masculine style. In Hemingway's case, a vast marketing scheme was built around associating his life with his literature, yet it is important to see that this connection between the male body and the masculine voice was nevertheless constructed. The vision of the masculine writer who writes masculine tales is a juxtaposition of the writer with his texts carefully orchestrated by Hemingway, his editor Maxwell Perkins, and the literary marketplace at large.[21]

The juxtaposition of life and text may account for some of the difficulty that critics have had getting beyond the seemingly narcissistic and self-promoting qualities of *Death in the Afternoon*. In his brief treatment of *Death in the Afternoon* in *The Wound and the Bow*, Edmund Wilson faults the book because it does not live up to ideals of normative masculinity. By actually writing in his own voice, Hemingway complicates the vision of the manly writer Wilson associates with Hemingway's texts: "[Hemingway] writes a book [*Death in the Afternoon*] not merely in the first person, but in the first person in his own character as Hemingway, and the results are unexpected and disconcerting."[22] After claiming that the book is a worthy "exposition of bullfighting," Wilson goes on to elaborate precisely what surprises and exasperates him:

> the book is partly infected by a queer kind of maudlin emotion, which sounds at once neurotic and drunken...He offsets the virility of the bullfighters by anecdotes of the male homosexuals that frequent Paris cafés, at the same time that he puts his chief celebration of the voluptuous excitement of the spectacle into the mouth of an imaginary old lady. The whole thing becomes a little hysterical.[23]

Wilson's critique casts Hemingway's book as hysterical, feminine, and effeminate, too proximate to queerness and too emotionally expressive. This critique, that Hemingway emasculates himself through his autobiographical approach, reifies the narrator's distance from characters provided by Hemingway's terse prose style. The autobiographical writing in *Death in the Afternoon* is, to Wilson, too close to the very sentimentality that Hemingway decries by advocating for "architecture" over "interior decoration." When Hemingway deals directly with his own biography, Wilson implies, his craft weakens. Only through the distant gaze can the masculine writer be properly masculine. This critique, of course, assumes that the male body is hermetically sealed off, at a safe remove from contamination from other bodies and, most importantly, feminizing emotion. By assuming that Hemingway's masculinity is stable, Wilson then critiques the ways in which *Death in the Afternoon* departs from that assumed stability.

But what if one approaches *Death in the Afternoon* as providing a model of masculinity that deploys a set of performative gestures, disciplines, and stylizations? What if we do not assume that masculinity is a thing but an always already incomplete set of behavioral and stylistic tropes? In a model of gender performativity, one can neither "be" nor "have" a gender. The seeming stability of the gendered body is an effect of the clusters of norms that construct our everyday lives. Gender exists through iteration and is consolidated only provisionally through acts. An intentional invocation of these norms, enacted through allegory or parody, can bring them into question, as Judith Butler has influentially argued, yet this questioning does not transcend gender but rather seeks to reconfigure it. Butler's discussion of drag has a bearing on Hemingway's overblown masculinity:

> At its best…drag can be read for the way in which hyperbolic norms are dissimulated as the heterosexual mundane. At the same time these same norms, taken not as commands to be obeyed, but as imperatives to be "cited," twisted, queered, brought into relief as heterosexual imperatives, are not, necessarily, subverted in the process.[24]

The masculinity represented in *Death in the Afternoon* is, like all genders, performative, yet it is performative in a particularly modernist way that self-consciously invokes repetition, public reception, and bodily disciplines. Following Butler, these citations do not undermine, subvert, or critique masculinity and its ties to heterosexuality but instead defamiliarize masculinity. Hemingway's gender is not natural but artificial, and gender cultivation, in Hemingway's *Death in the Afternoon*, endows the gendered subject with the agency, however limited, to discipline the gendered body. As Wyndham Lewis noticed, Hemingway's masculine persona is a clear performance of a role that requires a severe amount of control and discipline: "Ernest Hemingway is the Noble Savage of Rousseau, but a white version, the simple American man. That is at all events the rôle that he has chosen, and he plays it with an imperturbable art and grace beyond praise."[25] Lewis's faint praise contains a sense of the constructedness of the "natural" that has eluded many disparaging treatments of Hemingway's masculinity. By choosing to be "the simple American man," Hemingway chooses a role. For Hemingway, masculinity is performance art.

Figure 5.1 Juan Gris, *El Torero*, 1913. The painting appeared as the frontispiece to the first edition of Ernest Hemingway's *Death in the Afternoon*, 1932.

Death in the Afternoon implicitly connects style, masculinity, and modernism with its own frontispiece, Juan Gris's 1913 painting *El Torero*, or "the bullfighter" (figure 5.1). Printed in color in the first edition of the book, *El Torero* offers a visual example of how Hemingway treats gender.[26] The painting is a cubist portrait of a bullfighter against a wall plastered with bullfighting advertisements. The letters and words on the bullfighting posters, peeling up, take parts of the bullfighter with them, rendering the figure another mere signifier on a piece of paper. Through the cubist technique of breaking up the picture plane, the fracturing of the bullfighter's face and chest divides the portrait into a more conventionally representational bottom section, the coat and tie, and an abstract face produced through juxtaposition of colored planes and fonts.[27] By disfiguring the figure, Gris denies the bullfighter the personality and consciousness traditionally ascribed to the subject of a portrait. If Gris's *El Torero* blocks interiority by fracturing the human face, then more broadly it detaches externality from interiority, the body from the psychological self. Gris's portrait, which turns its central figure into shapes on a canvas, suggests that the self is also a surface, one that can be fragmented and reimagined as an aesthetic project. Gris is often categorized as one of the most logical of cubists, and *El Torero* seems to mark the difficulty of the move between "analytic" and "synthetic" cubism.[28] Emerging in the first decade of the twentieth century, analytic cubism dissects objects into shapes, colors, and forms.[29] Synthetic cubism, which emerges in the 1910s, uses objects, such as the bullfighting posters in *El Torero*, to create an abstract form. *El Torero* seems to straddle analytic and synthetic methods. The bullfighter's tie and blazer are clearly represented, yet the figure's face is a collage of posters and color planes that seem less to pick apart an already-existing figure than constitute the face. As I will argue, Hemingway's *Death in the Afternoon* presents masculinity as just such an aesthetic project, both a dismantling of the self and the production of the self as an abstraction.

Death in the Afternoon begins with the narrator's own ambivalence about the bullfight: "At the first bullfight I ever went to I expected to be horrified and perhaps sickened by what I had been told would happen to the horses."[30] This sentence is written in characteristic Hemingway style. It uses multiple verbs, packing in multiple actions and a series of temporal distances. The narrator is describing something that happened in the past, the bullfight he "went to," but this past event is narrated through expectations, projecting the sentence further back, and then even further back to what the narrator "had been told would happen." This layering of the past onto the recollection of and expectations for a singular experience bears an interesting relation to Hemingway's plea to the reader of *Death in the Afternoon* to approach bullfighting with an open mind. The sentence describes a complex, layered past that threatens to predetermine Hemingway's response to the bullfight, and this is precisely what Hemingway wants to shift away from. That is, Hemingway wishes to view the world with fresh emotions; he wants to watch events without scripted reactions and false sentiments. In this way, *Death in the Afternoon* takes Ezra Pound's injunction to "Make It New" and applies it to the self. Through discipline and practice, one can enter into the curious fraternity of the aficionados by leaving behind prejudice.

Hemingway explicitly links the emotional discipline one gains from watching bullfights to the types of emotional control and precision needed to write well. In his words:

> If a writer of prose knows enough about what he is writing about he may omit things that he knows and the reader, if the writer is writing truly enough, will have a feeling of those things as strongly as though the writer had stated them. The dignity of movement of an ice-berg is due to only one-eighth of it being above water. A writer who omits things because he does not know them only makes hollow places in his writing.[31]

This emphasis on producing "feeling" makes Hemingway sound much like a finely skilled sentimentalist. Hemingway argues here that literature should produce emotion in a reader and that this emotion must be crafted in words. The focus on the economy of the signifier, on minimizing words until only the most necessary remain, demonstrates Hemingway's reliance on Stein's stylistic interests in repetition and elision. It also shows his indebtedness to a longer tradition in American literature—usually associated with sentimentalism—that uses emotional responses to literature in the service of a social vision.[32] The intertwining of the author's emotional discipline and the reader's disciplining through the detection of hidden emotion in prose renders Hemingway's texts as whole objects, lacking any "hollow places." In this sense, Hemingway's texts are striking modernist artifacts. They aim for objecthood yet nonetheless gesture to some truth that makes them socially and politically meaningful. This interest in content, though, dovetails with style; Hemingway advocates for the objecthood of the self, that is, the metamorphosis of style into a container for both form and content.

Death in the Afternoon, then, is an attempt to construct a discipline of the sentiments, to move away from "what you were supposed to feel" to a state of refined emotional response.[33] Hemingway's explanation of why death is the proper object for this study is telling of the relation of disciplined sentiment to the production of stylized masculinity. The passage reads:

> I had seen certain things, certain simple things of this sort that I remembered, but in taking part in them, or, in other cases, having to write of them immediately after and consequently noticing the things I needed for instant recording, I had never been able to study them as a man might, for instance, study the death of his father or the hanging of some one, say, that he did not know and would not have to write of immediately after for the first edition of an afternoon newspaper.[34]

The juxtaposition of the death of one's father with the hanging of a complete stranger produces a unique view of what kinds of emotion Hemingway is interested in exploring. In simple Freudian terms, the death of the father allows for a son's entrance into adulthood, no longer under the yoke of the patriarch. Yet within this interest in "studying" the "death of his father" lies the possibility that the son will not follow Freud's schema of assuming the role of the dead father. Instead, by slowing down, by repeating death, Hemingway's method might open up new possibilities for the son outside of a simple progression to male dominance. Furthermore, there is a broader public sensibility involved in this masculine sentiment since the father is interchangeable with a total stranger. Closeness to death opens up new possibilities, as each death figures as the death of the father, the death of the dominant order. The repetition of "instant" and "instance" in this passage also foregrounds a crucial temporal inflection to *Death in the Afternoon*'s central focus on bullfighting. While the bullfight offers a singular event with each bull's death, the event is also restaged with a different bull each time. This iterative-yet-singular event shares a temporal logic with gender performativity.[35] While the ritual is, by definition, something that is repeated, each iteration of the performance is marked with a difference at its core, namely, that the bull will actually die and therefore not perform in the ritual again. In the same sense, a masculine subject has to get dressed every morning, yet that subject wears different clothes from day to day. The repeated activity of dressing oneself, which has a great deal to do with how gender is performed and perceived, is diffcrent each day. With this repeated-yet-differentiated activity, one can hone one's fashion sense, or merely become a creature of habit. Hemingway's emphasis on for-getting "what you were supposed to feel" advocates for the overthrow of conventional behavior. The bullfight's repetition and its staging of death disciplines the aficionado's and, ideally, the bullfighter's senti-ments. This temporal logic provides a framework for both casting off tired habits and the cultivation of masculinity as a style.

The bullfight, Hemingway claims, "is indefensible . . . from a moral point of view, that is, a Christian point of view."[36] This invocation of Christianity foreshadows Hemingway's account of the Catholic Church's regulation of bullfights in Spain. The regulation that Hemingway focuses on in particular is the rule that a bull must be killed during or after a bullfight so that it may never return to the bullfighting ring, knowledgeable of the ruse of the cape and sword.[37] This Christian influence forces the bullfight to be a ritual where the animal is at a disadvantage. As Cary Wolfe notices about the bull-fight, it is a space where the human asserts its power over the animal, reinforcing a species boundary:

> Violence and the threat of emasculation it harbors are not transmogri-fied into "tragedy" by the bullfight but are instead *fetishized* by it in a series of desperate therapeutic attempts to remedy, by compensa-tory domination of a weaker being, the constitutive internal difference of the Enlightenment subject—an internal difference of the symbolic order that opens it and that promises, sirenlike, to heal it.[38]

Wolfe's interest in the function of the human/animal divide as a way of producing or healing splits in the subject caused by modernity too quickly assumes that violence is a social ill, something that should be eliminated from the public sphere. What I find interesting about the centrality of violence to *Death in the Afternoon* is that it pro-vides a forum for a repetitive dislodging of the Enlightenment subject through the demystification of the public sphere as a venue cleansed of all violence. The bullfight, in this sense, literally founds a human public sphere on violence, rendering clear the constitutive violence that allows any assumption of human dominance.[39] Furthermore, the bullfight engages man and animal in an intimate struggle. As in Owen Wister's *The Virginian*, animals train human subjects in the ways of intimate relations. In Wister's novel, horses and men engage in intimate, romantic relationships, while in Hemingway's text bulls and men come together in death. For Hemingway, this training con-sists of a ritualized violence and closeness to the dirt and blood that constitute engagement with the world.

A short story included in *Death in the Afternoon*, "A Natural History of the Dead," further emphasizes the way in which the deaths of animals gesture to an engagement with the natural world rather than a transcendent dominance over lesser beings. The story contains a passage about dead mules:

> Most of those mules I saw dead were along mountain roads or lying at the foot of steep declivities whence they had been pushed to rid the road of their encumbrance. They seemed a fitting enough sight in the mountains where one was accustomed to their presence and looked less incongruous there than they did later, at Smyrna, where the Greeks broke the legs of all their baggage animals and pushed them off the quay into the shallow water to drown.[40]

This juxtaposition of mules pushed off of mountain roads and mules killed during a wartime evacuation resonates with the appeal of not only the bullfight but also war-torn Europe in general as a thoroughly primitive-yet-modern culture. This particular scene at Smyrna, present-day Izmir, occurred in 1922 at the end of the Greco-Turkish War.[41] In the 1930 edition of Hemingway's *In Our Time*, the introductory story in the volume, "On the Quai at Smyrna," also recounts this scene. Unlike "A Natural History of the Dead," which is written in Hemingway's voice, this story is told by a British officer:

> The Greeks were nice chaps, too. When they evacuated they had all their baggage animals they couldn't take off with them so they just broke their forelegs and dumped them into the shallow water. All those mules with their forelegs broken pushed over into the shallow water. It was all a pleasant business. My word yes a most pleasant business.[42]

This passage drips with cynicism, only magnified by the repetition of "pleasant" at the end of the paragraph. In the version quoted earlier, the passage from *Death in the Afternoon*, Hemingway excludes the British officer's cynicism. "A Natural History of the Dead" documents the lack of transcendence, the lack of triumph over the natural world, implied by the British officer's cynicism, which not only claims distance from a traumatic scene but also, in the passage, distances the British speaker from "the Greeks." By shifting the tone in "A Natural History of the Dead," Hemingway involves the reader more robustly by engaging the reader's sentiment rather than informing the reader of the "proper" attitude to take. Hemingway changes the mule scene to fit into *Death in the Afternoon*'s larger project, the cultivation of masculinity as a style that is involved with rather than dominant over others. While *Death in the Afternoon* does not take place in the American West, the masculine style here connotes the same play of the signifier and mobility within hierarchical relations evident in other works about the American West; Hemingway finds models for this masculine style in Spain and during wartime, analogs for the open and "primitive" frontier.

In addition to staging a constitutive act of violence, the bullfight also serves as an ideal scene for masculine performance in the text, what Thomas Strychacz has described as one of Hemingway's "theaters of masculinity."[43] Hemingway often writes of the bullfighter's training and discipline as a kind of ethic. In this passage, after a discussion of taste, wine drinking, and bullfighting, Hemingway elaborates his view of the good life:

> Our bodies all wear out in some way and we die, and I would rather have a palate that will give me the pleasure of enjoying completely a Chateaux Margaux or a Haut Brion, even though excesses indulged in in the acquiring of it has brought a liver that will not allow me to drink Richebourg, Corton, or Chambertin, than to have the corrugated iron internals of my boyhood when all red wines were bitter except port and drinking was the process of getting down enough of anything to make you feel reckless. The thing, of course, is to avoid having to give up wine entirely just as, with the eye, it is to avoid going blind. But there seems to be much luck in all these things and no man can avoid death by honest effort nor say what use any part of his body will bear until he tries it.[44]

This passage provides a remarkably condensed example of the appeal of Hemingway as a writer and celebrity. A figure who explicitly modeled his life to meld with his writings, Hemingway's ethic of living well with an acceptance of death implies a critique of a consumer culture overrun with goods designed for subjects that will never die. The commonality of mass cultural items—be it cheap wine or studio film—means that the consumer need no expertise to consume. Hemingway's appreciation of the "finer things" in life resists a consumer culture that caters to its members as if they are immortal consumers, that markets goods to lengthen life without qualitatively improving it, and that displaces violence to foreign lands. By endorsing quality over quantity, Hemingway produces a democratizing vision of the subject—one can, through discipline, come to appreciate things such as the bullfight, activities for which American culture has little or no appreciation.[45]

Self-Fashioning as Sentimental and Sexual Discipline

An interlocutor referred to only as the "Old Lady" frequently appears in the book and converses with the author. She usually asks questions about bullfighting that lead to aesthetic debates and demands for stories, and at one point, after being bored by a long description of bullfighting technique, the "Old Lady" asks for a story about "those unfortunate people."[46] By "those unfortunate people," the Old Lady is referring to homosexuals, a subject about which "she has been reading lately."[47] Hemingway responds that he knows "a few [stories about them], but in general they lack drama as do all tales of abnormality since no one can predict what will happen in the normal while all tales of the abnormal end much the same." The story Hemingway ends up telling to the "Old Lady" is not a moralizing tale of the "abnormal." Instead, he tells a story about two young men, one of whom has been invited to travel to Europe with the other, wealthier young man. While in a hotel room next door to the two young men, the story's narrator is disturbed by a frantic knocking. The poorer of the two young men is at his door in tears and threatens to kill himself rather than go back into the hotel room with his friend. After the wealthy friend coaxes his companion back into the room, the narrator overhears the young man yelling "I won't!" over and over again, followed by sobbing that lasts all night. The story ends with the narrator seeing the two young men at breakfast the next morning, "chatting together happily and reading copies of the Paris *New York Herald*."[48]

When Hemingway finishes the story with this image of banal contentment, the Old Lady is left unsatisfied. She asks, "Is there not to be what we called in my youth a wow at the end?" In response, Hemingway offers a coda to the story that again denies a "wow" ending:

> The last time I saw the two they were sitting on the terrace of the Café des Deux Magots, wearing well-tailored clothes, looking clean cut as ever, except that the younger of the two, the one who had said he would kill himself rather than go back in that room, had had his hair hennaed.[49]

Hemingway refuses to give a standard narrative of "the abnormal." By facing down death, here in the form of contemplated suicide, the young man who has dyed his hair, like the bullfighter, faced death and emerged as a subject embracing a new masculinity style. Through the sign of hennaed hair, Hemingway turns what many would believe to be a drastic overhaul of one's social and psychic life, parodically, into a change in style and fashion. Though it is told with Hemingway's characteristic homophobia, this story serves as an example of how the unpleasant reorientation and redisciplining of the emotions, the departure from what "one is supposed to feel," can produce different and more pleasurable forms of masculinity. Even when disparaging the young men, Hemingway's insistence on surpassing conventional sentiments, on training the body and mind to see and feel differently, turns the body and gender into aesthetic projects. For Hemingway and the man with hennaed hair, identity is malleable and changeable. This anecdote also points to the anxieties that surround masculine performativity for Hemingway. As in Owen Wister's *The Virginian*, masculinity exceeds Hemingway's own sense of propriety, and the homosexual couple, while mocked here, nonetheless partake in the same stylistic fashioning as Hemingway advises in other, less sarcastic sections of *Death in the Afternoon*.

Hemingway's statement that "prose is architecture, not interior decoration, and the Baroque is over" sits alongside many other aesthetic claims in *Death in the Afternoon* about how to create an artistic novel.[50] In keeping with a characteristically modernist endorsement of the original and the "new," Hemingway goes on in this section to claim that figures in novels should not be lifted from popular conceits,

> When writing a novel a writer should create living people; people not characters. A character is a caricature. If a writer can make people live there may be no great characters in his book, but it is possible that his book will remain as a whole; as an entity; as a novel.[51]

In this passage, fictional people and real people blur together; both are the products of style and, ultimately, become autonomous. It is worthwhile to reverse Hemingway's statement to fully grasp the writer's understanding of masculinity. Not only should characters in novels be real people, but real people should also be just as much the products of imagination, fantasy, and style as fictional characters. Writing well, for Hemingway, produces life, just as life itself, the stylization of selfhood, is a discursive act.

For Hemingway, masculine identity is formed through discipline. It is not certain acts—a pass of the bull, sex with a woman, or the winning of a safari trophy—that make one masculine but a discipline of the body, a series of acts that are repeated and performed over time.

Because masculinity is the product of repetition and connoisseurship, rather than a permanent possession, it bears the promise of coming unhinged from the sexed body as well as normative restrictions on the masculine as male and heterosexual. This modernist masculinity holds out possibilities for lived experience. *Death in the Afternoon* is, to use Hemingway's description, "practical," a handbook for self-fashioning that seizes upon the promise of cowboy masculinity to produce a new, more open, and more indecorous form of masculinity.[52]

CHAPTER 6

Specters of Masculinity: Collectivity in John Steinbeck's *The Grapes of Wrath*

> *I thought richly of you once; you grew to be a brazen figure of the night. And now—I find you a babbler, a speaker of sweet, condensed words, and rather clumsy about it. I find you are no realist at all, but only a bungling romancer.*
>
> —John Steinbeck, *Cup of Gold*

In his 1963 Nobel Prize acceptance speech, John Steinbeck claims literature as a field of public sentiment, not scholastic piety: "Literature was not promulgated by a pale and emasculated critical priesthood singing their litanies in empty churches—nor is it a game for the cloistered elect, the tin-horn mendicants of low-calorie despair."[1] Critical of the solitary author and the inaccessible work, Steinbeck envisions a literature that is neither penitent nor elitist. Literature that adheres to the "high duties and responsibilities" of the trade "is delegated to declare and to celebrate man's proven capacity for greatness of heart and spirit—for gallantry in defeat, for courage, compassion and love."[2] Steinbeck locates sentiment as a key factor in determining literary value. "Low-calorie despair" neglects the reader's somatic body, while "courage, compassion, and love" connect the bodies of authors, characters and readers in affective relationships.[3]

Steinbeck's ideal literature corresponds with the worst that has been said of his work. Critics find him broadly humanistic to the point of losing all political orientation, melodramatic in his celebration of heroic confrontations, and, particularly late in his career, lacking the social realism that defined his best work in the 1930s.[4] Steinbeck was and remains a middlebrow writer. Steinbeck's middlebrow status is confirmed by his many novels that became Book-of-the-Month Club selections, his large popular readership, and his eagerness to work with the culture industry as a journalist, magazine columnist, screenwriter, director, and playwright.[5] Consequently, Steinbeck's literary value has often come under attack, most notably by Leslie Fiedler, who expressed disgust at Steinbeck's Nobel Prize and who labeled *The Grapes of Wrath* "maudlin, sentimental and overblown."[6] In *Waiting for the End*, Fiedler sketches a common literary history of the masculinist, modernist American novel:

> Both Faulkner and Hemingway are dead, a slow suicide by the bottle in one case, and a quick one by the gun in the other, as seems appropriate to our tradition; and we must come to terms with our surviving selves; yet first, of course, with them. Their deaths have made eminently clear what the passage of time had already begun to establish (and our sense of outrage over the awarding of the Nobel Prize to John Steinbeck merely emphasizes the fact): that these two writers represent to us and to the world the real meaning and the true success of the novel in America during the first half of the twentieth century.[7]

Steinbeck, then, survives, like American readers after the death of Fiedler's successful novelists, without "coming to terms" with the literary dead. As opposed to the work of Hemingway and Faulkner, Steinbeck merely writes popular, trite fiction, unaware of that most significant modernist appendage to literary genius, what T. S. Eliot describes as "Tradition."[8] What Steinbeck does offer, though, is a clear example of both how inextricably connected modernism is to mass culture, especially in its representations of masculinity, and how the boundary between high and low culture is viciously policed to maintain the illusory purity of the modernist work of art. Like Hemingway's guide to cultivating modernist masculinity, *Death in the Afternoon*, Steinbeck's prose blends the popular with the elite, the stoic with the sentimental, to produce masculinities that can respond to modern circumstances.

Steinbeck's first novel, *Cup of Gold*, published in 1929, chronicles the life of Captain Morgan. The infamous pirate, driven by love, dedicates his life to the pursuit and capture of a beautiful woman named "La Santa Roja." After conquering Panama City, he encounters his beloved, only to be rejected by her for his overflow of sentiment. As the epigraph to this chapter states, she finds that the notorious pirate is "no realist at all, but only a bungling romancer."[9] This insult foreshadows Steinbeck's critical reputation. The common Steinbeck chronology privileges social realism as his central genre; he peaks with *Of Mice and Men* and *The Grapes of Wrath*, creates a melodramatic and flawed family saga in *East of Eden*, and then writes a series of minor works in the mid-1950s until his death in 1968. When he stopped writing about migrant workers and moved from his native California to New York in 1941, so the story goes, Steinbeck lost his territory and his style. His works after *The Grapes of Wrath*—including novels along with plays, a scientific log, novellas, film scripts, journalism, essays, and his rewrite of Malory's *Morte d'Arthur*—seem to suggest a writer out of touch, lost after the New Deal and unable to find a balance between the novelistic and the political during the Cold War.[10]

Those who want to decry Steinbeck as middlebrow, either politically or in the vocabulary of New Criticism, claim that he is sentimental and melodramatic. Malcolm Cowley's review of *The Grapes of Wrath*, for example, links Steinbeck's novel directly to Harriet Beecher Stowe's *Uncle Tom's Cabin*, the mainstay of sentimental fiction:

I can't agree with those critics who say that *The Grapes of Wrath* is the greatest novel of the last ten years; for example, it doesn't rank with the best of Hemingway or Dos Passos. But it belongs very high in the category of the great angry books like *Uncle Tom's Cabin* that have roused a people to fight against intolerable wrongs.[11]

In light of current critical treatments of sentimental novels, the claim of sentimentalism is not necessarily as damning as it once was. However, the counter to the claims of sentimentalism, which in Cowley is less derogatory and more of a reference to an alternate literary history running alongside realism and modernism, usually involves branding Steinbeck a social realist.[12] But as John Seelye argues, the radical separation between sentimentalism and realism might not apply to Steinbeck's novels:

In short, Steinbeck is a gravely misunderstood writer, as Leslie Fiedler's dismissal surely demonstrates. But that in some ways is his own fault, for much as Steinbeck, though a realist, often uses symbolic frameworks derived from archetypal sources, structures essentially romantic in implication, so as a realist he is anomalous in his use of sentimentality.[13]

As the large body of criticism surrounding sentimental fiction has shown, the clear demarcation between sentimentalism and realism is often drawn not on the basis of prose style but on the author's gender or a text's gendered readership.[14] However, the sentimental and the domestic are not necessarily distinct from the realistic and the public.[15] Sentimentalism contributes a valuable mode of political activism through its reliance on allegory and emotion to motivate social change.[16] Naturalist writers such as Stephen Crane, Jack London, and Frank Norris can be thought of as borrowing from the sentimental in their depictions of those left behind by capitalism, yet they are certainly not gendered as "feminine" or "domestic" writers.[17] This is not to claim that sentimentalism is a masculine form but rather that it is a gendered form. Masculine narratives from dime-novel Westerns through high modernism use sentimentality and emotional response to construct masculinity in different historical moments as fluid and modern. After all, the first dime novel is a traditional sentimental narrative: Ann S. Stephens's *Malaeska: The Indian Wife of the White Hunter*.[18] American modernism is in many ways a masculine-inflected version of sentimentalism.[19]

The critical bias against Steinbeck, then, stems from a misunderstanding of popular literary forms. Instead of thinking seriously about the tradition of popular literature and its interconnectedness with modernism, critics such as Fiedler merely assume that the sentimental novel and the romance are lesser "feminine" literary forms in twentieth-century American literature. Yet many Steinbeck critics have argued that Steinbeck's writing is surprisingly experimental in its use of narrative structure, and his involvement with film, journalism and theater, along with his eccentric sense of literary history, make him a formally interesting novelist. Steinbeck is, then, a middlebrow experimentalist.[20] In contrast to Hemingway's masculinist terseness and Faulkner's vertiginous narration, Steinbeck produces novels that openly adopt and complicate popular literary forms. Steinbeck draws heavily on the power of public sentiment and, particularly in *The Grapes of Wrath*, uses sentiment as a means to refashion gender and family relations as modes of performing belonging, rather than embodying hierarchy. Through a combination of gendered popular narrative forms, Steinbeck's *The Grapes of Wrath* reworks the masculine Western and the feminine sentimental novel into narratives that entail the production of public feeling and the destruction of traditional modes of kinship that limit familial belonging to the fruits of heteronormative reproduction. One of the effects of Steinbeck's emphasis on collective feeling is masculinity's metamorphosis from stylistic embodiment to spectral affect.

Masculinity, Collectivity, and Maternity

In *The Grapes of Wrath*, Steinbeck attempts to seize upon a mode of narrating protest that accounts for the individual, the family, and the social collective. The novel's experimental balance between abstract interchapters and chapters chronicling the Joad family's journey to California gives an allegorical sweep to the text. By explicitly collectivizing the plight of one family, Steinbeck turns masculinity—especially Tom Joad's activist masculinity—into a set of universal affects.[21] Masculinity in *The Grapes of Wrath* becomes both individual and universal, and it is counterbalanced by maternity in the novel's vision of an expansive, collective family. The novel begins with Tom Joad's release from prison. He finds his family in the process of packing up their belongings to move westward after the bank foreclosed on their small Oklahoma farm. The family then travels to California, where they meet with exploitative labor practices. The novel as a whole seeks to dramatize exploitation as both personal and collective, and the Joad family becomes the novel's focal point as it strives to account for one family's struggle during the Great Depression as exemplary of a larger, collective struggle.

Through the creation of affective bonds that surpass the conventional family unit, the Joad family's actions gesture to a utopian collective as the solution to the Great Depression, and this collectivity is thematized in the novel by expansive and critical notions of thought and the body. One of the major themes in the novel is the denigration of thought, of what the Joad family refers to as "figuring." Activity that stems from or accompanies thought is portrayed as helpless, futile, while activity that emerges out of passion, emotion, or affect sutures the disenfranchised together for survival. "Cold" instrumental logic allows exploitative owners to sever emotion from action, contributing to the treatment of the noble "Okies" in the novel as subhuman, mere objects:

> Some of the owner men were kind because they hated what they had to do, and some of them were angry because they hated to be cruel, and some of them were cold because they had long ago found that one could not be an owner unless one were cold. And all of them were caught in something larger than themselves. Some of them hated the mathematics that drove them, and some were afraid, and some worshiped the mathematics because it provided a refuge from thought and from feeling. If bank or a finance company owned the land, the owner man said, The Bank—or the Company—needs— wants—insists—must have—as though the Bank or the Company

were a monster, with thought and feeling, which had ensnared them.[22]

This movement between objectification and subjectification—between people becoming mere instruments of another's desire, and abstract institutions becoming feeling, thinking subjects—both expands and limits what qualifies as subject who has claims to rights. While this movement expands the field of the "human" by including large institutions, it also increasingly disenfranchises and denies rights to individuals. Corporations become people, while managers become mere instruments. Mathematics allows the manager to ignore his compassion for the disenfranchised Okies, and the very language of "thought and feeling" that the manager hides from also humanizes abstract institutions by giving corporations and banks the ability to desire.

The novel's depiction of bodies foregrounds this expansion of the category of the "human." In its reconceptualization of the family as an allegory for collective belonging, the narrative locates the human as a public feeling, acting body rather than a private rational mind. The novel begins with a famous description of a divided landscape that becomes flesh, emphasizing the universal expanse of feeling:

> To the red country and part of the gray country of Oklahoma, the last rains came gently, and they did not cut the scarred earth. The plows crossed and recrossed the rivulet marks. The last rains lifted the corn quickly and scattered weed colonies and grass along the sides of the roads so that the gray country and the dark red country began to disappear under a green cover. In the last part of May the sky grew pale and the clouds that had hung in high puffs for so long in the spring were dissipated. The sun flared down on the growing corn day after day until a line of brown spread along the edge of each green bayonet. The clouds appeared, and went away, and in a while they did not try any more. The weeds grew darker green to protect themselves, and they did not spread any more. The surface of the earth crusted, a thin hard crust, and as the sky became pale, so the earth became pale, pink in the red country and white in the gray country.[23]

The presence of agriculture, coupled with the drought, turns the land into a body, "scarred," "pale," "pink" and "white." This landscape description launches the novel both literally and thematically, for the novel troubles the distinction between the nonhuman—the objectified, laboring body—and the human—the feeling body that suffers under exploitative practices.

In *Antigone's Claim*, Judith Butler charts how kinship relations define and limit what counts as a human subject. In her reading of Sophocles's *Antigone*, Butler finds that Antigone uses kinship relations as a reason for breaking the law and burying her deceased brother Polynices against the orders of Creon. By accepting kinship as her primary duty, Antigone demonstrates how a claimed kinship relation can in fact turn someone, like her brother, into a human subject even after he has been denied that status. For Butler, Antigone's actions point to the way in which kinship relations can make a subject fully human, even when that subject has been formerly denied status as human: "If kinship is the precondition of the human, then Antigone is the occasion for a new field of the human, achieved through political catachresis, the one that happens when the less than human speaks as human, when gender is displaced, and kinship founders on its own founding laws."[24] This move of forcing the recognition of a human subject in what has otherwise been classed as "less than" occurs in *The Grapes of Wrath* repeatedly as the way in which the extended Joad family coheres, both as a family determined to survive and ultimately as a family open to others, unbound by kinship.

The remaking of the human is explicitly undertaken by Casy, a preacher who travels with the Joad family. When Tom Joad knocks out a policeman, Casy takes the blame and is hauled away by the police. As Casy is taken away, he "sat proudly, his head up and the stringy muscles of his neck prominent. On his lips there was a faint smile and on his face a curious look of conquest."[25] Casy forces the police to recognize him as a subject and not as a mere body. This scene is also key to John Ford's 1940 film adaptation of the novel. In the scene, Casy, played by John Carradine, holds his long arms out for the police to put cuffs on him, forcing the police to treat him as an agent rather than an object that will go where it is told.[26] Although he claims he will "go 'thout trouble," Casy troubles the police officers to cuff him, as they would cuff any rights-bearing subject.[27] Casy has forced the state to recognize him as a subject, as a subject who not only bears rights but more importantly bears the right to act against the state. In so doing, Casy's gesture conjures the possibility of action against the dominant order.

The Grapes of Wrath alternates between chapters dealing with the Joads and interchapters, philosophical and abstract sections that ruminate on the migrant workers as types within a social collective rather than distinct individuals. Early in the novel, this blurring of the individual into type is foregrounded by a truck driver's interest in being able to identify individuals by their appearance.[28] Tom Joad, just released from prison, hitches a ride with this trucker who meshes his love for reading people as types with a particular, scientific identification of specific individuals:

> "I train my mind all the time. I took a course in that two years ago." He patted the steering wheel with his right hand. "Suppose I pass a guy on the road. I look at him, an' after I'm past I try to remember ever'thing about him, kind a clothes an' shoes an' hat, an' how he walked an' maybe how tall an' what weight an' any scars. I do it pretty good. I can jus' make a whole picture in my head. Sometimes I think I ought to take a course to be a fingerprint expert. You'd be surprised how much a guy can remember."[29]

Tom's hands give away his class status and his place within the disciplinary system, causing the truck driver to notice, "I seen your hands. Been swinging a pick or an ax or a sledge."[30] While the trucker can place Tom, he cannot, through visual, objective evidence alone, answer the very question that he is dying to ask: what crime did Tom commit? In contrast to the trucker's limited powers of rational detection, Tom can sense desires rather than read bodies; Tom can "smell a question comin' from hell to breakfast."[31] Tom's ability to "smell" fuses the body and the mind together, while the trucker's reliance on physical clues has no access to interiority. Tom's mind and body are united through the flesh, and the trucker, like the manager who hides behind mathematics, "trains his mind" to be separate from his working body.

While the trucker views Tom as an object rather than a subject, and therefore reduces him to the status of a thing, *The Grapes of Wrath* figures masculinity as one possible way to reclaim one's humanity, to become more than a mere instrument of capital. In one of the abstract interchapters, a farmer being kicked off of his land interrogates a tractor driver about who he can confront: "Where does it stop? Who can we shoot? I don't aim to starve to death before I kill the man that's starving me."[32] The farmer's desire to confront someone, to strike out at the "man that's starving me," is tempered by the tractor driver's response, "I don't know. Maybe there's nobody to shoot. Maybe the thing isn't men at all. Maybe, like you said, the property's doing it."[33] While masculinity is central to the novel, it repeatedly fails as an allegory for violent confrontation with oppressive institutions. The displaced farmer simply cannot fight a subject without a body, "there's nobody to shoot." As both Casy's recognition by the police and the farmer's threats demonstrate, masculinity can symbolically resist state and corporate power but flounders when an individual acts alone.

The novel stages the death of its chief individual activist, Casy, who is killed because "he was a-leadin' the strike" of migrant farm workers.[34] Tom Joad, in turn, clubs one of Casy's attackers. Fearing that his presence will endanger his family, Tom becomes "an outlaw."[35] No longer content to work toward the realization of a bourgeois vision of personal success after being radicalized by Casy, Tom explains to his mother the impact Casy's politics have had on his worldview:

> An I got to thinkin', Ma—most of the preachin' is about the poor we shall have always with us, an' if you got nothin', why, jus' fol' your hands an to hell with it, you gonna git ice cream on gol' plates when you're dead. An' then this here Preacher says two get a better reward for their work.[36]

Tom vows to do "what Casy done," but his final explanation of what he will do and what he will become conflicts with Casy's nuts-and-bolts strike organization. Instead of becoming a pragmatic organizer, Tom becomes an allegorical masculine figure, a spectral presence. He will "be ever'where—wherever you look."[37]

No longer able to think of power as embodied in one person—a bank manager or tractor driver—Tom concludes in his final speech to Ma that power saturates everyday life:

> Wherever they's a fight so hungry people can eat, I'll be there. Wherever they's a cop beatin' up a guy, I'll be there. If Casy knowed, why, I'll be in the way guys yell when they're mad an'—I'll be in the way kids laugh when they're hungry an' they know supper's ready. An' when our folks eat the stuff they raise an' live in the houses they build—why, I'll be there.[38]

Tom democratizes masculinity by giving up his own individual body; after this speech, he leaves the Joad family and never appears in the novel again. This metafictive moment—a character in the novel acknowledging his own allegorical status as working-class hero—points to what actual collectivism would look like: the dispersal of the centered individual into heterogeneity, the death of the subject. Recognizing his inability to fight power through manly combat, Tom seeks to understand how power exists in everyday relations, in the disciplinary structure of the state, and even in the propertied happiness of his own class. Following Tom's realization that power has no center, Steinbeck portrays Tom's evaporation into everyday practice. Tom becomes a democratized, mobile presence, a specter of masculine style. This abstraction of masculinity into a ghostly presence is both nostalgic for a time when face-to-face confrontation with oppressors was possible and prophetic as Tom vows to watch over humanity. This spectral, protective masculinity becomes a dominant narrative device in the Cold War, as I will discuss in the conclusion.

Coupled with Tom's democratized, spectral masculinity, *The Grapes of Wrath* also dramatizes a politicized femininity. This reimagined femininity is best represented in the series of events that close the novel. Rose of Sharon, who has been pregnant throughout the novel and whose husband has left her, gives birth to a stillborn child. The remaining Joad men, Pa and Uncle John, send the baby's body down the river. While others in the novel have died, the stillborn baby is the first body that the Joads have not properly buried. As he places the baby's body in the river, Uncle John speaks to the corpse: "Go down an' tell 'em. Go down in the street an' rot an' tell 'em that way. That's the way you can talk. Don' even know if you was a boy or a girl. Ain't gonna find out. Go on down now, an' lay in the street. Maybe they'll know then."[39] Playing on the Biblical story of the baby Moses, the genderless body functions as a new figure of protest. The public, distant from the suffering of these marginal migrant workers, will be reminded of their existence through the silent presence of the baby's corpse. Simply flesh, the dead baby complicates and expands the human; its silent speech is evidence of the flesh of the "less than," of the humanity of those denied status as human subjects and those denied access to rights. Typically a trope of renewal, the child in this moment registers the erosion of the traditional family and the crisis of maternal care that will be resolved in the novel's concluding moment.

Finally, in the closing scene of *The Grapes of Wrath*, having found a barn for shelter, the Joads stumble upon a starving old man and his son. Pa and Uncle look on "helplessly" while Ma and Rose of Sharon decide what to do, how to act. After asking all of the men to leave the room, thus averting the gazes of her father and uncle, Rose of Sharon breastfeeds the old stranger:

> For a minute Rose of Sharon sat still in the whispering barn. Then she hoisted her tired body up and drew her comfort about her. She moved slowly to the corner and stood looking down at the wasted face, into the wide, frightened eyes. Then slowly she lay down beside him. He shook his head slowly from side to side. Rose of Sharon loosened one

side of the blanket and bared her breast. "You got to," she said. She squirmed closer and pulled his head close. "There!" she said. "There." Her hand moved behind his head and supported it. Her fingers moved gently in his hair. She looked up and across the barn, and her lips came together and smiled mysteriously.[40]

This final scene is allegorical, collective, sentimental, and utopian at once. The narration details the minute motions of Rose of Sharon's body, her slow movements toward the anonymous old man, her gentle cradling of his head, and her mysterious smile. This act of maternal care, this public act of sentiment and sentimentalism, does not so much consolidate a family as move beyond the familial bonds dictated by kinship. The breast-feeding image, like Tom's final speech, figures gender as a way of performing belonging, of expanding the category of the human by opening up private acts to others.

In *Labor and Desire*, Paula Rabinowitz argues that the masculinist rhetoric of proletarian literature shifts into a rhetoric of maternity as the Popular Front emerges as a large-scale social movement: "If women became Communists out of their maternal instincts, men could become mothers out of their communistic experiences."[41] The novel's conclusion reinstates a trope of sentimentalism, but in a radically altered context. Maternity figures prominently in classic sentimental literature, but Steinbeck's take on maternity is unconventional. Michael Szalay finds Steinbeck's representation of maternity, particularly breast-feeding, troubling: "Women in *The Grapes of Wrath* are taught by anxious men around them to not distinguish between strangers and blood relations, to extend even the most personal forms of maternal aid to those who are not kin but are nevertheless compatriots in a national enterprise."[42] Szalay then reads maternity as a function of patriarchy in *The Grapes of Wrath*. Paula Rabinowitz's analysis of women's proletarian fiction, however, finds that maternity is not merely an inheritance from a flawed sentimentalism:

> Female writers who sought to construct the female working-class subject within the proletarian narrative reembodied metaphors of gender governing the genre through the trope of maternal collectivity. They resurrected the narrative of desire and made of it a means for women to enter history by removing it from the realm of the purely domestic, personal, and psychological where it had traditionally been located. In these novels, the working-class woman's body is inscribed through the dual constructs of labor and desire; the maternal trope, though, however, liberating, still carries traces of the bourgeois motherhood depicted in domestic fiction.[43]

Rather than endorsing the patriarchal control of women, as Szalay argues, *The Grapes of Wrath* uses the "trope of maternal collectivity" along with Tom's spectral masculine activism in an attempt to avoid the very patriarchal residue of "bourgeois motherhood." Indeed, maternity in *The Grapes of Wrath* occurs within a notably reworked familial structure, one that seems very distant from both bourgeois sentiment and patriarchal marriage relations.

The novel's title, *The Grapes of Wrath,* is borrowed from Julia Ward Howe's "Battle-Hymn of the Republic," a song with a transnational, revolutionary, even eschatological message. Howe's "Battle-Hymn" envisions a collective through the "glory in [Christ's] bosom that transfigures you and me," and the hymn mobilized both soldiers and abolitionists, ultimately blurring masculine and feminine forms of activism together in a narrative of redemptive violence.[44] *The Grapes of Wrath* also insists on an emergent collectivity that supercedes the family unit. As Ma states, the Joad family's disintegration ushers in a larger sense of obligation: "Use ta be the fambly was fust. It ain't so now. It's anybody. Worse off we get, the more we got to do."[45] Ma envisions a collective moment removed from traditional kinship structures, where one must work not for one's immediate family but for an expansive, collective good. Like Howe's "Battle-Hymn of the Republic," *The Grapes of Wrath* mobilizes gendered modes of activism, but in an effort to unite the exploited into an active public. In both texts, violence and the "bosom" have the ability to "transfigure," to remake the social. *The Grapes of Wrath*, though, dramatizes not only the sentimental power of gendered activism but also its limitations: femininity connotes maternal care, while masculinity evaporates into spectral promise.

"A Clumsy Vehicle at Best"

After completing the *Grapes of Wrath*, John Steinbeck declared that he was through with novels: "I must make a new start. I've worked the novel—I know it as far as I can take it. I never did think much of it—a clumsy vehicle at best."[46] This "clumsy vehicle," like the modified Model T the Joads used to traverse the Southwest, relies on a tradition of gendered popular literary forms. In reworking family and gender, *The Grapes of Wrath* clumsily moves toward a type of affective belonging that attempts to undo ever-expansive alienation and recognizes that "the worse off we get, the more we got to do."[47] In his review of *The Grapes of Wrath* for the *New Masses*, Granville Hicks describes the novel as the best example of proletarian literature: "We can now say, 'Proletarian literature? Oh, that means a book like John Steinbeck's *The Grapes of Wrath*. Of course, that isn't the only kind of novel that deserves to be called proletarian literature, but it has all the qualities proletarian literature has to have. That is the real thing.' "[48] Barbara Foley sees the imagination of a collective novelistic form, despite the fact that the novel seems to require individuality on a formal level, as the major goal of the proletarian novel.[49] *The Grapes of Wrath* imagines that collectivity through the workings of gender more so than it does through class. While *The Grapes of Wrath* gestures to a radical notion of collectivity, Steinbeck's film and nonfiction writing during World War II seeks to reinscribe an explicitly masculine collectivity into national boundaries. In so doing, Steinbeck foreshadows the ways in which masculinity's role in American literature and culture will be increasingly produced in relation to and in tension with the family after 1945.

Published in 1941 and 1942 respectively, *The Forgotten Village*, a screenplay, and *Bombs Away: The Story of a Bomber Team*, a piece of military propaganda, evidence Steinbeck's attempt to recuperate a place for masculine activity and masculine community from within an increasingly militarized nation by using new textual forms. *The Forgotten Village*, a documentary scripted by Steinbeck and directed by Herbert Kline that was also published as a book containing the script and stills from the film, takes place in Santiago, Mexico, where the local community well is infected with bacteria. Juan Diego, a boy, travels to the city to find a cure. He returns with a team of doctors, but the local medicine woman, fearing that they will ruin her livelihood, turns the villagers against modern medicine, calling the doctors "horse-blood men," since the cure is derived from an infected horse.[50] Juan Diego then sneaks the "horse-blood" cure to his ailing sister, and for doing so is exiled from the village. He ventures to the city, where he goes to medical school. The narrator claims, reassuringly, "The change will come, is coming, as surely as there are thousands of Juan Diegos in the villages of Mexico."[51] The text's final words are uttered by Juan Diego, who states his own name, "I am Juan Diego."[52] He marks himself as one of the "thousands of Juan Diegos" in the villages of Mexico, alienated and suffering, but willing to participate in modernization. Much like the New Deal, this educational narrative endorses participation in a national project rather than clinging to older forms of collectivity. *The Forgotten Village*'s championing of the modernization of Mexico finds a new mode of collective belonging in professionalism. This is a distinct form of masculinity that will become dominant, especially in the United States, in the postwar era. Rather than insisting on social mobility and the disruption of convention, the figure of the technocrat remakes masculinity into an achievement of education, social stability, and prestige.

Published in 1942, *Bombs Away: The Story of a Bomber Team* bears the subtitle "Written for the U.S. Army Air Forces." This book details and glorifies the training and operations of a bomber team, the relatively new mode of warfare employed during World War II.[53] Steinbeck makes no qualms about the book's overt nationalistic purpose.[54] The first sentences read: "A book should have a dedication, I suppose, but this book is a dedication. It is a dedication to the men who have gone through the hard and rigid training of members of a bomber crew and who have gone away to defend the nation."[55] While the book is dedicated to these men fighting for the nation, it is directed to a domestic readership: "this book is intended to be read by the mothers and fathers of the prospective Air Force men, to the end that they will have some idea of the training their sons have undertaken."[56] *Bombs Away* is designed to fuse the family to the militarized nation.

As in *The Forgotten Village*, Steinbeck struggles to find a utopian masculine community in *Bombs Away*. Describing a nation that had lost direction in the 1930s and 1940s, the book's introduction cites frontier expansion as proof of the American citizenry's readiness for war:

> With the very techniques required for this war, our people explored a continent and peopled it and developed it, threw rails across it, drove highways north and south, burrowed for metals, and dammed rivers for power. And the energy and versatility and initiative which developed this continent have not died. Perhaps some of our difficulty before the beginning of this war was caused by the aliveness and the versatility without the goal.[57]

Steinbeck employs a common narrative of American masculinity: after the settling of the frontier, men are domesticated and, without a theater for strenuous exertion, lose their vitality. Hearkening back to Theodore Roosevelt's democratic vision of military service, Steinbeck argues that a resurgence of national feeling will galvanize the populace and reignite progress. As Steinbeck goes on to claim later in the text, the bomber team stands out because every member is necessary:

> This is truly a team, each member responsible to the whole and the whole responsible to the members. And only with its teamlike quality can the bomber successfully function. Here is no commander with subordinates, but a group of responsible individuals functioning as a unit while each member exercises individual judgment and foresight and care. [58]

The utopian community of the bomber team functions without a hierarchy; each member, pulled from different class and regional backgrounds, functions within the collective. The bomber team and the technology around which the team is organized emerge from within the nation, but Steinbeck's rhetoric emphasizes communal action while repressing the violence and hierarchy that structure the nation and America's involvement in World War II.[59]

In his efforts to locate new sites of collective possibility in *The Forgotten Village* and *Bombs Away,* Steinbeck anticipates the shape that masculinity will take in postwar America. The masculinity steeped in styles of self-fashioning that runs throughout American modernism, from the working-class advocacy of dime-novel bandits to Hemingway's democratized connoisseurship, becomes the enforcer of and a threat to normative familial belonging in postwar America. After World War II, masculinity, particularly as dramatized in the Western genre, becomes a trope for "containment," that is, the rigorous policing of domestic and national belonging central to Cold War culture. What is striking about *The Grapes of Wrath*, then, is its radically collective vision, especially compared to the insular forms of belonging in *The Forgotten Village* and *Bombs Away.* Tom Joad universalizes masculinity in his final speech even as he disappears from the novel. This moment points to modernist masculinity's significance as an aesthetic project that is bound to everyday life, namely, the drive to remake the subject into a work of art, yet it also marks a shift in the history of masculinity as that aesthetic impulse is detached from everyday life.

"There Never Was a Man Like Shane"

First published in 1949 for an adult readership, adapted in 1953 into a film directed by George Stevens, and reprinted in 1954 as juvenile literature with all of the dirty words removed, Jack Schaefer's *Shane* tells a familiar story.[1] Similar to other postwar Westerns such as *The Man Who Shot Liberty Valance* or *High Noon, Shane* dramatizes a central tenet of Cold War culture, that the selective use of force is needed to secure domestic stability. What makes *Shane* stand out among the many 1950s Westerns that register various components of Cold War America is its focus on both masculinity and the family. Accordingly, *Shane* seems remarkably clean as far as postwar Westerns go. It has a body count of only four and references none of the gritty realities of frontier life often ubiquitous to the Western: Indian massacre, prostitution, alcoholism, gambling. But, for a narrative almost obsessively antiseptic, where a major confrontation develops over Shane's right to order a soda pop at the local saloon, *Shane* repeatedly and anxiously defines and redefines the threat of "dirty business." Claiming that someone has or participates in "dirty business," whether it is raising livestock or hiring gunfighters, is the ultimate insult in *Shane* and often leads to those most central of Western confrontations, the gunfight and the saloon brawl. I conclude with *Shane* because it dramatizes so well how modernist masculinity is eclipsed by the family in Cold War America. In *Shane,* it is the family unit itself that participates in "dirty business" by excluding masculinities that do not participate within its rigid structures of national—and familial—belonging.[2]

Shane is a historical narrative, ostensibly about the 1892 Johnson Country War in Wyoming. The most frequently accused of "dirty business" in *Shane* are homesteaders, families recently settled in Wyoming on federal land grants to start small farms and raise cattle. The land that the homesteaders settle upon, however, is not vacant wilderness. A rancher—named Fletcher in the novel and Riker in the film—uses the land for free-range cattle grazing. Because the homesteaders interfere with his access to water and land, the rancher and his cowboys terrorize the settlers, hoping to scare them away. One of their central tactics is insult; the rancher's men call the homesteaders "pig farmers."[3] This accusation—that the homesteaders are unclean because they raise an animal that lives in filth—points to *Shane*'s ideological function as a transitional narrative. The true difference between *Shane*'s ranchers and the homesteaders is the production not of pigs or cattle, but of subjects on the frontier. As such, this classic Western has just as much to do with postwar U.S. culture as it does with the late nineteenth century, and it indeed dramatizes the dominance of the family in Cold War America. As James Gilbert argues, crises of masculinity are often thought to peak in both the late nineteenth century and the 1950s: "the basic account of the history of masculinity in the twentieth century has become one of crisis and response, rapid change, problematic compromise, and shifting definitions of manliness with the 1890s and 1950s as key moments of transition."[4] Gilbert goes on to argue that this narrative of crisis is best viewed skeptically, owing to its myopic construction of a universal, essential masculinity. I share Gilbert's skepticism of the crisis model of masculinity. As I have argued throughout this project, masculinity is multiple and malleable. The language of crisis assumes that there is some fixed masculine identity, when in fact masculinity is remade throughout the late nineteenth and twentieth centuries. What is telling about the 1950s, as evidenced through *Shane*, is the increasing importance of the family and the imperative to create a safe, secure domestic space for children. While works such as *The Life and Adventures of Nat Love*, *The Virginian*, even *My Àntonia* conclude with domestic stability, the narratives themselves focus not on the family and the home but instead spend a great deal of their narratives chronicling mobility. In striking contrast, *Shane*'s entire narrative hinges upon threats to and the protection of domestic space.

Shane narrates the way in which masculine individuals give way to—and even help entrench the dominance of—the stable family. The rancher's insult of "pig farming" is apropos of this transition, for the homesteaders raise children unable to think of conditions other than those of their parents. The homesteaders work to create a safe, quiet environment for their children to learn how to behave responsibly as citizens. In the economy of private property and secure homes ultimately triumphant in *Shane*, one remains in the same place, in stark contrast to the obsolete cowpuncher or gunfighter, who lives in no particular place and has no particular home.

This binary, threatening homosocial nomadism and wholesome heterosexual domesticity, was quite common in 1950s America. As Gilbert argues, the 1950s "crisis" in masculinity was narrated as an "initial male preponderance—a homosocial world—that eventually everywhere gave way to a female majority."[5] This narrative of masculinity in crisis is not specific to the 1950s but is instead repeated through the late nineteenth and twentieth centuries, and *Shane* allegorizes a shift away from mobility and toward stability in American culture. The significance of stability and legibility has been discussed by Alan Nadel as "containment culture," a dominant trope in Cold War America that "equated containment of communism with containment of atomic secrets, of sexual license, of gender roles, of nuclear energy, and of artistic expression."[6] The Western is a central genre to "containment culture," especially owing to its dramatization of the way in which, according to Nadel, "the success of the Western man...is measured by his ability to create a place in which there is no longer any place for him."[7] That is, masculinity contains and secures domestic space while excluding itself from that containment. Stanley Corkin also links the postwar Western to containment, and he suggests similarly that "the heroes of these films compete with the forces of atavism to see if they can bring those with ordinary characteristics—the mass of bystanders—definitively into the family of civilized, socially responsible humanity."[8] By providing a secure normative domesticity, masculinity comes to be both constitutive of and a danger to the family. In *Shane*, this mode of representing masculinity is explicitly played out in the context of domestic space, and masculinity comes to signify less a style than a necessary threat to the social fabric of America.

Jack Schaefer's *Shane* is narrated by Bob, who appears as a child in the narrative. He is, however, narrating the story many years after he "has had a chance to live out his boyhood and grow straight inside as a man should."[9] Speaking from the secure vantage point of the normative "straight" man, Bob describes the development of his town in Wyoming from the first arrival of miners, its boost as a stagecoach stop, the construction of a saloon and general store, to the eventual presence of a schoolhouse. The narrative, shared by both novel and film, opens with the title character's appearance at the Starrett farm, which is in close proximity to town. Shane emerges from open grazing land and enters into the Starrett family's private property, the fences rendered obscene and scant in the film compared to the broad landscape surrounding them. Shane is a mysterious figure; he carries guns, and the villainous rancher and his hired guns know him by reputation. However, Shane also has a soft spot for young Bob—or little Joey in the film, which further emphasizes the insularity of the family unit through the repeated patronym—as well as for Joe and Marian Starrett, Bob/Joey's homesteader parents. The story follows Shane's employment by Joe Starrett as a farmhand, and his eventual gunfight with the villains, Stark Wilson, a hired gunfighter, and Fletcher/Riker, the old rancher who attempts to drive Joe Starrett and the other homesteaders off of their riverside properties. In the end, Shane kills the bad men and rides off, mortally wounded. This concluding moment casts masculinity as useful only insofar as it erases itself. Shane successfully removes the possibility of life outside of conventional domestic space.

Shane is residual, a member of the old and now obsolete order. His origin is ambiguous in both the novel and the film, but the two versions use his ambiguous origin to different ends. In the novel, when Shane arrives, young Bob first notices his worn yet strikingly fancy clothes:

> As he came near, what impressed me first was his clothes. He wore dark trousers of some serge material tucked into tall boots and held at the waist by a wide belt, both of a soft black leather and tooled in intricate design. A coat of the same dark material as the trousers was neatly folded and strapped to his saddle-roll. His shirt was finespun linen, rich brown in color. The handkerchief knotted loosely around his throat was black silk. His hat was not the familiar Stetson, not the familiar gray or muddy tan. It was a plain black, soft in texture, unlike any hat I had ever seen, with a creased crown and a wide curling brim swept down in front to shield the face. All trace of newness was long since gone from these things. The dust of distance was beaten into them. They were worn and stained and several new patches showed on the shirt. Yet a kind of magnificence remained and with it a hint of men and manners alien to my limited boy's experience.[10]

Shane's dress connotes an alien way of life. Bob can only describe him with opposites: his clothes are "worn" yet "magnificent," "finespun" and "stained." Like Deadwood Dick, Shane is a contradictory and elusive figure; he is at ease, but "even in this easiness was a suggestion of tension. It was the easiness of a coiled spring, of a trap set."[11] Shane is portrayed as a formal mechanism, an agent in place to mediate between his own obsolete, nomadic style and the newly stable homestead. The novel's depiction of Shane likens him to a chivalrous Southerner; Joe and Marian guess that he is from Tennessee and "was shaped in some firm forging of past circumstance for other things," an educated and civilized man who defends the homesteaders in lieu of "past" causes.[12] Furthering this allusion to the South, Shane defends the homesteaders against claims of miscegenation. Wilson, the hired gunfighter, accuses Ernie Wright, a homesteader, of being a "crossbreed squatter."[13] Shane defends the homesteaders from insults and allegations as to their purity and purges the frontier of the impure, including Fletcher, who notably shares his name with the maker of arrowheads. The novel, then, consolidates the homesteaders through a shared racial identity, one that is distinctly and aggressively white, in opposition to the rancher and cowboys, who are associated with Native Americans, animals, and the uncultivated land of the open prairie. Importantly, though, for all of Shane's work to unite the homesteaders against the ranchers, he cannot fully participate in their consolidated community. He is marked by his outsider status, and this resonates not only with his familiarity with gunfights but also with his strange black and brown clothes.

While the novel emphasizes racial solidarity, the film is more explicitly nationalist in its portrayal of the homesteaders. In the film, Shane is dressed in buckskin, a kind of Natty Bumppo figure posing as a Native American; he does not represent Southern chivalry and civilized whiteness but instead mythological Western primitivism. The film further emphasizes the homesteader's solidarity through national belonging by remaking Ernie Wright, the homesteader accused of being a "crossbreed" in the novel, into Stonewall Torrey, a devout Southerner from Alabama who is accused of being "rebel trash." When Torrey is shot and killed, the homesteaders bury him and are further galvanized to resist the threats of the ranching organization. The burial of the Civil War veteran serves to unite the homesteaders as members of the same nation through an imaginary reconciliation between North and South. Tellingly, the rancher in the film is renamed Riker, associating him not with Native Americans, as he is in the novel, but with Nazism. Thus, the film version of *Shane* portrays the homesteaders as first and foremost national subjects and uses national belonging as the basis for collective identification. This nationalism is, of course, still tied to racial homogeneity. The discourse of nationalism merely masks the white supremacy that underlies the narrative, made clear when Shane, associated with the primitive by his buckskin suit, rides off into the distance at the end of the film and leaves the more indisputably white settlers to their safe, quiet town.

While the novel and film versions of *Shane* differ in their privileging of race and nation as rallying points for the settlers, both texts figure the creation of a home as a national endeavor. Shane's first activity on the Starrett farm—in both the novel and film—is the removal of a large tree stump. Shane and Joe Starrett work together, clearing the land in a heroic act of physical exertion. The removal of the stump signifies the homesteaders' civilizing mission; the old ways, no matter how permanent they may seem, must be uprooted. By overturning the stump, the Starrett family takes possession of the land; it undergoes a transition from wilderness to private home. Afterward, the men eat Marian's apple pie. The apple pie inducts Shane into national belonging, distancing him from the rancher and cowboys, with whom he has much more in common.

Shane's presence in the Starrett household also troubles their stability, especially with his ubiquitous six-shooters. In the film, when Shane teaches Joey how to use a revolver, Mrs. Starrett scolds him: "Guns aren't going to be my boy's life…We'd all be much better off if there wasn't a single gun in this valley." This sentiment puts child-raising, particularly in an environment free of violence, above all other values. Paradoxically, then, *Shane* is a story about the necessity of violence for the production of the safe, violence-free family space that Mrs. Starrett desires. This seeming contradiction—that violence is required to end violence—casts Shane as a necessity to domestic security yet also a threat to its permanence. The film ultimately resolves this through Shane's disappearance at the end of the narrative.[14] In order for the family to survive, Shane's mode of being as a single male content to work the land and own nothing but what is on his back must vanish. The code by which Shane and the rancher live is obsolete; violence is no longer the means by which one is expected to resolve conflicts.

In *A Singular Modernity*, Fredric Jameson emphasizes the importance of transitional narratives that make use of a "vanishing mediator" and that give an ideological reason for social change.[15] With this in mind, *Shane* serves an ideological purpose. The narrative contours the shift in the late nineteenth century from large-scale and openly competitive cattle ranching to fenced-in farms, legitimized by property rights rather than violent force. This development also brings commodities to the frontier in an entirely new magnitude, facilitating the industrialization of the agrarian economy, one of the markers of late capitalism. Shane then functions as a "vanishing mediator" who facilitates change but ultimately renders himself obsolete. Without any Indians or bad men to kill, Shane has made the frontier safe for the civilized; his job done, he rides off into the sunset, never to return. Speaking from the position of the man who has grown "straight,"

Bob embraces the stable manhood left in Shane's absence yet also notes the lingering appeal of a more fluid masculinity that exists as stories and imaginings: "I guess that is all there is to tell. The folks in town and the kids at school liked to talk about Shane, to spin tales and speculate about him. I never did."[16]

Shane repeatedly emphasizes that the "safe" place, the only place in which one can be oneself, is the private home. The novel contains a telling symbol of Shane's ideological function as a mediator between a masculinity that thrives on mobility and instability and a domestic organization of the nation's citizens. In a fit of frustration after Shane's disappearance, Joe Starrett attempts to remove one of the fence posts Shane set on the family farm:

> He took hold of the post and pulled it. He shook his head and braced his feet and strained at it with all his strength. The big muscles of his shoulders and back knotted and bulged till I thought this shirt, too, would shred. Creakings ran along the rails and the post moved ever so slightly and the ground at the base showed little cracks fanning out. But the rails held and the post stood.[17]

In his wake, Shane leaves private property as a structural, legal, and economic certainty. The homesteader's claim to the land, tenuous throughout the narrative, is now absolute. The family's fences are permanent.

Shane marks the mediation from one brand of masculinity, the lone hero who must constantly enact masculinity through confrontations, to another, the paternal stability of Joe Starrett. Furthermore, the narrative is told from the viewpoint of a child, the new ideal postwar American citizen. Held in a strange, ungendered space—he wears a long nightgown for nearly half of the film—Joey does not have a clear mode of gender performance. The narrative repeatedly foregrounds his function as a consumer, as a passive spectator who loves soda and fetishizes guns, but who is never deemed responsible enough to act on his own. The Starrett boy, then, marks the rise of what Lauren Berlant refers to as "the infant citizen," the American citizen who is incapable of making rational decisions for himself because, as Joe says of his son, "he ain't quite of age."[18] *Shane* narrates the policing of masculinity within Cold War America, as the family and the child become the increasingly dominant figures for national belonging.[19] Masculinity serves as a mediator for these shifting concerns, and Shane stands out as a doomed alternative to the dominant order. Neither a grisly rancher nor a family man,

Shane embodies masculine style; he is a man who changes roles with changes of clothes.

The film's final scene, in which little Joey plaintively cries "Come Back, Shane!" as the eponymous hero rides off in the distance, provides a glimpse of the persistent appeal of masculine style, even in its obsolescence. Joey both identifies with and desires Shane; in the words of Willa Cather's Ántonia, he "[likes] to be like a man."[20] Indeed, the fact that Shane performs rather than possesses masculinity is why he is so appealing. As the film's promotional trailer asserts, "There never was a man like Shane." Indeed, Shane is not a man in any stable sense. Joey's longing for Shane's return gestures to both the nature of masculinity as a style solidified through repetition and our common misunderstanding of what masculinity is. The child grows up "straight inside as a man should" at the end of the novel version of *Shane*, and in so doing, masculinity becomes the site of melancholic attachment.[21] Shane leaves Joey, never to return, yet this absence is also full of unrealized possibility. Because "there never was a man like Shane," Joey has not lost anything at all. Instead, masculinity remains a matter of performance, style, and affect, rather than a concrete object to be lost or found. The possibilities opened up by masculinity persist, creating new constellations of fantasy, intimacy, and belonging. Unfortunately for Joey, and for us, masculinity's unruliness in postwar American culture is too often viewed as threatening when it is so full of possibility.

Notes

Introduction: Masculinity, Modernism, and the West

1. My argument about masculinity here and throughout is influenced by Judith Butler's work on gender performativity and Eve Kosofsky Sedgwick's work on masculinity, which separates masculinity from a binary relationship with femininity. See Judith Butler, *Bodies that Matter: On the Discursive Limits of "Sex"* (New York: Routledge, 1993), 1–55; and *Gender Trouble: Feminism and the Subversion of Identity* (1990; New York: Routledge, 1999), 163–80; and Eve Kosofsky Sedgwick, "Gosh, Boy George, You Must Be Awfully Secure in Your Masculinity!," *Constructing Masculinity*, ed. Maurice Berger, Brian Wallis, and Simon Watson (New York: Routledge, 1995), 11–20. The growing body of scholarship on masculinity has been usefully anthologized in a handful of volumes, including Rachel Adams and David Savran, eds., *The Masculinity Studies Reader* (New York: Blackwell, 2002); Maurice Berger, Brian Wallis, and Simon Watson, eds., *Constructing Masculinity* (New York: Routledge, 1995); and Judith Kegan Gardiner, ed., *Masculinity Studies and Feminist Theory: New Directions* (New York: Columbia UP, 2002).

2. Frederick Jackson Turner begins his "The Significance of the Frontier in American History" (*Does the Frontier Make America Exceptional?*, ed. Richard Etulain (Boston: Bedford, 1999), 18–43) by citing the 1890 census as evidence of the closing of the frontier and, therefore, as a moment of crisis for American nationalism and American masculinity.

3. Constance Penley and Sharon Willis, "Introduction," *Male Trouble*, ed. Constance Penley and Sharon Willis (Minneapolis: U of Minnesota P, 1993), xviii.

4. Gail Bederman, *Manliness and Civilization: A Cultural History of Gender and Race in the United States, 1880–1917* (Chicago: U of Chicago P, 1995), 42.

5. For further treatments of manhood and nineteenth-century America, see Amy S. Greenberg, *Manifest Manhood and the Antebellum American Empire* (Cambridge: Cambridge UP, 2005); Dana D. Nelson, *National Manhood: Capitalist Citizenship and the Imagined Fraternity of White Men* (Durham: Duke UP, 1998); Alexander Saxton, *The Rise and Fall of the White Republic: Class Politics and Mass Culture in Nineteenth-Century America* (1990; New York: Verso, 2003); and Shelley Streeby, *American Sensations: Class, Empire, and the Production of Popular Culture* (Berkeley: U of California P, 2002).

6. There is a growing body of scholarship that looks closely at nineteenth-century male sentimentalism, a complex phenomenon that has been overlooked by the public/private distinction's mapping out of gender roles. This body of

scholarship provides a valuable backdrop to my work here in its interrogation of the supposedly rational, public manhood of the nineteenth century. See Mary Chapman and Glenn Hendler, eds., *Sentimental Men: Masculinity and the Politics of Affect in American Culture* (Berkeley: U of California P, 1999); David Greven, *Men beyond Desire: Manhood, Sex, and Violation in American Literature* (New York: Palgrave, 2005); Glenn Hendler, *Public Sentiments: Structures of Feeling in Nineteenth-Century American Literature* (Chapel Hill: U of North Carolina P, 2001); Milette Shamir and Jennifer Travis, eds., *Boys Don't Cry?: Rethinking Narratives of Masculinity and Emotion in the U.S.* (New York: Columbia UP, 2002); and Jennifer Travis, *Wounded Hearts: Masculinity, Law, and Literature in American Culture* (Chapel Hill: U of North Carolina P, 2005). For a critique of the public/private distinction and its gendered connotations, see Cathy N. Davidson and Jessamyn Hatcher, eds., *No More Separate Spheres!: A Next Wave American Studies Reader* (Durham: Duke UP, 2002).

7. Judith Halberstam, *Female Masculinity* (Durham: Duke UP, 1998), 2.

8. Along with Halberstam, Jean Bobby Noble's *Masculinities Without Men?: Female Masculinity in Twentieth-Century Fictions* (Vancouver: U of British Columbia P, 2004). has also influenced my thinking here. Like Halberstam's *Female Masculinity*, Noble's work is concerned with masculinities that are not male.

9. Butler, *Bodies that Matter*, 187.

10. Wendy Brown, *States of Injury: Power and Freedom in Late Modernity* (Princeton: Princeton UP, 1995), 167.

11. Butler, *Bodies that Matter*, 122.

12. Fredric Jameson, *The Political Unconscious: Narrative as Socially Symbolic Act* (Ithaca: Cornell UP, 1981), 102.

13. Ibid., 286.

14. The high/low divide is often thought to be constituted in part on the masculine/feminine binary. The influential account of the high/low divide's gendering is Andreas Huyssen's "Mass Culture as Woman: Modernism's Other" in Andreas Huyssen, *After the Great Divide: Modernism, Mass Culture, Postmodernism* (Bloomington: Indiana UP, 1986), 44–62.

15. Sedgwick, "Gosh, Boy George...," 15.

16. Rita Felski, *The Gender of Modernity* (Cambridge: Harvard UP, 1995), 114.

17. For example, Aaron Jaffe analyzes the marketing and celebrity-making devices of writers, publishers, and editors, yet these structures are held separate from culture more broadly defined. See Aaron Jaffe, *Modernism and the Culture of Celebrity* (New York: Cambridge UP, 2005). Other works that seek to analyze modernism's mode of production include Loren Glass, *Authors, Inc.: Literary Celebrity in the Modern United States, 1880–1980* (New York: New York UP, 2004); Lawrence Rainey, *The Institutions of Modernism: Literary Elites and Public Culture* (New Haven: Yale UP, 1998); and Catherine Turner, *Marketing Modernism between the Two World Wars* (Amherst: U of Massachusetts P, 2003).

18. Michael North, *Reading 1922: A Return to the Scene of the Modern* (New York: Oxford UP, 1999), 11.

19. Felski, *Gender of Modernity*, 144.

20. Douglas Mao and Rebecca L. Walkowitz, "The New Modernist Studies," *PMLA* 123.3 (May 2008), 737.

21. Raymond Williams, "When Was Modernism?," *The Politics of Modernism: Against the New Conformists*, ed. Tony Pinkney (1989; New York: Verso, 2007), 35.

22. E. E. Cummings, "Buffalo Bill's," *100 Selected Poems* (New York: Grove P, 1994), 7. I regret that I can only quote two lines from this poem due to copyright restrictions.

23. For accounts of the divisions between high and low, the avant-garde and the bourgeois, and other binaries for approaching modernist art and its tensions with mass culture, see Peter Bürger, *Theory of the Avant-Garde*, trans. Michael Shaw (Minneapolis: U of Minnesota P, 1984); Matei Calinescu, *Five Faces of Modernity: Modernism, Avant-Garde, Decadence, Kitsch, Postmodernism* (Durham: Duke UP, 1987); and Huyssen, *After the Great Divide*.

24. For a cultural history of Buffalo Bill and his Wild West Show, see Joy S. Kasson, *Buffalo Bill's Wild West: Celebrity, Memory, and Popular History* (New York: Hill & Wang, 2000).

25. For an account of American masculinity that focuses on emasculation as a product of modernity, see Michael S. Kimmel, *Manhood in America* (New York: Free P, 1996). For theories of masculinity that focus on woundedness, see David Savran, *Taking it Like a Man: White Masculinity, Masochism, and Contemporary American Culture* (Princeton: Princeton UP, 1998); Kaja Silverman, *Male Subjectivity at the Margins* (New York: Routledge, 1992); and Paul Smith, *Clint Eastwood: A Cultural Production* (Minneapolis: U of Minnesota P, 1993).

26. T. S. Eliot, *The Waste Land*, 1922, *Selected Poems* (New York: Harcourt, 1964), lines 69–76.

27. For a very convincing reading of "Stetson" in *The Waste Land* as a reference to the Western hat, see Donald J. Childs, "Stetson in *The Waste Land*," *Essays in Criticism* 38.2 (April 1988): 131–48. Childs's reading makes this link explicit by pointing out that Australian soldiers were known for wearing Stetson hats and that this reference would have linked the "Stetson" figure to the Gallipoli Campaign, where Eliot's close friend Jean Verdenal was killed. "Stetson" then signifies loss and homosocial affection, and those affects are relayed through a sign—the Stetson hat—that connotes the American West.

28. For a recent critical treatment of heteronormativity and polemical endorsement of queerness as alternative to "reproductive futurity," see Lee Edelman, *No Future: Queer Theory and the Death Drive* (Durham: Duke UP, 2004).

29. F. Scott Fitzgerald, *The Great Gatsby* (1925; New York: Collier, 1992), 184.

30. Michael T. Gilmore, *Surface and Depth: The Quest for Legibility in American Culture* (New York: Oxford UP, 2003), 139.

31. William Faulkner, *Light in August* (1932; New York: Vintage, 1990), 111–12.

32. Ibid., 112.

33. For a reading of the importance of pulp and popular magazines to modernism, see David M. Earle, *Re-Covering Modernism: Pulps, Paperbacks, and the Prejudice of Form* (Burlington: Ashgate, 2009).

34. Bill Brown, *A Sense of Things: The Object Matter of American Literature* (Chicago: U of Chicago P, 2003), 3.

35. Willa Cather, "The Novel Démeublé," *Willa Cather: Stories, Poems, and Other Writings*, ed. Sharon O'Brien (New York: Library of America, 1992), 834; and Ernest Hemingway, *Death in the Afternoon* (1932; New York: Touchstone, 1996), 191.

36. I was initially drawn to dime novels by Michael Denning's *Mechanic Accents.* Denning's interest in class, in both *Mechanic Accents* and *The Cultural Front,* seemed to occlude the fact that in both works activism was explicitly gendered masculine. This study, in a way, is an attempt to account for why masculinity is so crucial to the American Left and provides, I hope, a kind of connective tissue between Denning's two studies. See Michael Denning, *Mechanic Accents: Dime Novels and Working-Class Culture in America* (1987; New York: Verso, 1998); and *The Cultural Front* (New York: Verso, 1997).

1   MASCULINITY FOR THE MILLION: GENDER IN DIME-NOVEL WESTERNS

1. Anthony Comstock, *Traps for the Young,* ed. Robert Bremmer (1883; Cambridge: Harvard UP, 1967), 21.
2. Ibid., 21–22.
3. Ibid., 22.
4. Dana D. Nelson argues that white manhood, "an abstracting group marker," dominated post-Revolutionary America. National manhood serves to "effectively undercut the radicalizing energy of local democratic practices and effectively [reroute] the conceptualization of democracy in the new nation, atomizing the idea of participation and fitting citizens out for market competition." Nelson's argument grounds the presidency in this "imagined fraternity" and convincingly traces the messianic promise of radical democracy run aground through the American Renaissance to the Clinton administration. Nelson's construction of "manhood" differs from "masculinity" in that the former refers to a stable, classist, usually white identity, while the latter is a narrative form and not a stable identity grounded in an essential classed, raced, or gendered body. See Nelson, *National Manhood: Capitalist Citizenship and the Imagined Fraternity of White Men* (Durham: Duke UP, 1998), 28, 34. The historical shift from manhood to the more performance-based masculinity is discussed in broader terms in Michael Kimmel, *Manhood in America: A Cultural History* (New York: Free P, 1996), 117–55. This distinction, between character-based manhood and performative masculinity, is supported by Warren I. Susman's argument about the difference between character and personality. See Warren I. Susman, "'Personality' and the Making of Twentieth-Century Culture," *Culture as History: The Transformation of American Society in the Twentieth Century* (1973; Washington, DC: Smithsonian, 2003), 271–85. There is a large body of scholarship that deals with nineteenth-century manhood. The sources particularly useful for this study are: Gail Bederman, *Manliness and Civilization: A Cultural History of Gender and Race in the United States, 1880–1917* (Chicago: U of Chicago P, 1995); Paul Gilmore, *The Genuine Article: Race, Mass Culture, and American Literary Manhood* (Durham: Duke UP, 2001); Kimmel, *Manhood in America*; Nelson, *National Manhood*; and E. Anthony Rotundo, *American Manhood: Transformations in Masculinity from the Revolution to the Modern Era* (New York: Basic, 1993).
5. William Everett, "Beadle's Dime Books," *North American Review* 99 (July 1864), 308.
6. A reading of "the genteel tradition" in American culture, from Alexis de Tocqueville through George Santayana, is offered in Robert Dawidoff, *The*

Genteel Tradition and the Sacred Rage: High Culture vs. Democracy in Adams, James, & Santayana (Chapel Hill: U of North Carolina P, 1992).

7. For an extended discussion of Comstock's use of demonic images and his anxieties about pornography, see Mark I. West, "The Role of Sexual Repression in Anthony Comstock's Campaign to Censor Children's Dime Novels," *Journal of American Culture* 22.4 (Winter 1999): 45–49.

8. "She Wants to Be a Cowboy," *New York Times*, October 23, 1888, 6.

9. Ibid.

10. Ibid.

11. For a dime novel that features Calamity Jane as a masculine heroine, see Edward Wheeler's *Deadwood Dick on Deck; or, Calamity Jane, the Heroine of Whoop-Up, Seth Jones by Edward S. Ellis and Deadwood Dick on Deck by Edward J. Wheeler: Dime Novels*, ed. Philip Durham (New York: Odyssey, 1966), 97–188. This dime novel originally appeared in *Beadle's Half-Dime Library* 73 (December 13, 1878). In his chapter on the "Dime Novel Heroine" in *Virgin Land,* Henry Nash Smith remarks that the masculine heroine is "distinguished from the hero solely by the physical fact of her sex," which I find less interesting than the fluidity of masculinity afforded to characters in dime novels. See Henry Nash Smith, *Virgin Land: The American West as Symbol and Myth* (1950; Cambridge: Harvard UP, 1978), 119. For a reading of Calamity Jane as an unconventional figure, see Janet Dean, "Calamities of Convention in a Dime Novel Western," *Scorned Literature: Essays on the History and Criticism of Popular and Mass-Produced Fiction in America*, ed. Lydia Cushman Schurman and Deidre Johnson (Westport: Greenwood, 2002), 37–50.

12. It is my contention here and throughout that masculinity is a mode of embodiment that does not have a necessary relation to patriarchal, imperialist, or racist politics but that is often associated with these traits in dominant culture. Judith Halberstam also argues for this view in the context of female masculinity. She rightly claims that one can see the alternative uses of masculinity "by turning a blind eye to conventional masculinities and refusing to engage." By avoiding a critical template that relegates Westerns and the masculinity produced therein to facets of imperialism, this chapter will try to disengage the gender and class politics of the dime-novel Western from conventional nineteenth-century manhood. See Halberstam, *Female Masculinity* (Durham: Duke UP, 1998), 6.

13. An account of the collecting scene surrounding dime novels in the first half of the twentieth century is provided by the indispensable dime-novel reference, Albert Johannsen, *The House of Beadle and Adams and its Dime and Nickel Novels: The Story of a Vanished Literature*, 3 vols. (Norman: U of Oklahoma P, 1950–1962). A journal for collectors of dime novels also exists, *The Dime Novel Round-Up*, initially *Reckless Ralph's Dime Novel Round-up* from 1931 through 1955. This journal features bibliographies of dime-novel authors and publishers.

14. Nelson, *National Manhood*.

15. The historical information regarding dime-novel publishers comes from a handful of reference sources. A short but very useful account of dime-novel publishing is given in Bill Brown, "Introduction: Reading the West," *Reading the West: An Anthology of Dime Westerns*, ed. Bill Brown (Boston: Bedford, 1997), 1–40. The definitive work on dime-novel publishers Beadle and Adams is Johannsen, *The House of Beadle and Adams*. For a history of Street and Smith, another dime-novel publisher, see Quentin Reynolds, *The*

Fiction Factory or from Pulp Row to Quality Street: The Story of 100 Years of Publishing at Street & Smith (New York: Random House, 1955). For an account of story papers, the predecessors to the dime novel, see Mary Noel, *Villains Galore…: The Heyday of the Popular Story Weekly* (New York: Macmillan, 1954) and E. S. Turner, *Boys Will Be Boys: The Story of Sweeney Todd, Deadwood Dick, Sexton Blake, Dick Barton, et al.* (London: Michael Joseph, 1948). An autobiographical account of Street and Smith can also be found in Gilbert Patten, *Frank Merriwell's "Father": An Autobiography by Gilbert Patten ("Burt L. Standish")*, ed. Harriet Hinsdale (Norman: U of Oklahoma P, 1964). The most recent reference work on dime novels is J. Randolph Cox, *The Dime Novel Companion: A Sourcebook* (Westport: Greenwood, 2000). Another valuable resource that traces the development of the dime-novel Western from its roots in Cooper's Leatherstocking Tales to narratives about cowboys and bandits is Daryl Jones, *The Dime Novel Western* (Bowling Gree: Bowling Green U Popular P, 1978).

16. The character-driven dime novel regularly features this open-ended narrative form. For other examples of this in the Western genre, see the James Boys dime novels published in Frank Tousey's *New York Detective Library*, the Buffalo Bill stories that appeared in *Beadle's Boys Library of Sport*, and Street and Smith's *Diamond Dick Library*. The detective genre also capitalized on recurring characters, especially in Street and Smith's *Nick Carter Library*, Frank Tousey's *Secret Service: Old and Young King Brady*, and Norman Munro's *Old Cap Collier Library*. Another very popular recurring character was Frank Merriwell, who appeared in Street and Smith's *Tip Top Weekly*. The narrative structure I am detailing in this essay occurs in all of these series through repeated avoidance of stabilizing endings. This is a narrative strategy that would have a direct impact on the pulp magazines and superhero comic books that followed the dime novels in the twentieth century.

17. As Janet Dean notes, some of the most exciting new scholarship on Western literature has focused on "the West as an imagined space where gender boundaries are blurred." See Janet Dean, "Searching for the New Western Literary Criticism," *Modern Fiction Studies* 46.4 (2000), 957. There are a number of studies that look at the complexities of masculinity in the Western. The most influential studies for my project have been Blake Allmendinger, *The Cowboy: Representations of Labor in an American Work Culture* (New York: Oxford UP, 1992); *Ten Most Wanted: The New Western Literature* (New York: Routledge, 1998); Christine Bold, *Selling the Wild West: Popular Western Fiction, 1860–1960* (Bloomington: Indiana UP, 1987); Melody Graulich and Stephen Tatum, eds., *Reading The Virginian in the New West* (Lincoln: U of Nebraska P, 2003); William Handley, *Marriage, Violence, and the Nation in the American Literary West* (Cambridge: Cambridge UP, 2002); Michael K. Johnson, *Black Masculinity and the Frontier Myth in American Literature* (Norman: U of Oklahoma P, 2002); Lee Clark Mitchell, *Westerns: Making the Man in Fiction and Film* (Chicago: U of Chicago P, 1996); Forrest G. Robinson, *Having it Both Ways: Self-Subversion in Western Popular Classics* (Albuquerque: U of New Mexico P, 1993); and Barbara Will, "The Nervous Origins of the American Western," *American Literature* 70.2 (1998): 293–316. The classic and still very useful study of the West as a mythological space is Smith, *Virgin Land*.

18. Johannsen, *House of Beadle and Adams*, 31–33.

19. Edward S. Ellis's *Seth Jones; or, The Captives of the Frontier* was first printed in *Beadle's Dime Novels* 8 (October 2, 1860). It was reprinted in the London-based *Beadle's American Library* 1 (February 15, 1861), and in *American Library Tales* 1 (April 1862), which was a bound collection of three novels from the *Beadle's American Library* Series. The novel was also reprinted in *Beadle's Fifteen Cent Novels* 8 (1860); *New & Old Friends* 1 (January 25, 1873); *Beadle's Half-Dime Library* 8 (November 9, 1877); *Beadle's New Dime Novels* 519 (June 20, 1882); *Beadle's Pocket Library* 82 (August 5, 1885); and *Beadle's Half-Dime Library* 1104 (August 1900). Further citations of this text refer to Edward S. Ellis, *Seth Jones; or, the Captives of the Frontier, Reading the West: An Anthology of Dime Westerns*, ed. Bill Brown (Boston: Bedford, 1997), 172–268.

20. Ellis, *Seth Jones*, 173.

21. Ibid., 209.

22. In his canonical 1893 address to the American Historical Association, "The Significance of the Frontier in American History," Frederick Jackson Turner defines American masculinity as the synthesis of a dialectic between the European and the Native American, or "civilized" and "savage." Arguing that the frontier makes America exceptional, Turner asserts that the European immigrant adopts Native American practices and becomes an American, a new type of man. The Native American influence begins with dress and then moves on to agriculture, for the settler "has gone to planting Indian corn and plowing with a sharp stick." After this agricultural influence, the settler "shouts the war cry and takes the scalp in orthodox Indian fashion. In short, at the frontier the environment is at first too harsh for the man. He must accept the conditions which it furnishes or perish, and so he fits himself into the Indian clearings and follows the Indian trails." See Frederick Jackson Turner, "The Significance of the Frontier in American History," *Does the Frontier Experience Make America Exceptional?* ed. Richard W. Etulain (Boston: Bedford, 1999), 20.

23. Ellis, *Seth Jones*, 217.

24. Haldidge is an "Indian-hater" character much like those discussed in Richard Slotkin, *Regeneration Through Violence: The Mythology of the American Frontier, 1600–1860* (1973; New York: Harper Perennial, 1996); and Richard *The Fatal Environment: The Myth of the Frontier in the Age of Industrialization, 1800–1890* (1985; New York: Harper Perennial, 1994). It is important to note, though, that the dime novel as a genre does not have a consistent attitude toward Indians. In fact, the first dime novel published by Beadle and Adams, Ann S. Stephens's *Malaeska; or, the Indian Wife of the White Hunter*, is a sentimental romance that features a sympathetic, though ultimately self-sacrificing, Indian woman, the title character Malaeska. As Bill Brown points out, Deadwood Dick eventually befriends and protects Indians, who have "[joined] the ranks of the oppressed who need to be defended by the hero." For a dime novel where Deadwood Dick fights for Indian land rights, see Edward L. Wheeler, *Deadwood Dick's Claim; or, The Fairy Face of Faro Flats, Beadle's Half-Dime Library* 362 (July 1, 1884). Ann S. Stephens's *Malaeska; or, the Indian Wife of the White Hunter* was published as *Beadle's Dime Novels* 1 (June 9, 1860). See Brown, "Introduction," 34 and Ann S. Stephens, *Malaeska; or, the Indian Wife of the White Hunter*, 1860, *Reading the West: An Anthology of Dime Westerns*, ed. Bill Brown (Boston: Bedford, 1997), 57–164.

25. Ellis, *Seth Jones*, 258.
26. For evidence that dime novelists did in fact think in these formal terms, see this guide to writing fiction, written by a former dime novelist, which literally maps out various mechanical plot points for the aspiring novelist: William Wallace Cook, *Plotto: A New Method of Plot Suggestion for Writers of Creative Fiction* (Battle Creek: Ellis Publishing, 1928).
27. Michael Denning, *Mechanic Accents: Dime Novels and Working-Class Culture in America* (Revised Ed. New York: Verso, 1998).
28. Ellis, *Seth Jones*, 262–64.
29. Pauline Hopkins's *Winona: A Tale of Negro Life in the South and Southwest* offers an interesting variation on the dime novel. Originally serialized in 1902 in the *Colored American Magazine*, the captivity narrative features John Brown as bandit hero and ends with the title character, Winona, realizing her aristocratic heritage and moving to England. See Pauline Hopkins, *Winona: A Tale of Negro Life in the South and Southwest, The Magazine Novels of Pauline Hopkins* (New York: Oxford UP, 1988), 285–437. For a comparison of *Winona* to *Deadwood Dick on Deck*, see Nicole Tonkovich, "Guardian Angels and Missing Mothers: Race and Domesticity in *Winona* and *Deadwood Dick on Deck*," *Western American Literature* 32.3 (1997): 241–64.
30. Richard Slotkin, *Gunfighter Nation: The Myth of the Frontier in Twentieth-Century America* (New York: Harper Perennial, 1992), 145.
31. Class identity becomes even more important in later bandit dime novels as a way not of ennobling the hero but of detecting the villain. For example, W. B. Lawson's *Diamond Dick, Jr.'s Call Down; or, the King of the Silver Box* features an aristocratic villain, "the Don," who impersonates Diamond Dick while passing off counterfeit money. Diamond Dick does not even consider marriage at the end of the dime novel but instead, after the Don's escape from prison, vows to continue foiling his plans. See W. B. Lawson, *Diamond Dick, Jr.'s Call Down; or, the King of the Silver Box*, *Diamond Dick Library* 175 (March 7, 1896).
32. Ellis, *Seth Jones*, 267.
33. Ibid., 268.
34. Christine Bold, "Malaeska's Revenge; or, the Dime Novel Tradition in Popular Fiction," *Wanted Dead or Alive: The American West in Popular Culture*, ed. Richard Aquila (Chicago: U of Illinois P, 1996), 32.
35. Edward L. Wheeler's *Deadwood Dick, The Prince of the Road; or, the Black Rider of the Black Hills* first appeared in *Beadle's Half-Dime Library* 1 (October 15, 1877). It was reprinted in *Beadle's Half-Dime Pocket Library* 1 (January 1884). Beadle and Adams's business failed in 1897, but the Arthur Westbrook Company of Cleveland, Ohio, reprinted sixty-four of Beadle and Adams's Deadwood Dick stories in *The Deadwood Dick Library*, which ran from 1899 to 1900. *Deadwood Dick, The Prince of the Road; or, the Black Rider of the Black Hills* was reprinted as the first number in Westbrook's *Deadwood Dick Library* 1.1 (March 15, 1899). Further citations of this text refer to Edward L. Wheeler, *Deadwood Dick, the Prince of the Road; or, the Black Rider of the Black Hills*, *Reading the West: An Anthology of Dime Westerns*, ed. Bill Brown (Boston: Bedford, 1997), 273–358.
36. Wheeler, *Deadwood Dick*, 282.
37. Ibid., 279.

38. This refers to Henry Nash Smith's foundational work on the mythology of the West. However, Smith argues that the dime novel served as a mass entertainment that distracted readers from industrialization and exploitation in urban centers. Contrary to Smith's reading, my reading locates industrialization as a central force in dime-novel Westerns. For Smith's argument, see Smith, *Virgin Land*, 90–120.
39. Denning, *Mechanic Accents*, 163.
40. Wheeler, *Deadwood Dick*, 280.
41. Ibid.
42. Ibid., 281. For an account of racial consolidation within labor unions in the nineteenth century, see David Roediger, *Wages of Whiteness: Race and the Making of the American Working Class* (New York: Verso, 1991).
43. Ibid., 279.
44. For an analysis of historical bandits and the communities that support them, particularly as they emerge in peasant communities, see Eric Hobsbawm, *Bandits* (1969; New York: New P, 2000). Interestingly, Hobsbawm's thesis that bandits emerge in feudal economies seems to support the dime novel's use of aristocratic language to describe bandits, as if their resistance of wage labor places them in a distant feudal economy.
45. Wheeler, *Deadwood Dick*, 281.
46. Ibid., 284.
47. Ibid.
48. Ibid.
49. Philip Fisher, *Hard Facts: Setting and Form in the American Novel* (New York: Oxford UP, 1985), 48.
50. Jane Tompkins, *Sensational Designs: The Cultural Work of American Fiction, 1790–1860* (New York: Oxford UP, 1985), 118.
51. Wheeler, *Deadwood Dick*, 286.
52. Ibid., 287.
53. Ibid., 288.
54. Ibid., 353.
55. Ibid., 357.
56. Ibid., 188. For another marriage, see Edward L. Wheeler, *Deadwood Dick's Doom; or, Calamity Jane's Last Adventure*, *Beadle's Half-Dime Library* 205 (June 25, 1881). In this novel, Deadwood Dick rescues Calamity Jane from Mormons and marries her. However, in a later dime novel, Calamity Jane appears as Deadwood Dick's enemy. See Wheeler, *Deadwood Dick's Claim*.
57. Interestingly, the plot of *Deadwood Dick on Deck* itself proves this point. The dime novel's villain, Cecil Grosvenor, proposes to Madame Minnie Majilton, the keeper of a dance-hall in Deadwood. It turns out that Minnie is actually Marie Lydia Galton, who was married to Cecil Grosvenor and fled his tyranny as a husband. Believing Marie dead, Cecil marries again and arrives in Deadwood to murder his current wife and remarry. Marriage in this dime novel is extraordinarily strategic and unconventional. The marriage that does close the dime novel is between Sandy, a young miner, and Cecil's wronged wife who has been posing as a man named Dusty Dick. At the end of the dime novel, the narrator remarks that the married couple is "still universally known in their home in the mines" as Sandy and Dusty Dick, i.e., as two men. See Wheeler, *Deadwood Dick on Deck*, 187.

58. For treatments of butch performance and its relation to working-class iden-
    tifications, see Halberstam, *Female Masculinity*, 111–39, and Jean Bobby
    Noble, *Masculinities Without Men?: Female Masculinity in Twentieth-century
    Fictions* (Vancouver: U of British Columbia P, 2004), 90–141.

59. By avoiding heteronormative rhythms of marriage and reproduction and
    plunging into a more expansive temporal horizon of adventure, Deadwood
    Dick offers an intriguing example of gender's ability to rework temporal-
    ity. For recent treatments of time and how gender can be both normal-
    ized through time and also subversive of social conventions, see Elizabeth
    Freeman, "Time Binds, or, Erotohistoriography," *Social Text* 84–85 (Fall/
    Winter 2005): 57–68; Elizabeth Grosz, *The Nick of Time: Politics, Evolution,
    and the Untimely* (Durham: Duke UP, 2004); and Judith Halberstam, *In a
    Queer Time and Place: Transgender Bodies, Subcultural Lives* (New York: New
    York UP, 2005).

61. Comstock, *Traps for the Young*, 22.

62. Robert Peabody Bellows, "The Degeneration of the Dime Novel," *The Writer*
    7.7 (July 1899), 99.

63. D. H. Lawrence, "Calendar of Modern Letters, April 1927," *Ernest
    Hemingway: The Critical Heritage*, ed. Jeffrey Myers (New York: Routledge,
    1997), 73.

2 BETWEEN ANARCHY AND HIERARCHY: NAT LOVE'S AND THEODORE ROOSEVELT'S MANLY FEELINGS

1. For a reading of Nat Love's autobiography that critiques his racial awareness, see Blake Allmendinger, *Ten Most Wanted: The New Western Literature*
   (New York: Routledge, 1998), 17–31. For an analysis of Love's similarities to
   Booker T. Washington, see Michael K. Johnson, *Black Masculinity and the
   Frontier Myth in American Literature* (Norman: U of Oklahoma P, 2002),
   98–146. Readings of Roosevelt's complicity with nativism and imperialism
   are Gail Bederman *Manliness and Civilization: A Cultural History of Gender
   and Race in the United States, 1880–1917* (Chicago: U of Chicago P, 1995),
   170–216; Amy Kaplan, *The Anarchy of Empire in the Making of U.S. Culture*
   (Cambridge: Harvard UP, 2002), 121–45; and Donna Haraway, "Teddy Bear
   Patriarchy: Taxidermy in the Garden of Eden, New York City, 1908–1936,"
   Social Text 11 (Winter 1984–1985): 20–64.

2. For more lengthy treatments of Roosevelt's life, see Kathleen Dalton,
   Theodore Roosevelt: A Strenuous Life (New York: Vintage, 2004); Edmund
   Morris, *The Rise of Theodore Roosevelt*, revised ed. (New York: Modern
   Library, 2001); Edmund Morris, *Theodore Rex* (New York: Modern Library,
   2002); and Sarah Watts, *Rough Rider in the White House: Theodore Roosevelt
   and the Politics of Desire* (Chicago: U of Chicago P, 2003).

3. Roosevelt, Theodore. *An Autobiography.* 1913. *Theodore Roosevelt: The
   Rough Riders, An Autobiography.* Ed. Louis Auchincloss (New York: Library
   of America, 2004), 588.

4. Ibid., 590.

5. Ibid., 282.

6. For a provocative historical account of Social Darwinism that argues persuasively that it might have been more of myth or reaction to industrialization

rather than the scientific, cultural, racial, and economic doctrine it is often characterized as, see Robert C. Bannister, *Social Darwinism: Science and Myth in Anglo-American Social Thought* (Philadelphia: Temple UP, 1979).

7. For a reading of theories of childhood development that emphasize the importance of environment and aesthetics, and how these theories came to dominate late nineteenth- and twentieth-century Europe and America, see Douglas Mao, *Fateful Beauty: Aesthetic Environments, Juvenile Development, and Literature, 1860–1960* (Princeton: Princeton UP, 2008).

8. For a reading of neurasthenia's importance to the Western, see Tom Lutz, *American Nervousness, 1903: An Anecdotal History* (Ithaca: Cornell UP, 1993) and Barbara Will, "The Nervous Origins of the American Western." *American Literature* 70.2 (1998): 293–316.

9. Richard Slotkin, *Gunfighter Nation: The Myth of the Frontier in Twentieth-Century America* (New York: Harper Perennial, 1992), 61.

10. Theodore Roosevelt, *The Rough Riders*, 1899, *Theodore Roosevelt: The Rough Riders, An Autobiography*, ed. Louis Auchincloss (New York: Library of America, 2004), 90.

11. Ibid., 25.

12. Ibid., 167.

13. Roosevelt, *Rough Riders*, 33.

14. See Kaplan, *Anarchy of Empire*.

15. The essays referred to are: Bill Brown, "Science Fiction, the World's Fair, and the Prosthetics of Empire"; Donna Haraway, "Teddy Bear Patriarchy: Taxidermy in the Garden of Eden, New York, 1908-1936"; Amy Kaplan, "Black and Blue on San Juan Hill"; and Richard Slotkin, "Buffalo Bill's 'Wild West' and the Mythologization of the American Empire." All appear in Amy Kaplan and Donald E. Pease, eds., *The Cultures of United States Imperialism* (Durham: Duke UP, 1993).

16. Haraway, "Teddy Bear Patriarchy," 23.

17. Bederman, *Manliness and Civilization*, 184.

18. For another study that equates masculinity with imperialism and especially violence, treating them all three as synonyms, see Carroll Smith-Rosenberg's reading of Davy Crockett frontier tales in Carroll Smith-Rosenberg, *Disorderly Conduct: Visions of Gender in Victorian America* (New York: Oxford UP, 1986).

19. Kaplan, *Anarchy of Empire*, 141.

20. Ibid., 121–45.

21. Roosevelt, *Rough Riders*, 90.

22. Roosevelt, *An Autobiography*, 642.

23. Roosevelt, *Rough Riders*, 43–44.

24. In this sense, Theodore Roosevelt can be seen as sharing in Thomas Jefferson's vision of democracy as the creation of a multitude rather than a sovereign power. For an account of Jeffersonian democracy, see Michael Hardt, "Jefferson and Democracy," *American Quarterly* 59.1 (March 2007): 41–78.

25. Roosevelt, *Rough Riders*, 179–81.

26. Ibid., 181.

27. Ibid., 182.

28. An account of the use of manhood to spur on America's involvement in the Spanish-American War is in Kristin L. Hoganson, *Fighting for American*

Manhood: How Gender Politics Provoked the Spanish-American and Philippine-American Wars (New Haven: Yale UP, 1998).

29. Roosevelt, *An Autobiography*, 602, 596.

30. See Kenneth B. Kidd, *Making American Boys: Boyology and the Feral Tale* (Minneapolis: U of Minnesota P, 2004).

31. Theodore Roosevelt, "To Granville Stanley Hall," November 29, 1899, *Theodore Roosevelt: Letters and Speeches*, ed. Louis Auchincloss (New York: Library of America, 2004), 183.

32. Nat Love, *The Life and Adventures of Nat Love* (1907; Lincoln: U of Nebraska P, 1995), 142.

33. Allmendinger, *Ten Most Wanted*, 4.

34. Ibid., 28.

35. For other treatments of the West that emphasize the roles played by African Americans, see Blake Allmendinger, *Imagining the African-American West* (Lincoln: U of Nebraska P, 2005); Johnson, *Black Masculinity and the Frontier Myth*; and Quintard Taylor, *In Search of the Racial Frontier: African Americans in the American West, 1528–1990* (New York: Norton, 1998).

36. Love, *Life and Adventures*, 14.

37. Ibid., 39.

38. Susan Scheckel, "Home on the Train: Race and Mobility in *The Life and Adventures of Nat Love*," *American Literature* 74.2 (2002), 225.

39. Love, *Life and Adventures*, 70.

40. Ibid., 162.

41. Ibid., 45.

42. Ibid., 70.

43. For a reading of the varieties of "self-making" in Nat Love's text, see Kenneth Speirs, "Writing Self (Effacingly): E-race-d Presences in *The Life and Adventures of Nat Love*," *Western American Literature* 40.3 (Fall 2005): 301–20.

44. Love, *Life and Adventures*, 105.

45. Michael Warner, "What Like a Bullet Can Undeceive?," *Public Culture* 15.1 (2003), 51.

46. Georgina Dodge, "Claiming Narrative, Disclaiming Race: Negotiating Black Masculinity in *The Life and Adventures of Nat Love*," *a/b: Auto/Biography Studies* 16.1 (2001), 122.

47. Johnson, *Black Masculinity and the Frontier Myth*, 115.

3   Marrying Men: Intimacy in Owen Wister's *The Virginian*

1. Owen Wister, *The Virginian: A Horseman of the Plains* (1902; New York: Oxford UP, 1998), 6. For an analysis of film adaptations of *The Virginian*, see Richard Huston, "Early Film Versions of *The Virginian*," *Reading the Virginian in the New West*, ed. Melody Graulich and Stephen Tatum (Lincoln: U of Nebraska P, 2003), 126–47.

2. Wister, *Virginian*, 6.

3. Quoted in Darwin Payne, *Owen Wister: Chronicles of the West, Gentleman of the East* (Dallas: Southern Methodist UP, 1985), 21.

4. Forrest G. Robinson, *Having it Both Ways: Self-Subversion in Western Popular Classics* (Albuquerque: U of New Mexico P, 1993), 53.

5. Lee Clark Mitchell, *Westerns: Making the Man in Fiction and Film* (Chicago: U of Chicago P, 1996), 118.

6. "The Evolution of the Cow-Puncher" was first published in the September 1895 issue of *Harper's Magazine*. See Owen Wister, "The Evolution of the Cow-Puncher," 1895, *The Virginian: A Horseman of the Plains* (New York: Oxford UP, 1998), 329–44.

7. William R. Handley, *Marriage, Violence, and the Nation in the American Literary West* (Cambridge: Cambridge UP, 2002), 96.

8. Wister, *Virginian*, 7.

9. Ibid.

10. For a treatment of Wister's relation to Theodore Roosevelt and Frederic Remington, particularly their use of the West as a way to reinvigorate American nationalism, see G. Edward White, *The Eastern Establishment and the Western Experience: The West of Frederic Remington, Theodore Roosevelt, and Owen Wister* (New Haven: Yale UP, 1968). For an account of Wister's neurasthenia and S. Weir Mitchell's diagnosis of exertion on the frontier, see Barbara Will, "The Nervous Origins of the American Western," *American Literature* 70.2 (1998): 293–316.

11. Wister, *Virginian*, 95.

12. Will, "Nervous Origins of the American Western," 310.

13. David Greven, *Men beyond Desire: Manhood, Sex, and Violation in American Literature* (New York: Palgrave, 2005), 89, 103.

14. Owen Wister, *Owen Wister Out West: His Journals and Letters*, ed. Fanny Kemble Wister (Chicago: U of Chicago P, 1958), 112–13.

15. Amy Kaplan, *The Social Construction of American Realism* (Chicago: U of Chicago P, 1988), 17.

16. Wister, *Owen Wister Out West*, 118.

17. For an insightful account of realism and Western American literature that positions the West centrally within American realism, see Nicolas Witschi, *Traces of Gold: California's Natural Resources and the Claim to Realism in Western American Literature* (Tuscaloosa: U of Alabama P, 2002).

18. Wister, *Owen Wister Out West*, 124.

19. Martha A. Sandweiss, *Print the Legend: Photography and the American West* (New Haven: Yale UP, 2002), 250–51.

20. Peter Henry Emerson, "Hints on Art," 1889, *Classic Essays on Photography*, ed. Alan Trachtenberg (New Haven: Leete's Island, 1980), 103. Emphasis in original.

21. Sandweiss, *Print the Legend*, 235.

22. Jennifer S. Tuttle, "Indigenous Whiteness and Wister's Invisible Indians," *Reading The Virginian in the New West*, ed. Melody Garulich and Stephen Tatum (Lincoln: U of Nebraska P, 2003), 95.

23. For a reading of homoeroticism and Western photography, including Wister's photographs, see Chris Packard, *Queer Cowboys: And Other Erotic Male Friendships in Nineteenth-Century American Literature* (New York: Palgrave, 2005).

24. John D. Dorst, *Looking West* (Philadelphia: U of Pennsylvania P, 1999), 65.

25. Wister, *Virginian*, 12.

26. Ibid., 13.

27. Ibid., 14.
28. Many Western states, including Utah and Indiana, passed laws making it quite easy to obtain a divorce. For an account of the anxiety this produced in the nation in the late nineteenth century, see Sarah Barringer Gordon, *The Mormon Question: Polygamy and Constitutional Conflict in Nineteenth-Century America* (Chapel Hill: U of North Carolina P, 2002), 172–81. For a broader reading of marriage and its ties to national identity, see Nancy Bentley, "Marriage as Treason: Polygamy, Nation, and the Novel," *The Futures of American Studies*, ed. Donald E. Pease and Robyn Wiegman (Durham: Duke UP, 2002), 341–70.
29. Wister, *Virginian*, 240.
30. Ibid., 182.
31. Ibid.
32. Ibid., 212–13.
33. For a theoretical and philosophical explication of emotion as working through otherness and the decentered subject, see Rei Terada, *Feeling in Theory: Emotion After "The Death of the Subject"* (Cambridge: Harvard UP, 2001).
34. For a reading of the importance of verbal skills in *The Virginian*, see Mitchell, *Westerns*, 94–119.
35. Wister, *Virginian*, 176.
36. Nancy F. Cott, *Public Vows: A History of Marriage and the Nation* (Cambridge: Harvard UP, 2000), 155. For another reading of marriage that has influenced my reading of marriage and intimacy in *The Virginian*, see Elizabeth Freeman, *The Wedding Complex: Forms of Belonging in Modern American Culture* (Durham: Duke UP, 2002).
37. Wister, *Virginian*, 191.
38. Ibid., 193.
39. Ibid., 196.
40. The definitive statement of this escapist masculinity can be found in Leslie Fiedler, *Love and Death in the American Novel* (1960; Normal: Dalkey Archive P, 1997).
41. Wister, *Virginian*, 199.
42. For an account of Wister and Roosevelt's exchange concerning "Balaam and Pedro," see Don D. Walker, "Wister, Roosevelt and James: A Note on the Western," *American Quarterly* 12.3 (Autumn 1960): 358–66.
43. Wister, *Virginian*, 203.
44. Ibid., 209.
45. Ibid., 7.
46. Ibid., 260.
47. Ibid.
48. Ibid., 269.
49. Ibid., 272.
50. Lauren Berlant, *The Female Complaint: The Unfinished Business of Sentimentality in American Culture* (Durham: Duke UP, 2008), 66.
51. Wister, *Virginian*, 91.
52. Ibid., 92.
53. Ibid., 93.
54. Ibid., 99.
55. Ibid., 72.

56. Ibid., 98.
57. Ibid., 295.
58. Ibid., 309.
59. Ibid.
60. Ibid., 313.
61. Ibid., 327.
62. Ibid., 342.
63. Kaplan, *Anarchy of Empire*, 106.
64. Jane Kuenz, "The Cowboy Businessman and 'The Course of Empire': Owen Wister's *The Virginian*," *Cultural Critique* 48.1 (2001): 102.
65. For an account of Theodore Roosevelt's advocacy of reproduction and fear of "race suicide," see Gail Bederman, *Manliness and Civilization: A Cultural History of Gender and Race in the United States, 1880–1917* (Chicago: U of Chicago P, 1995), 170–215.
66. Cary Wolfe, "In the Shadow of Wittgenstein's Lion: Language, Ethics, and the Question of the Animal," *Zoontologies: The Question of the Animal*, ed. Cary Wolfe (Minneapolis: U of Minnesota P, 2003), 41.
67. Wister, *Virginian*, 55.
68. Jane Tompkins, *West of Everything: The Inner Life of Westerns* (New York: Oxford UP, 1992), 141.
69. Wister, *Virginian*, 60.
70. Wister, *Virginian*, 59.
71. Wister, *Virginian*, 62.
72. Wister, *Owen Wister Out West*, 183.

4 "I LIKE TO BE LIKE A MAN": FEMALE MASCULINITY IN WILLA CATHER'S *O PIONEERS!* AND *MY ÁNTONIA*

1. Willa Cather, "My First Novels (There Were Two)," 1931, *Willa Cather: Stories, Poems, and Other Writings*, ed. Sharon O'Brien (New York: Library of America, 1992), 964.
2. Cather, "The Novel Démeublé," 834.
3. Willa Cather, *My Ántonia*, ed. Charles Mignon and Kari A. Ronning (1918; Lincoln: U of Nebraska P, 1997), 133.
4. Judith Halberstam *Female Masculinity* (Durham: Duke UP, 1998), 46.
5. Gayle Rubin, "Thinking Sex: Notes for a Radical Theory of the Politics of Sexuality," *The Lesbian and Gay Studies Reader*, ed. Henry Abelove, Michèle Aina Barale, and David M. Halperin (New York: Routledge, 1993), 34.
6. For readings of *My Ántonia* as relaying lesbian desire through Jim Burden, the male narrator, see Judith Fetterley, "*My Ántonia*, Jim Burden, and the Dilemma of the Lesbian Writer," *Lesbian Texts and Contexts*, ed. Karla Jay and Judith Glasgow (New York: New York UP, 1990), 145–63; Katrina Irving, "Displacing Homosexuality: The Use of Ethnicity in Willa Cather's *My Ántonia*," *Modern Fiction Studies* 36.1 (Spring 1990): 91–102; and Deborah Lambert, "The Defeat of the Hero: Autonomy and Sexuality in *My Ántonia*," *American Literature* 53 (1982): 76–90.

7. Blanche Gelfant, "The Forgotten Reaping-Hook: Sex in *My Ántonia*," *American Literature* 43.1 (March 1971), 76.
8. For an analysis of how tomboyism is treated as a developmental stage rather than the staging of female masculinity, and how literature has undone this heteronormative narrative, see the reading of Carson McCullers's *The Member of the Wedding* in Halberstam, *Female Masculinity*, 5–9.
9. Sharon O'Brien, *Willa Cather: The Emerging Voice* (1987; Cambridge: Harvard UP, 1997), 425.
10. Janis P. Stout's work on Cather's early journalism and endorsement of "manly" prose is a valuable alternative to the dominant paradigm of Cather studies, especially for the suggestion that Cather's masculinity informs her movement between "male and female narrative perspectives." See Janis P. Stout, "Willa Cather's Early Journalism: Gender, Performance, and the 'Manly Battle Yarn,'" *Arizona Quarterly* 55.3 (Autumn 1999), 78. Stout has also argued that Cather creates a "gender-neutral aesthetic of the West." See Janis P. Stout, *Picturing a Different West: Vision, Illustration, and the Tradition of Cather and Austin* (Lubbock: Texas Tech UP, 2007), 136. This claim is similar to David Leverenz's argument that Alexandra Bergson "takes up Emersonian selflessness." See David Leverenz, *Paternalism Incorporated: Fables of American Fatherhood, 1865–1940* (Ithaca: Cornell UP, 2003), 88. It is my contention here that the kind of abstraction necessary for self-fashioning is connoted as masculine in Cather's novels, not as gender-neutral or transcendent. For a reading of dominant masculinity in Cather, see Domna Pastourmatzi, "Willa Cather and the Cult of Masculinity," *Willa Cather Pioneer Memorial Newsletter* 38.4 (Winter 1995): 2–14.
11. Eve Kosofsky Sedgwick, "Across Gender, Across Sexuality: Willa Cather and Others," *South Atlantic Quarterly* 88.1 (Winter 1989), 65–66.
12. Judith Butler, *Bodies That Matter: On the Discursive Limits of "Sex"* (New York: Routledge, 1993), 145.
13. Christopher Nealon, *Foundlings: Lesbian and Gay Emotion Before Stonewall* (Durham: Duke UP, 2001), 62.
14. Ibid., 87.
15. In his reading of "Paul's Case," Scott Herring claims that Cather's central interest is in "depersonalizing aesthetics" in a way that confounds sexological classification. This depersonalization, though, occurs not outside of but within gender. My argument here is that Cather's characters engage in masculine self-fashioning precisely because it allows for the kind of abstraction and depersonalization Herring charts in Cather's story. See Scott Herring, *Queering the Underworld: Slumming, Literature, and the Undoing of Lesbian and Gay History* (Chicago: U of Chicago P, 2007), 100. For a reading of Cather's *The Professor's House* and the author's relationship to Sarah Orne Jewett that likewise focuses on impossibility, loss, and illegibility, see Heather Love, *Feeling Backward: Loss and the Politics of Queer History* (Cambridge: Harvard UP, 2007), 72–99.
16. Willa Cather, *O Pioneers!*, ed. Susan Rosowski, Charles W. Mignon, and Kathleen Danken (1913; Lincoln: U of Nebraska P, 1992), 5.
17. My reading of time as central to gender normativity and thus a site for reworking gender owes much to Judith Halberstam's *In a Queer Time and Place*. Willa Cather's interest in the philosophy of Henri Bergson, I think, informed her thinking about time. For a cultural history of Bergson's popularity in

pre–World War I America that traces the philosopher's influence on Cather, see Tom Quirk, *Bergson and American Culture: The Worlds of Willa Cather and Wallace Stevens* (Chapel Hill: U of North Carolina P, 1990). Quirk's study provides a great account of this often overlooked moment in American literary history.

18. See Walter Benn Michaels, *Our America: Nativism, Modernism, and Pluralism* (Durham: Duke UP, 1995), 1–16.

19. Marilee Lindemann, *Willa Cather: Queering America* (New York: Columbia UP, 1999), 44.

20. Jonathan Goldberg, *Willa Cather and Others* (Durham: Duke UP, 2001), 14.

21. Lindemann, *Willa Cather*, 38.

22. Cather, *O Pioneers!*, 12.

23. I owe thanks to the Willa Cather Seminar audience member who convinced me that it is not the flannel dress but the description of the dress that is feminine in this passage. As one sees with little Joey in *Shane*, discussed in the conclusion to this volume, flannel dresses were common children's clothing in the nineteenth century.

24. Cather, *O Pioneers!*, 13–14.

25. Ibid., 13.

26. Ibid., 11.

27. Ibid., 15.

28. Ibid., 16.

29. Ibid., 202.

30. Ibid., 80.

31. Ibid., 81.

32. Cather, "The Novel Démeublé," 834.

33. Ibid., 837.

34. Cather, "The Novel Démeublé," 837. See Butler, *Bodies That Matter*, 143–66 and Nealon, *Foundlings*, 61–97.

35. This stance on mass culture and its negative relation to high art echoes in Andrea Huyssen's argument about the masculinism of modernist art. See Andreas Huyssen, *After the Great Divide: Modernism, Mass Culture, Postmodernism* (Bloomington: Indiana UP, 1986), 44–62.

36. Nealon, *Foundlings*, 64.

37. Herring, *Queering the Underworld*, 102.

38. Cather, *O Pioneers!*, 92.

39. Ibid., 28.

40. Ibid., 29.

41. Ibid., 28.

42. Ibid., 29.

43. Ibid., 69.

44. Ibid., 30.

45. Ibid., 31.

46. Ibid., 32.

47. Ibid., 150.

48. Ibid., 151.

49. Ibid., 154.

50. Ibid., 152.

51. Susan Rosowski, *Birthing a Nation: Gender, Creativity, and the West in American Literature* (Lincoln: U of Nebraska P, 1999), 79.

52. Mary Paniccia Carden, "Creative Fertility and the National Romance in Willa Cather's *O Pioneers!* and *My Ántonia*," *Modern Fiction Studies* 45.2 (1999), 283.

53. Cather, *O Pioneers!*, 154.

54. For more on reproductive futurity as a fixture of heteronormativity, see Lee Edelman, *No Future: Queer Theory and the Death Drive* (Durham: Duke UP, 2004), 1–32. For a reading of the significance of the child as the ideal unit in the American political imaginary, see Lauren Berlant, *The Queen of America Goes to Washington City: Essays on Sex and Citizenship* (Durham: Duke UP, 1997), 25–54.

55. Cather, *O Pioneers!*, 197.

56. Ibid., 200.

57. Ibid., 201

58. Ibid., 202

59. Ibid., 185.

60. Ibid., 223–24.

61. Ibid., 241.

62. Ibid., 185.

63. Ibid., 185–86.

64. Melissa Ryan, "The Enclosure of America: Civilization and Confinement in Willa Cather's *O Pioneers!*," *American Literature* 75.2 (2003), 295. For another reading of Cather's relation to American imperialism and the frontier, see Mike Fischer, "Pastoralism and its Discontents: Willa Cather and the Burden of Imperialism," *Mosaic* 23.1 (Winter 1990): 31–44.

65. The classic reading of primitivism as renewal in the American novel is Leslie Fiedler's *Love and Death in the American Novel* (1960. Normal, IL: Dalkey Archive P, 1997). The desire for the primitive is part of the appeal of escapism, in Fielder's account, for masculine characters.

66. Cather, *O Pioneers!*, 251.

67. Ibid., 273.

68. Ibid., 272–73.

69. Ibid., 274.

70. Cather, *My Ántonia*, ix–x.

71. Michael Kimmel, *Manhood in America: A Cultural History* (New York: Free P, 1996), 171.

72. Ibid., 173.

73. Cather, *My Ántonia*, xi.

74. Sharon O'Brien, "Introduction," *New Essays on My Ántonia*, ed. Sharon O'Brien (Cambridge: Cambridge UP, 1999), 15.

75. Cather, *My Ántonia*, xii.

76. Ibid., xii-xiii.

77. Butler, *Bodies That Matter*, 148.

78. Cather, *My Ántonia*, 133.

79. Judith Butler, "Melancholy Gender/Refused Identification," *The Psychic Life of Power: Theories in Subjection* (Stanford: Stanford UP, 1997), 132–50.

80. Cather, *My Ántonia*, 81.

81. Ibid., 312.

82. Ibid., 321.

83. Ibid., 321–22.

84. Ibid., 341, 347, 355.

85. Ibid., 342.
86. Ibid., 329.
87. Ibid., 339.
88. Cather, *O Pioneers!*, 108.
89. Cather, *My Ántonia*, 360.

5   A DISCIPLINE OF SENTIMENTS: MASCULINITY
    IN ERNEST HEMINGWAY'S *DEATH*
    IN THE AFTERNOON

1. D. A. Miller, *Jane Austen, or the Secret of Style* (Princeton: Princeton UP, 2003), 29.
2. Michael North's account of Hemingway's "authenticity," as wedded to reporting "truth determined by social practice," grounds my reading in this chapter. While North is concerned with Hemingway's early journalism and short stories, I am interested in how Hemingway's treatment of fashion as truth morphs into an understanding that fashion can be remade. Therefore, truth itself, or at least the truth of the individual subject, is malleable through "social practice," which includes literary form. See Michael North, *Camera Works: Photography and the Twentieth-century Word* (New York: Oxford UP, 2005), 202.
3. For an account of the way in which Hemingway was marketed as a masculine writer, see David M. Earle, *All Man!: Hemingway, 1950s Men Magazines, and the Masculine Persona* (Kent: Kent State UP, 2009) and Catherine Turner, *Marketing Modernism: Between the Two World Wars* (Amherst: U of Massachusetts P, 2003), 145–72. Also of interest in this regard is this wonderful collection of Hemingway's advertisements and public statements: Matthew Bruccoli and Judith S. Baughman, eds., *Hemingway and the Mechanism of Fame: Statements, Public Letters, Introductions, Forewords, Prefaces, Blurbs, Reviews, And Endorsements* (Columbia: U of South Carolina P, 2005).
4. Cary Wolfe, *Animal Rites: American Culture, the Discourse of Species, and Posthumanist Theory* (Chicago: U of Chicago P, 2003), 123.
5. For psychoanalytic approaches to Hemingway, see Carl Eby, *Hemingway's Fetishism: Psychoanalysis and the Mirror of Manhood* (Albany: SUNY P, 1999); and Debra Moddelmog, *Reading Desire: In Pursuit of Ernest Hemingway* (Ithaca: Cornell UP, 1999). An early, well-known psychoanalytic study of Hemingway is Philip Young, *Ernest Hemingway: A Reconsideration*, revised ed. (University Park: Pennsylvania State UP, 1966). For an analysis of the controversy around Young's study, see Loren Glass, *Authors Inc.: Literary Celebrity in the Modern United States, 1880–1980* (New York: New York UP, 2004), 139–74.
6. James Plath argues that Hemingway's heroes are modeled on the archetypal Western, with a particular focus on Owen Wister and Hemingway's correspondence about *A Farewell to Arms*. His account of masculinity as a set of archetypal traits differs from my own argument here, which focuses on masculinity's performativity and relationship to depersonalizing aesthetics. See James Plath, "Shadow Rider: The Hemingway Hero as Western Archetype,"

Hemingway and the Natural World, ed. Robert E. Fleming (Moscow: U of Idaho P, 1999), 69–85.

7. This reading of *Death in the Afternoon* builds upon Thomas Strychacz's work on Hemingway and masculinity. Strychacz argues that in Hemingway's bull-fighting book, "masculine writing...emerges when men and language are staged rhetorically before a watching eye." I aim to push this insight further by locating a discipline of the self in that staged performance of masculinity. See Thomas Strychacz, *Hemingway's Theaters of Masculinity* (Baton Rouge: Louisiana State UP, 2003), 166.

8. Malcolm Cowley, *Exile's Return: A Literary Odyssey of the 1920s*, revised ed. (1951; New York: Penguin, 1994), 3.

9. Gertrude Stein, *The Autobiography of Alice B. Toklas* (1933; New York: Vintage, 1961), 216–17.

10. For a close reading of Stein and Hemingway's stylistic similarities, particularly their focus on repetition and the ways in which Hemingway modifies and popularizes Stein's method, see Marjorie Perloff, " 'Ninety Percent Rotarian': Gertrude Stein's Hemingway," *American Literature* 62.4 (December 1990): 668–83.

11. For a reading of the various power struggles surrounding Hemingway's characters in *The Sun Also Rises*, with a particular focus on gender and ethnicity in the context of World War I, see Keith Gandal, *The Gun and the Pen: Hemingway, Fitzgerald, Faulkner, and the Fiction of Mobilization* (New York: Oxford UP, 2008), 123–50.

12. Ernest Hemingway, *The Sun Also Rises* (1926; New York: Scribners, 2006), 39.

13. Ibid., 38.

14. This is not to say that Hemingway should be read as a writer who eschews hierarchal distinction—quite the contrary. Hemingway's racism is discussed and critiqued in Walter Benn Michaels, *Our America: Nativism, Modernism, and Pluralism* (Durham: Duke UP, 1995), 26–29. For Michaels, Jake's wartime injury is also the result of ethnic immigration and the waning of white supremacy in the United States. For a corrective to Michaels's view that nonetheless locates racism as central to Hemingway's aesthetic, see Gandal, *The Gun and the Pen*, 123–50. Michael Szalay's account of Hemingway's resistance to the New Deal focuses on his texts' hostilities to public consumption more generally. See Michael Szalay, *New Deal Modernism: American Literature and the Invention of the Welfare State* (Durham: Duke UP, 2000), 94–119. These critics read Hemingway as an elite writer, in relation to an increasingly meritocratic America and middlebrow literary marketplace. It is my contention that Hemingway's masculinity is both elitist and democratic.

15. "Vanity Fair's Own Paper Dolls—no. 5," *Vanity Fair* (March 1934), 29. The *Vanity Fair* paper dolls have been reprinted in Bruccoli and Bauchman, eds., *Hemingway and the Mechanism of Fame*, 26. They can also be viewed online, as part of a Smithsonian Institution Libraries' exhibition on "Celebrity Caricature": http://www.sil.si.edu/exhibitions/Celeb/gallery05.htm.

16. In his study of the celebrity author, Loren Glass focuses on *Death in the Afternoon* as the text in which "Hemingway began to establish his hyper-masculine public persona that he would present to the international public sphere for the rest of his life." See Glass, *Authors Inc.*, 143. My work here is building upon a recent wave of interest in androgyny in Hemingway's writing, inspired by the publication of his posthumous novel *Garden of*

Eden. See Nancy Comley and Robert Scholes, *Hemingway's Genders: Rereading the Hemingway Text* (New Haven: Yale UP, 1994); Kenneth S. Lynn, *Hemingway* (New York: Simon & Schuster, 1987); and Mark Spilka. *Hemingway's Quarrel with Androgyny* (Lincoln: U of Nebraska P, 1990). I aim to extend this interest in androgyny to an interest in masculinity's own possibilities when thought of as another mode of gender performance rather than a default, natural position.

17. I am indebted to Michael Thurston's reading of *Death in the Afternoon*'s experimental approach to genre. See Michael Thurston, "Gender, Genre, and Truth in *Death in the Afternoon*," *Hemingway Review* 17.2 (Spring 1998): 47–63.

18. Hemingway, *Death in the Afternoon*, 191.

19. See Hugh Kenner, *A Homemade World: The American Modernist Writers* (1975; Baltimore: Johns Hopkins UP, 1989).

20. For a reading of modernism as a literature explicitly interested in the tension and play between surface and depth, and as ultimately preoccupied with surface, see Michael T. Gilmore, *Surface and Depth: The Quest for Legibility in American Culture* (New York: Oxford UP, 2003), 128–58.

21. Accounts of Hemingway as a celebrity figure are Earle, *All Man!*; Glass, *Authors Inc.*, 139–74; and Turner, *Marketing Modernism*, 145–72.

22. Edmund Wilson, *The Wound and the Bow: Seven Studies in Literature* (1941; Athens: Ohio UP, 1997), 181.

23. Ibid.

24. Butler, *Bodies That Matter*, 237.

25. Wyndham Lewis, *Men without Art* (1934; Santa Rosa: Black Sparrow P, 1987), 20.

26. For an account of *Death in the Afternoon*'s publication history and studies of its reception, see Miriam B. Mandel, ed., *A Companion to Hemingway's Death in the Afternoon* (Rochester: Camden House, 2004).

27. For Rosalind Krauss, the fracturing of space is indicative of cubism in general: "Cubism was, after all, the painstaking and thoroughgoing dismantling of unified, perspectival space." Krauss's reading of Picasso has informed my account of Hemingway. For Krauss, Picasso's use of pastiche produces the sense that a secret or inner truth exists within the free play of the signifier. This secret, of course, is an effect of the signifier and does not exist prior to pastiche. I am similarly arguing that Hemingway's style locates masculinity on the surface and, while it posits that surface as truth, does not rely upon some hidden signified. See Rosalind Krauss, *The Picasso Papers* (New York: Farrar, Straus and Giroux, 1998), 114, 240–41.

28. For an informative discussion of Gris as "the demon of logic," with a focus on the period during which he painted *El Torero*, see Christopher Green, *Juan Gris* (New Haven: Whitechapel Art Gallery/Yale UP, 1992), 29–46.

29. David Cottington has influenced my understanding of analytic and synthetic cubism. See David Cottington, *Cubism and its Histories* (New York: Manchester UP, 2004), 172–81.

30. Hemingway, *Death in the Afternoon*, 1.

31. Ibid., 192.

32. The now classic treatment of sentimentalism is Jane Tompkins, *Sensational Designs: The Cultural Work of American Fiction, 1790–1860* (New York: Oxford UP, 1985). A more recent work that analyzes the novel's connections

to social reform is Amanda Claybaugh, *The Novel of Purpose: Literature and Social Reform in the Anglo-American World* (Ithaca: Cornell UP, 2006).

33. Hemingway, *Death in the Afternoon*, 2.
34. Ibid., 3.
35. For a discussion of iteration and gender, see Judith Butler, *Gender Trouble: Feminism and the Subversion of Identity* (1990; New York: Routledge, 1999), 163–80.
36. Hemingway, *Death in the Afternoon*, 1.
37. For a brief account of the bullfight and its contentious relation with Spanish Catholicism, see Marc Shell, *Children of the Earth: Literature, Politics, and Nationhood* (New York: Oxford UP, 1993).
38. Wolfe, *Animal Rites*, 141.
39. Michael Warner gives an account of this abstraction of violence, albeit in the context of the Civil War, when he claims that "naming violence . . . mobilizes a complex structure of feeling." See Michael Warner, "What Like a Bullet Can Undeceive?" *Public Culture* 15.1 (2003): 53.
40. Hemingway, *Death in the Afternoon*, 135.
41. For the historical context of the story, see Matthew Stewart, "It Was All a Pleasant Business: The Historical Context of 'On the Quai at Smyrna,'" *Hemingway Review* 23.1 (Fall 2003): 58–71.
42. Ernest Hemingway, *In Our Time*, revised ed. (1930; New York: Scribners, 1986), 12.
43. See Strychacz, *Hemingway's Theaters of Masculinity.*
44. Hemingway, *Death in the Afternoon*, 11.
45. Hemingway's emphasis on qualitative value echoes Owen Wister's articulation, in *The Virginian*, of the importance of "quality" over "quantity," discussed in chapter three.
46. Hemingway, *Death in the Afternoon*, 179.
47. Ibid., 180.
48. Ibid., 182.
49. Ibid.
50. Ibid., 191.
51. Ibid.
52. Ibid., 278.

6 SPECTERS OF MASCULINITY: COLLECTIVITY IN JOHN STEINBECK'S *THE GRAPES OF WRATH*

1. John Steinbeck, "Nobel Prize Acceptance Speech," 1963, *America and Americans and Selected Nonfiction*, ed. Susan Shillinglaw and Jackson J. Benson (New York: Penguin, 2003), 172.
2. Ibid., 173.
3. In her treatment of sentimentalism and sentimentality, June Howard argues that sentimentalism has a broader formal influence on the literary tradition than commonly acknowledged. Tracing the "literary" through Henry James to Cleanth Brooks and Robert Penn Warren, Howard finds that "the whole conceptual landscape of criticism, particularly the system of genres, is organized according to gender-inflected values." This gendering tends to obfuscate the impact of the "feminine" on the "literary." See June Howard, "What is Sentimentality?," *American Literary History* 11.1 (Spring 1999), 75.

4. This narrative of Steinbeck was developed during the 1950s, when the writer was experimenting with new forms and when his earlier works (*Grapes of Wrath*, *Of Mice and Men*, *Tortilla Flat*) had already attained the status of both bestsellers and contemporary classics. As John Ditsky comments, when he approached Steinbeck's oeuvre in the 1950s, he was "completely unaware that somewhere in the 1940s there was supposed to be some moment when Steinbeck as an author 'declined.'" See John Ditsky, *John Steinbeck and the Critics* (Rochester: Camden House, 2000), 9.

5. Steinbeck's status as a popular and even sentimental writer seems to have been recapitulated by his placement in Oprah's Book Club. *East of Eden* was chosen to restart Oprah's Book Club in September 2003.

6. Quoted in John Seelye, "Come Back to the Boxcar, Leslie Honey: Or, Don't Cry for Me, Madonna, Just Pass the Milk: Steinbeck and Sentimentality," *Beyond Boundaries: Rereading John Steinbeck*, ed. Susan Shillinglaw and Kevin Hearle (Tuscaloosa: U ofAlabama P, 2002), 12. Leslie Fiedler gave the keynote address at the 1989 Steinbeck conference in San Jose, California. Ditsky summarizes this talk with the following scornful sentence: "acknowledging the right of *Grapes* to continue to be read, [Fiedler earned] himself (all unknowing) the year's Harold Bloom award for graceless patronization." Ditsky, *John Steinbeck*, 99.

7. Leslie Fiedler, *Waiting for the End: A Portrait of Twentieth-century American Literature and its Writers* (New York: Stein & Day, 1964), 9.

8. See T. S. Eliot, "Tradition and the Individual Talent," 1919, *Selected Prose of T.S. Eliot*, ed. Frank Kermode (New York: Harcourt, 1975), 33–44.

9. John Steinbeck, *Cup of Gold: A Life of Sir Henry Morgan, Buccaneer, with Occasional Reference to History* (1929; New York: Penguin, 1995), 167.

10. This narrative is present in the major Steinbeck biographies, which make it clear that after *The Grapes of Wrath*, critics tended to judge his new material against the "classic" work. Two major Steinbeck biographies are Jackson J. Benson, *John Steinbeck, Writer: A Biography* (1984; New York: Penguin, 1990); and Jay Parini, *John Steinbeck: A Biography* (New York: Henry Holt, 1995).

11. Malcolm Cowley, "American Tragedy," 1938, *Critical Essays on Steinbeck's The Grapes of Wrath*, ed. John Ditsky (Boston: G.K. Hall, 1989), 29. Cowley's review was initially published in the *New Republic* 98 (May 1938).

12. The most frequent argument for Steinbeck's social realism focuses on his work as a journalist and his involvement with "documentary expression" in the 1930s. For example, William Howarth reads the final scene of *The Grapes of Wrath* as dramatizing Steinbeck's claim that journalism is "the mother of literature," thus "rescuing" the novel from sentimentalism: *"The Grapes of Wrath* endures as literature because it sprang from journalism." See William Howarth, "The Mother of Literature: Journalism and *The Grapes of Wrath*," *New Essays on The Grapes of Wrath*, ed. David Wyatt (Cambridge: Cambridge UP, 1990), 96. For an account of the documentary aesthetic in the 1930s, see William Stott, *Documentary Expression and Thirties America* (New York: Oxford UP, 1973). For more on Depression-era documentary style and photojournalism—as well as a treatment of *The Grapes of Wrath*'s ties to these forms of reportage, see Charles J. Shindo, *Dust Bowl Migrants in the American Imagination* (Lawrence: UP of Kansas, 1997). For a treatment of "documentary fiction" that doesn't mention Steinbeck but deals with a broad swath of American novelists, see Barbara Foley, *Telling the*

Truth: The Theory and Practice of Documentary Fiction (Ithaca: Cornell UP, 1986).

13. Seelye, "Come Back to the Boxcar, Leslie Honey," 23.

14. For accounts of sentimentalism and gender, see Suzanne Clark, *Sentimental Modernism: Women Writers and the Revolution of the Word* (Bloomington: Indiana UP, 1991); Howard, "What is Sentimentality?"; and Jane Tompkins, *Sensational Designs: The Cultural Work of American Fiction, 1790–1860* (New York: Oxford UP, 1985). For an account of sentimentalism in "masculine" literature, see Nina Baym, "Narratives of Beset Manhood: How Theories of American Fiction Exclude Women Authors," *American Quarterly* 33.2 (1981): 123–39.

15. For a forceful argument that the gendered division of sentimentalism and realism, and with it the corollary division between private and public, collapses far too many complexities into simple binaries, see Cathy N. Davidson and Jessamyn Hatcher, "Introduction," *No More Separate Spheres!: A Next Wave American Studies Reader*, ed. Cathy N. Davidson and Jessamyn Hatcher (Durham: Duke UP, 2002), 7–26.

16. For discussion of sentimentalism's ties to emotional responses, see Howard, "What is Sentimentality?"

17. For an excellent treatment of Jack London as a "manly" writer, see Jonathan Auerbach, *Male Call: Becoming Jack London* (Durham: Duke UP, 1996). Steinbeck, along with the 1930s proletarian writers, is often thought of as a naturalist. See John J. Conder, *Naturalism in American Fiction: The Classic Phase* (Lexington: UP of Kentucky, 1984); and Warren French, *The Social Novel at the End of Era* (Carbondale: Southern Illinois UP, 1966).

18. This novel was initially serialized in *Ladies' Home Companion* in 1839 was reprinted on July 9, 1860, as number 1 in *Beadle's Dime Novels.*

19. In *The Cultural Front*, Michael Denning argues that activist literature and film in the 1930s was often sentimental. From those sympathetic to the New Deal, like Steinbeck, "an official, mainstream, populist rhetoric emerged in the New Deal state and in the culture industry, perhaps best represented by the fireside chats of Franklin Roosevelt and the films of Frank Capra. This populism might well be called sentimental, for, unlike the populisms of the right and the left, its narratives avoided the depiction of enemies, villains, or scapegoats." See Michael Denning, *The Cultural Front* (New York: Verso, 1997), 127.

20. An interesting anthology of critical essays, emerging out of the 1997 Fourth International Steinbeck Conference, is Susan Shillinglaw and Kevin Hearle, eds., *Beyond Boundaries: Rereading John Steinbeck* (Tuscaloosa: U of Alabama P, 2002). The essays in this volume span from readings of Bruce Springsteen's reliance on Steinbeck's imagery to readings of Steinbeck's popularity in other nations, and they demonstrate both Steinbeck's influence and the heterogeneity of his work.

21. In his controversial essay "Third World Literature," Fredric Jameson argues that allegory functions as a mode emergent with the modern nation: "Third-world texts, even those which are seemingly private and invested with a properly libidinal dynamic—necessarily project a political dimension in the form of national allegory: *the story of the private individual destiny is always an allegory of the embattled situation of the public third-world culture and society.*" To qualify this claim, this allegorical structure is not limited to the "third-world" but is instead repressed in "first-world" texts: "Such allegorical

structures, then, are not so much absent from first-world cultural texts as they are *unconscious*, and therefore they must be deciphered by interpretive mechanisms that necessarily entail a whole social and historical critique of our first-world situation." Jameson's argument places allegory within all cultural texts, and in the case of Steinbeck, allegory seems to be less "unconscious" and more of a conscious manifestation of the breakdown of national culture—and the New Deal's project for rebuilding the nation—in the 1930s and 1940s. See Fredric Jameson, "Third-World Literature in the Era of Multinational Capitalism," *Social Text* 15 (Autumn 1986), 69, 79.

22. John Steinbeck, *The Grapes of Wrath* (1939; New York: Penguin, 1999), 31–32.
23. Ibid., 1.
24. Judith Butler, *Antigone's Claim: Kinship Between Life and Death* (New York: Columbia UP, 2000), 82.
25. Steinbeck, *Grapes of Wrath*, 267.
26. *The Grapes of Wrath*, dir. John Ford, perf. Henry Fonda, Jane Darwell, John Carradine, Charley Grapewin, and Dorris Bowdon (1940; 20th Century Fox DVD, 2004).
27. Steinbeck, *Grapes of Wrath*, 267.
28. This trucker's interest in identifying people seems to borrow from the popularity of the detective figure in the 1930s. As Sean McCann argues, the New Deal-era detective discloses private relations just as the state becomes increasingly involved in managing its citizens' lives. The hard-boiled detective, resistant to the law-affirming structure of the "classic detective story," instead occupies oppositional poles of "utopian vision of a collective, 'public taste' and a realization of the irresolvable plurality of contemporary society." The detective, then, operates with an eye toward the collective, but affirms individualism as a necessary condition of modernity's chaotic social organization. See Sean McCann, *Gumshoe America: Hard-Boiled Crime Fiction and the Rise and Fall of New Deal Liberalism* (Durham: Duke UP, 2000), 32.
29. Steinbeck, *Grapes of Wrath*, 11.
30. Ibid., 9.
31. Ibid., 13.
32. Ibid., 38.
33. Ibid.
34. Ibid., 390.
35. Ibid., 419.
36. Ibid., 418.
37. Ibid., 419.
38. Ibid.
39. Ibid., 448.
40. Ibid., 455.
41. Paula Rabinowitz, *Labor and Desire: Women's Revolutionary Fiction in Depression America* (Chapel Hill: U of North Carolina P, 1990), 55.
42. Michael Szalay, *New Deal Modernism: American Literature and the Invention of the Welfare State* (Durham: Duke UP, 2000) 181.
43. Rabinowitz, *Labor and Desire*, 137.
44. Julia Ward Howe, "Battle-Hymn of the Republic," 1862, *American Poetry: The Nineteenth Century*, Vol. 1, ed. John Hollander (New York: Library of America, 1993), 710.
45. Steinbeck, *Grapes of Wrath*, 445.

46. John Steinbeck, "To Carlton A. Sheffield," November 13, 1939, *Steinbeck: A Life in Letters*, ed. Elaine Steinbeck and Robert Wallsten (New York: Viking, 1975), 194.

47. Steinbeck, *Grapes of Wrath*, 445.

48. Granville Hicks, "Steinbeck's Powerful New Novel," 1939, *Granville Hicks in the New Masses*, ed. Jack Alan Robbins (Port Washington: Kennikat P, 1974), 139.

49. In her monumental study of proletarian fiction in the 1930s, *Radical Representations*, Barbara Foley summarizes the postmodernist critique of realism as being particularly damning to American social realists in the 1930s:

> The logic of the postmodernist critique of realism is that, hard as they might have tried to make realism serve the ends of an oppositional— even a revolutionary—politics, the proletarian novelists were doomed in advance by their adherence to an intrinsically conservative and repressive mode of writing. The political line explicitly urged in a text—the necessity for militant participation in class struggle, the falsity of petty bourgeois aspirations, even the desirability of Communism as an alternative to capitalism—cannot move the reader leftward if it is embedded in a discursive mode premised upon a bourgeois epistemology and bourgeois assumptions about selfhood.

After voicing this position, Foley then goes on to endorse a "tendency position," arguing that one must "grant the limitations of conventional realism in articulating an oppositional politics but...still argue that many proletarian texts do manage to give fictional embodiment to such a politics." The genre within proletarian fiction most successful at this "embodiment" is "the collective novel," opposed to the other three generic distinctions Foley makes between proletarian novels: fictional autobiography, Bildungsroman, and social novel. The collective novel, by not focusing on one individual character's development or one particular labor strike, attempts to "fix more attention on the 'big picture' as a political construct." By shifting focus from the reified bourgeois individual subject and on to the politics and movements of a group or groups of subjects, the collective novel, in Foley's estimation, is the most successful at freeing the proletarian novel's politics from the politics of the novel. See Barbara Foley, *Radical Representations: Politics and Form in U.S. Proletarian Fiction, 1929–1941* (Durham: Duke UP, 1993), 255, 261, 402.

50. John Steinbeck, *The Forgotten Village* (New York: Viking, 1941), 108.

51. Steinbeck, *Forgotten Village*, 142.

52. Ibid., 143.

53. For a biographical account of Steinbeck's literary production after *The Grapes of Wrath* and during World War II, see Roy Simmonds, *John Steinbeck: The War Years, 1939–1945* (Lewisburg: Bucknell UP, 1996).

54. As Caren Irr argues in *The Suburb of Dissent*, 1930s radicals used nationalism as a weapon in their critique of capitalism, but in the 1940s, the "nation" as a concept shifts, barring the radicalism of its deployment in the 1930s, due to the impending crisis in Germany: "One element of this crisis was that national culture began to be defined in terms of space (if not actual territory) rather than time, and form rather than content." National culture, then, becomes dissociated from the revolutionary critique mobilized by writers and critics of

the 1930s. Steinbeck's migrant workers cease to stand in for the nation, and, as the 1940s begin, Steinbeck begins to locate national culture within state institutions rather than in groups left behind by the state. See Caren Irr, *The Suburb of Dissent: Cultural Politics in the United States and Canada During the 1930s* (Durham: Duke UP, 1998), 42.

55. John Steinbeck, *Bombs Away: The Story of a Bomber Team* (1942; New York: Paragon House, 1990), 5.

56. Ibid.

57. Ibid., 14–15.

58. Ibid., 23.

59. This piece of propaganda certainly participates in what Marianna Torgovnick has described as "the war complex," the cluster of discourses, memories, and histories that cast war as a redemptive event that elicits a sense of belonging, even citizenship, among a group of survivors. What is compelling about Steinbeck's vision here is the way in which it so clearly morphs 1930s collectivism into World War II military nationalism. See Marianne Torgovnick, *The War Complex: World War II in Our Time* (Chicago: U of Chicago P, 2005), 7–11.

CONCLUSION: "THERE NEVER WAS A MAN LIKE SHANE"

1. For an account of the changes made to the novel when it was reprinted in 1954, see James C. Work, "Preface," *Shane: The Critical Edition*, by Jack Schaefer, ed. James C. Work (Lincoln: U of Nebraska P, 1984), xiv–xvi.

2. *Shane* participates, then, in Cold War "containment culture." See Alan Nadel, *Containment Culture: American Narratives, Postmodernism, and the Atomic Age* (Durham: Duke UP, 1995), 1–9.

3. *Shane*, dir. George Stevens, perf. Jean Arthur, Brandon De Wilde, Van Heflin, Alan Ladd, and Jack Palance (1953; Paramount DVD, 2000).

4. James Gilbert, *Men in the Middle: Searching for Masculinity in the 1950s* (Chicago: U of Chicago P, 2005), 21.

5. Ibid., 216.

6. Nadel, *Containment Culture*, 5.

7. Ibid., 193.

8. Stanley Corkin, *Cowboys as Cold Warriors: The Western and U.S. History* (Philadelphia: Temple UP, 2004), 152. For a reading of Roosevelt's frontier rhetoric and the Cold War, see Suzanne Clark, *Cold Warriors: Manliness on Trial in the Rhetoric of the West* (Carbondale: Southern Illinois UP, 2000).

9. Jack Schaefer, *Shane: The Critical Edition*, ed. James C. Work (Lincoln: U of Nebraska P, 1984), 273.

10. Ibid., 62–63.

11. Ibid., 64.

12. Ibid., 121.

13. Ibid., 214.

14. George Stevens, the director of *Shane*, intended the film to critique violence. Stemming in part from his experiences working on a film crew during World War II, he went to great lengths to render the violence in the film unappealing and less than heroic. For a detailed reading of Stevens's thoughts about

Shane and violence, see Marilyn Ann Moss, *Giant: George Stevens, a Life on Film* (Madison: U of Wisconsin P, 2004), 177–200.

15. The term "vanishing mediator" was coined by Max Weber, and I am using it here in the way outlined by Fredric Jameson. This concept refers to a figure in a narrative who comes from an older order but somehow ushers in a new order that renders that figure obsolete. The "Vanishing Mediator" is a device often used to narrate "natural" transitions in the economic, political, and social systems. Here, I am interested in how the Western hero ushers in a family-centered national imaginary that, in turn, casts the Western hero as dangerous, unruly, even effete. Philip Fisher reads Natty Bumppo in the Leatherstocking Tales as a kind of mediator figure, too, between lawless and lawful violence, in the context of the nineteenth century. Shane, then, has a same function, but within a different historical context. See Philip Fisher, *Hard Facts: Setting and Form in the American Novel* (New York: Oxford UP, 1985), 51–61; Fredric Jameson, *A Singular Modernity: Essay on the Ontology of the Present* (New York: Verso, 2002); and "The Vanishing Mediator; or, Max Weber as Storyteller," 1973, *Ideologies of Theory: Essays 1971–1986, Volume 2: The Syntax of History* (Minneapolis: U of Minnesota P, 1988), 3–34.

16. Schaefer, *Shane*, 272.

17. Ibid., 271.

18. For an account of the centrality of the "infant citizen" to American culture, see Lauren Berlant, *The Queen of American Goes to Washington City: Essays on Sex and Citizenship* (Durham: Duke UP, 1997), 25–54.

19. James Gilbert's work on 1950s masculinity speaks to the tensions and complexities of this shift, particularly in its impact on notions of fatherhood and religiosity. See the chapters on Billy Graham and *Ozzie and Harriet* in Gilbert, *Men in the Middle*, 106–63.

20. Willa Cather, *My Ántonia*. 1918. Ed. Charles Mignon and Kari A. Ronning (Lincoln: U of Nebraska P, 1997), 133.

21. Schaefer, *Shane*, 273.

BIBLIOGRAPHY

Adams, Rachel, and David Savran, eds. *The Masculinity Studies Reader*. New York: Blackwell, 2002.

Allmendinger, Blake. *The Cowboy: Representations of Labor in an American Work Culture*. New York: Oxford UP, 1992.

———. *Imagining the African American West*. Lincoln: U of Nebraska P, 2005.

———. *Ten Most Wanted: The New Western Literature*. New York: Routledge, 1998.

Auerbach, Jonathan. *Male Call: Becoming Jack London*. Durham: Duke UP, 1996.

Bannister, Robert C. *Social Darwinism: Science and Myth in Anglo-American Social Thought*. Philadelphia: Temple UP, 1979.

Baym, Nina. "Narratives of Beset Manhood: How Theories of American Fiction Exclude Women Authors." *American Quarterly* 33.2 (1981): 123–39.

Bederman, Gail. *Manliness and Civilization: A Cultural History of Gender and Race in the United States, 1880–1917*. Chicago: U of Chicago P, 1995.

Bellows, Robert Peabody. "The Degeneration of the Dime Novel." *The Writer* 7.7 (July 1899): 97–99.

Benson, Jackson J. *John Steinbeck, Writer: A Biography*. 1984. New York: Penguin, 1990.

Bentley, Nancy. "Marriage as Treason: Polygamy, Nation, and the Novel." *The Futures of American Studies*. Ed. Donald E. Pease and Robyn Wiegman. Durham: Duke UP, 2002. 341–70.

Berger, Maurice, Brian Wallis, and Simon Watson, eds. *Constructing Masculinity*. New York: Routledge, 1995.

Berlant, Lauren. *The Female Complaint: The Unfinished Business of Sentimentality in American Culture*. Durham: Duke UP, 2008.

———. *The Queen of America Goes to Washington City: Essays on Sex and Citizenship*. Durham: Duke UP, 1997.

Bold, Christine. "Malaeska's Revenge; or, The Dime Novel Tradition in Popular Fiction." *Wanted Dead or Alive: The American West in Popular Culture*. Ed. Richard Aquila. Chicago: U of Illinois P, 1996. 21–42.

———. *Selling the Wild West: Popular Western Fiction, 1860 to 1960*. Bloomington: Indiana UP, 1987.

Brown, Bill. "Introduction: Reading the West." *Reading the West: An Anthology of Dime Westerns*. Ed. Bill Brown. Boston: Bedford, 1997. 1–40.

———. *A Sense of Things: The Object Matter of American Literature*. Chicago: U of Chicago P, 2003.

Brown, Wendy. *States of Injury: Power and Freedom in Late Modernity*. Princeton: Princeton UP, 1995.

Bruccoli, Matthew, and Judith S. Baughman, eds. *Hemingway and the Mechanism of Fame: Statements, Public Letters, Introductions, Forewords, Prefaces, Blurbs, Reviews, and Endorsements*. Columbia: U of South Carolina P, 2005.

Bürger, Peter. *Theory of the Avant-Garde*. Michael Shaw, trans. Minneapolis: U of Minnesota P, 1984.

Butler, Judith. *Antigone's Claim: Kinship between Life and Death*. New York: Columbia UP, 2000.

———. *Bodies That Matter: On the Discursive Limits of "Sex."* New York: Routledge, 1993.

———. *Gender Trouble: Feminism and the Subversion of Identity*. 1990. New York: Routledge, 1999.

———. "Melancholy Gender/Refused Identification." *The Psychic Life of Power: Theories in Subjection*. Stanford: Stanford UP, 1997. 132–50.

Calinescu, Matie. *Five Faces of Modernity: Modernism, Avant-Garde, Decadence, Kitsch, Postmodernism*. Durham: Duke UP, 1987.

Carden, Mary Paniccia. "Creative Fertility and the National Romance in Willa Cather's *O Pioneers!* and *My Ántonia*." *Modern Fiction Studies* 45.2 (1999): 275–302.

Cather, Willa. *My Ántonia*. 1918. Ed. Charles Mignon and Kari A. Ronning. Lincoln: U of Nebraska P, 1997.

———. "My First Novels (There Were Two)." 1931. *Willa Cather: Stories, Poems, and Other Writings*. Ed. Sharon O'Brien. New York: Library of America, 1992. 963–65.

———. "The Novel Démeublé." 1922. *Willa Cather: Stories, Poems, and Other Writings*. Ed. Sharon O'Brien. New York: Library of America, 1992. 834–37.

———. *O Pioneers!* 1913. Ed. Susan J. Rosowski, Charles W. Mignon, and Kathleen Danken. Lincoln: U of Nebraska P, 1992.

Chapman, Mary, and Glenn Hendler, eds. *Sentimental Men: Masculinity and the Politics of Affect in American Culture*. Berkeley: U of California P, 1999.

Childs, Donald J. "Stetson in *The Waste Land*." *Essays in Criticism* 38.2 (April 1988): 131–48.

Clark, Suzanne. *Cold Warriors: Manliness on Trial in the Rhetoric of the West*. Carbondale: Southern Illinois UP, 2000.

———. *Sentimental Modernism: Women Writers and the Revolution of the Word*. Bloomington: Indiana UP, 1991.

Claybaugh, Amanda. *The Novel of Purpose: Literature and Social Reform in the Anglo-American World*. Ithaca: Cornell UP, 2006.

Comley, Nancy, and Robert Scholes. *Hemingway's Genders: Rereading the Hemingway Text*. New Haven: Yale UP, 1994.

Comstock, Anthony. *Traps for the Young*. 1883. Ed. Robert Bremner. Cambridge: Harvard UP, 1967.

Conder, John J. *Naturalism in American Fiction: The Classic Phase*. Lexington: UP of Kentucky, 1984.

Cook, William Wallace. *Plotto: A New Method of Plot Suggestion for Writers of Creative Fiction*. Battle Creek: Ellis Publishing, 1928.

Corkin, Stanley. *Cowboys as Cold Warriors: The Western and U.S. History*. Philadelphia: Temple UP, 2004.

Cott, Nancy F. *Public Vows: A History of Marriage and the Nation*. Cambridge: Harvard UP, 2000.

Cottington, David. *Cubism and its Histories*. New York: Manchester UP, 2004.

Cowley, Malcolm. "American Tragedy." 1938. *Critical Essays on Steinbeck's The Grapes of Wrath*. Ed. John Ditsky. Boston: G.K. Hall, 1989. 27–29.

———. *Exile's Return: A Literary Odyssey of the 1920s*. Revised ed. 1951. New York: Penguin, 1994.

Cox, J. Randolph. *The Dime Novel Companion: A Sourcebook*. Westport: Greenwood, 2000.

Cummings, E. E. "Buffalo Bill's." 1923. *100 Selected Poems*. New York: Grove P, 1954. 7.

Dalton. Kathleen. *Theodore Roosevelt: A Strenuous Life*. New York: Vintage, 2004.

Davidson, Cathy N., and Jessamyn Hatcher. "Introduction." *No More Separate Spheres!: A Next Wave American Studies Reader*. Ed. Cathy N. Davidson and Jessamyn Hatcher. Durham: Duke UP, 2002. 7–26.

———, eds. *No More Separate Spheres!: A Next Wave American Studies Reader*. Durham: Duke UP, 2002.

Dawidoff, Robert. *The Genteel Tradition and the Sacred Rage: High Culture vs. Democracy in Adams, James, and Santayana*. Chapel Hill: U of North Carolina P, 1992.

Dean, Janet. "Calamities of Convention in a Dime Novel Western." *Scorned Literature: Essays on the History and Criticism of Popular and Mass-Produced Fiction in America*. Ed. Lydia Cishman Schurman and Deidre Johnson. Westport: Greenwood, 2002. 37–50.

———. "Searching for the New Western Literary Criticism." *Modern Fiction Studies* 46.4 (2000): 949–58.

Denning, Michael. *The Cultural Front*. New York: Verso, 1997.

———. *Mechanic Accents: Dime Novels and Working-Class Culture in America*. Revised ed. New York: Verso, 1998.

Ditsky, John. *John Steinbeck and the Critics*. Rochester: Camden House, 2000.

Dodge, Georgina. "Claiming Narrative, Disclaiming Race: Negotiating Black Masculinity in *The Life and Adventures of Nat Love*." *a/b: Auto/Biography Studies* 16.1 (2001): 109–26.

Dorst, John D. *Looking West*. Philadelphia: U of Pennsylvania P, 1999.

Earle, David M. *All Man!: Hemingway, 1950s Men Magazines, and the Masculine Persona*. Kent: Kent State UP, 2009.

———. *Re-Covering Modernism: Pulps, Paperbacks, and the Prejudice of Form*. Burlington: Ashgate, 2009.

Eby, Carl. *Hemingway's Fetishism: Psychoanalysis and the Mirror of Manhood*. Albany: SUNY P, 1999.

Edelman, Lee. *No Future: Queer Theory and the Death Drive*. Durham: Duke UP, 2004.

Eliot, T. S. "Tradition and the Individual Talent." 1919. *Selected Prose of T.S. Eliot*. Ed. Frank Kermode. New York: Harcourt, 1975. 33–44.

———. *The Waste Land*. 1922. *Selected Poems*. New York: Harcourt Brace, 1964. 49–74.

Ellis, Edward S. *Seth Jones; or, the Captives of the Frontier*. 1860. In *Reading the West: An Anthology of Dime Westerns*. Ed. Bill Brown. Boston: Bedford, 1997. 172–268.

Emerson, Peter Henry. "Hints on Art." 1889. *Classic Essays on Photography*. Ed. Alan Trachtenberg. New Haven: Leete's Island, 1980. 99–105.

Everett, William. "Beadle's Dime Books." *North American Review* 99 (July 1864): 303–309.

Faulkner, William. *Light in August*. 1932. New York: Vintage, 1990.

Feslki, Rita. *The Gender of Modernity*. Cambridge: Harvard UP, 1995.

Fetterley, Judith. "*My Ántonia*, Jim Burden, and the Dilemma of the Lesbian Writer." *Lesbian Texts and Contexts*. Ed. Karla Jay and Judith Glasgow. New York: New York UP, 1990. 145–63.

Fiedler, Leslie. *Love and Death in the American Novel*. 1960. Normal, IL: Dalkey Archive P, 1997.

————. *Waiting for the End: A Portrait of Twentieth-Century American Literature and its Writers.* New York: Stein & Day, 1964.

Fischer, Mike. "Pastoralism and its Discontents: Willa Cather and the Burden of Imperialism." *Mosaic* 23.1 (Winter 1990): 31–44.

Fisher, Philip. *Hard Facts: Setting and Form in the American Novel.* New York: Oxford UP, 1985.

Fitzgerald, F. Scott. *The Great Gatsby.* 1925. New York: Collier, 1992.

Foley, Barbara. *Radical Representations: Politics and Form in U.S. Proletarian Fiction, 1929–1941.* Durham: Duke UP, 1993.

————. *Telling the Truth: The Theory and Practice of Documentary Fiction.* Ithaca: Cornell UP, 1986.

Freeman, Elizabeth. "Time Binds, or, Erotohistoriography." *Social Text* 84–85 (Fall/ Winter 2005): 57–68.

————. *The Wedding Complex: Forms of Belonging in Modern American Culture.* Durham: Duke UP, 2002.

French, Warren. *The Social Novel at the End of Era.* Carbondale: Southern Illinois UP, 1966.

Gandal, Keith. *The Gun and the Pen: Hemingway, Fitzgerald, Faulkner, and the Fiction of Mobilization.* New York: Oxford UP, 2008.

Gardiner, Judith Kegan, ed. *Masculinity Studies and Feminist Theory: New Directions.* New York: Columbia University Press, 2002.

Gelfant, Blanche. "The Forgotten Reaping-Hook: Sex in *My Ántonia.*" *American Literature* 43.1 (March 1971): 60–82.

Gilbert, James. *Men in the Middle: Searching for Masculinity in the 1950s.* Chicago: U of Chicago P, 2005.

Gilmore, Michael T. *Surface and Depth: The Quest for Legibility in American Culture.* New York: Oxford UP, 2003.

Gilmore, Paul. *The Genuine Article: Race, Mass Culture, and American Literary Manhood.* Durham: Duke UP, 2001.

Glass, Loren. *Authors Inc.: Literary Celebrity in the Modern United States, 1880–1980.* New York: New York UP, 2004.

Goldberg, Jonathan. *Willa Cather and Others.* Durham: Duke UP, 2001.

Gordon, Sarah Barringer. *The Mormon Question: Polygamy and Constitutional Conflict in Nineteenth-Century America.* Chapel Hill: U of North Carolina P, 2002.

The Grapes of Wrath. Dir. John Ford. Perf. Henry Fonda, Jane Darwell, John Carradine, Charley Grapewin, and Dorris Bowdon. 1940. 20th Century Fox, 2004. DVD.

Graulich, Melody, and Stephen Tatum, eds. *Reading* The Virginian *in the New West.* Lincoln: U of Nebraska P, 2003.

Green, Christopher. *Juan Gris.* New Haven: Whitechapel Art Gallery/Yale UP, 1992.

Greenberg, Amy S. *Manifest Manhood and the Antebellum American Empire.* Cambridge: Cambridge UP, 2005.

Greven, David. *Men Beyond Desire: Manhood, Sex, and Violation in American Literature.* New York: Palgrave, 2005.

Grosz, Elizabeth. *The Nick of Time: Politics, Evolution, and the Untimely.* Durham: Duke UP, 2004.

Halberstam, Judith. *Female Masculinity.* Durham: Duke UP, 1998.

———. *In a Queer Time and Place: Transgender Bodies, Subcultural Lives*. New York: New York UP, 2005.

Handley, William R. *Marriage, Violence, and the Nation in the American Literary West*. Cambridge: Cambridge UP, 2002.

Haraway, Donna. "Teddy Bear Patriarchy: Taxidermy in the Garden of Eden, New York City, 1908–1936." *Social Text* 11 (Winter 1984–1985): 20–64.

Hardt, Michael. "Jefferson and Democracy." *American Quarterly* 59.1 (March 2007): 41–78.

Hawthorne, Nathaniel. *The Scarlet Letter*. 1850. New York: Modern Library, 2000.

Hemingway, Ernest. *Death in the Afternoon*. 1932. New York: Touchstone, 1996.

———. *In Our Time*. Revised ed. 1930. New York: Scribners, 1986.

———. *The Sun Also Rises*. 1926. New York: Scribners, 2006.

Hendler, Glenn. *Public Sentiments: Structures of Feeling in Nineteenth-Century American Literature*. Chapel Hill: U of North Carolina P, 2001.

Herring, Scott. *Queering the Underworld: Slumming, Literature, and the Undoing of Lesbian and Gay History*. Chicago: U of Chicago P, 2007.

Hicks, Granville. "Steinbeck's Powerful New Novel." 1939. *Granville Hicks in the New Masses*. Ed. Jack Alan Robbins. Port Washington: Kennikat P, 1974. 138–43.

Hobsbawm, Eric. *Bandits*. 1969. New York: New P, 2000.

Hoganson, Kristin L. *Fighting for American Manhood: How Gender Politics Provoked the Spanish-American and Philippine-American Wars*. New Haven: Yale UP, 1998.

Hopkins, Pauline. *Winona: A Tale of Negro Life in the South and Southwest*. 1902. *The Magazine Novels of Pauline Hopkins*. New York: Oxford UP, 1988. 285–437.

Howard, June. "What is Sentimentality?" *American Literary History* 11.1 (Spring 1999): 63–81.

Howarth, William. "The Mother of Literature: Journalism and *The Grapes of Wrath*." *New Essays on The Grapes of Wrath*. Ed. David Wyatt. New York: Cambridge UP, 1990. 71–99.

Howe, Julia Ward. "Battle-Hymn of the Republic." 1862. *American Poetry: The Nineteenth Century*. Vol. 1. Ed John Hollander. New York: Library of America, 1993. 709–10.

Howells, William Dean. *The Rise of Silas Lapham*. 1885. New York: Penguin, 1986.

Huston, Richard. "Early Film Versions of *The Virginian*." *Reading* The Virginian *in the New West*. Ed. Melody Graulich and Stephen Tatum. Lincoln: U of Nebraska P, 2003. 126–47.

Huyssen, Andreas. *After the Great Divide: Modernism, Mass Culture, Postmodernism*. Bloomington: Indiana UP, 1986.

Irr, Caren. *The Suburb of Dissent: Cultural Politics in the United States and Canada during the 1930s*. Durham: Duke UP, 1998.

Irving, Katrina. "Displacing Homosexuality: The Use of Ethnicity in Willa Cather's *My Ántonia*." *Modern Fiction Studies* 36.1 (Spring 1990): 91–102.

Jaffe, Aaron. *Modernism and the Culture of Celebrity*. New York: Cambridge UP, 2005.

Jameson, Fredric. *The Political Unconscious: Narrative as Socially Symbolic Act*. Ithaca: Cornell UP, 1981.

———. *A Singular Modernity: Essay on the Ontology of the Present*. New York: Verso, 2002.

Jameson, Fredric. "Third-World Literature in the Era of Multinational Capitalism." *Social Text* 15 (Autumn 1986): 65–88.

———. "The Vanishing Mediator; or, Max Weber as Storyteller." 1973. *The Ideologies of Theory: Essays 1971–1986, Volume 2: The Syntax of History.* Minneapolis: U of Minnesota P, 1988. 3–34.

Johannsen, Albert. *The House of Beadle and Adams and Its Dime and Nickel Novels: The Story of a Vanished Literature.* 3 Vols. Norman: U of Oklahoma P, 1950–1962.

Johnson, Michael K. *Black Masculinity and the Frontier Myth in American Literature.* Norman: U of Oklahoma P, 2002.

Jones, Daryl. *The Dime Novel Western.* Bowling Green: Bowling Green U Popular P, 1978.

Kaplan, Amy. *The Anarchy of Empire in the Making of U.S. Culture.* Cambridge: Harvard UP, 2002.

———. *The Social Construction of American Realism.* Chicago: U of Chicago P, 1988.

Kaplan, Amy, and Donald E. Pease, eds. *Cultures of United States Imperialism.* Durham: Duke UP, 1993.

Kasson, Joy S. *Buffalo Bill's Wild West: Celebrity, Memory, and Popular History.* New York: Hill & Wang, 2000.

Kenner, Hugh. *A Homemade World: The American Modernist Writers.* 1975. Baltimore: Johns Hopkins UP, 1989.

Kidd, Kenneth B. *Making American Boys: Boyology and the Feral Tale.* Minneapolis: U of Minnesota P, 2004.

Kimmel, Michael. *Manhood in America: A Cultural History.* New York: Free P, 1996.

Krauss, Rosalind E. *The Picasso Papers.* New York: Farrar, Straus and Giroux, 1998.

Kuenz, Jane. "The Cowboy Businessman and 'The Course of Empire': Owen Wister's *The Virginian.*" *Cultural Critique* 48.1 (2001): 98–128.

Lambert, Deborah. "The Defeat of the Hero: Autonomy and Sexuality in *My Ántonia.*" *American Literature* 53 (1982): 76–90.

Lawrence, D. H. "A Calendar of Modern Letters, April 1927." *Ernest Hemingway: The Critical Heritage.* Ed. Jeffrey Meyers. New York: Routledge, 1997. 72–74.

———. *Studies in Classic American Literature.* 1923. New York: Penguin, 1977.

Lawson, W. B. *Diamond Dick, Jr.'s Call-Down; or, the King of the Silver Box. Diamond Dick Library* 175 (March 7, 1896).

Leverenz, David. *Paternalism Incorporated: Fables of American Fatherhood, 1865–1940.* Ithaca: Cornell UP, 2003.

Lewis, Wyndham. *Men Without Art.* 1934. Ed. Seamus Cooney. Santa Rosa: Black Sparrow P, 1987.

Lindemann, Marilee. *Willa Cather: Queering America.* New York: Columbia UP, 1999.

Love, Heather. *Feeling Backward: Loss and the Politics of Queer History.* Cambridge: Harvard UP, 2007.

Love, Nat. *The Life and Adventures of Nat Love.* 1907. Lincoln: U of Nebraska P, 1995.

Lutz, Tom. *American Nervousness, 1903: An Anecdotal History.* Ithaca: Cornell UP, 1993.

Lynn, Kenneth S. *Hemingway.* New York: Simon & Schuster, 1987.

Mandel, Miriam B., ed. *A Companion to Hemingway's Death in the Afternoon.* Rochester: Camden House, 2004.

Mao, Douglas. *Fateful Beauty: Aesthetic Environments, Juvenile Development, and Literature, 1860–1960*. Princeton: Princeton UP, 2008.

Mao, Douglas, and Rebecca L. Walkowitz. "The New Modernist Studies." *PMLA* 123.3 (May 2008): 737–48.

McCann, Sean. *Gumshoe America: Hard-Boiled Crime Fiction and the Rise and Fall of New Deal Liberalism*. Durham: Duke UP, 2000.

Michaels, Walter Benn. *Our America: Nativism, Modernism, and Pluralism*. Durham: Duke UP, 1995.

Miller, D. A. *Jane Austen, or the Secret of Style*. Princeton: Princeton UP, 2003.

Mitchell, Lee Clark. *Westerns: Making the Man in Fiction and Film*. Chicago: U of Chicago P, 1996.

Moddelmog, Debra. *Reading Desire: In Pursuit of Ernest Hemingway*. Ithaca: Cornell UP, 1999.

Morris, Edmund. *The Rise of Theodore Roosevelt*. Revised ed. New York: Modern Library, 2001.

———. *Theodore Rex*. New York: Modern Library, 2002.

Moss, Marilyn Ann. *Giant: George Stevens, a Life on Film*. Madison: U of Wisconsin P, 2004.

Nadel, Alan. *Containment Culture: American Narratives, Postmodernism, and the Atomic Age*. Durham: Duke UP, 1995.

Nealon, Christopher. *Foundlings: Lesbian and Gay Emotion Before Stonewall*. Durham: Duke UP, 2001.

Nelson, Dana D. *National Manhood: Capitalist Citizenship and the Imagined Fraternity of White Men*. Durham: Duke UP, 1998.

Noble, Jean Bobby. *Masculinities Without Men?: Female Masculinity in Twentieth-century Fictions*. Vancouver: U of British Columbia P, 2004.

Noel, Mary. *Villains Galore…: The Heyday of the Popular Story Weekly*. New York: Macmillan, 1954.

North, Michael. *Camera Works: Photography and the Twentieth-Century Word*. New York: Oxford UP, 2005.

———. *Reading 1922: A Return to the Scene of the Modern*. New York: Oxford UP, 1999.

O'Brien, Sharon. "Introduction." *New Essays on My Ántonia*. Ed. Sharon O'Brien. Cambridge: Cambridge UP, 1999. 1–29.

———. *Willa Cather: The Emerging Voice*. 1987. Cambridge: Harvard UP, 1997.

Packard, Chris. *Queer Cowboys: And Other Erotic Male Friendships in Nineteenth-century American Literature*. New York: Palgrave, 2005.

Parini, Jay. *John Steinbeck: A Biography*. New York: Henry Holt, 1995.

Pastourmatzi, Domna. "Willa Cather and the Cult of Masculinity." *Willa Cather Pioneer Memorial Newsletter* 38.4 (Winter 1995): 2–18.

Patten, Gilbert. *Frank Merriwell's "Father": An Autobiography by Gilbert Patten ("Burt L. Standish")*. Ed. Harriet Hinsdale. Norman: University of Oklahoma Press, 1964.

Payne, Darwin. *Owen Wister: Chronicler of the West, Gentleman of the East*. Dallas: Southern Methodist UP, 1985.

Penley, Constance, and Sharon Willis. "Introduction." *Male Trouble*. Ed. Constance Penley and Sharon Willis. Minneapolis: U of Minnesota P, 1993. vii–xix.

Perloff, Marjorie. "'Ninety Percent Rotarian': Gertrude Stein's Hemingway." *American Literature* 62.4 (December 1990): 668–83.

Plath, James. "Shadow Rider: The Hemingway Hero as Western Archetype." *Hemingway and the Natural Word.* Ed. Robert E. Fleming. Moscow, ID: U of Idaho P, 1999. 69–85.

Quirk, Tom. *Bergson and American Culture: The Worlds of Willa Cather and Wallace Stevens.* Chapel Hill: U of North Carolina P, 1990.

Rabinowitz, Paula. *Labor and Desire: Women's Revolutionary Fiction in Depression America.* Chapel Hill: U of North Carolina P, 1991.

Rainey, Lawrence. *Institutions of Modernism: Literary Elites and Public Culture.* New Haven: Yale UP, 1998.

Reynolds, Quentin. *The Fiction Factory or From Pulp Row to Quality Street: The Story of 100 Years of Publishing at Street & Smith.* New York: Random House, 1955.

Robinson, Forrest G. *Having it Both Ways: Self-Subversion in Western Popular Classics.* Albuquerque: U of New Mexico P, 1993.

Roediger, David. *The Wages of Whiteness: Race and the Making of the American Working Class.* New York: Verso, 1991.

Roosevelt, Theodore. *An Autobiography.* 1913. *Theodore Roosevelt: The Rough Riders, An Autobiography.* Ed. Louis Auchincloss. New York: Library of America, 2004. 241–851.

———. *The Rough Riders.* 1899. *Theodore Roosevelt: The Rough Riders, An Autobiography.* Ed. Louis Auchincloss. New York: Library of America, 2004. 1–239.

———. "To Granville Stanley Hall." November 29, 1899. *Theodore Roosevelt: Letters and Speeches.* Ed. Louis Auchincloss. New York: Library of America, 2004. 183.

Rosowski, Susan. *Birthing a Nation: Gender, Creativity, and the West in American Literature.* Lincoln: U of Nebraska P, 1999.

Rotundo, E. Anthony. *American Manhood: Transformations in Masculinity from the Revolution to the Modern Era.* New York: Basic, 1993.

Rubin, Gayle S. "Thinking Sex: Notes for a Radical Theory of the Politics of Sexuality." 1984, 1992. *The Lesbian and Gay Studies Reader.* Ed. Henry Abelove, Michèle Aina Barale, and David M. Halperin. New York: Routledge, 1993. 3–44.

Ryan, Melissa. "The Enclosure of America: Civilization and Confinement in Willa Cather's *O Pioneers!*" *American Literature* 75.2 (2003): 275–303.

Sandweiss, Martha A. *Print the Legend: Photography and the American West.* New Haven: Yale UP, 2002.

Savran, David. *Taking it Like a Man: White Masculinity, Masochism, and Contemporary American Culture.* Princeton: Princeton UP, 1998.

Saxton, Alexander. *The Rise and Fall of the White Republic: Class Politics and Mass Culture in Nineteenth-Century America.* 1990. New York: Verso, 2003.

Schaefer, Jack. *Shane: The Critical Edition.* Ed. James C. Work. Lincoln: U of Nebraska P, 1984.

Scheckel, Susan. "Home on the Train: Race and Mobility in *The Life and Adventures of Nat Love.*" *American Literature* 74.2 (2002): 219–50.

Sedgwick, Eve Kosofsky. "Across Gender, Across Sexuality: Willa Cather and Others." *South Atlantic Quarterly* 88.1 (Winter 1989): 53–72.

———. "'Gosh, Boy George, You Must Be Awfully Secure in Your Masculinity!'" *Constructing Masculinity.* Ed. Maurice Berger, Brian Wallis, and Simon Watson. New York: Routledge, 1995. 11–20.

Seelye, John. "Come Back to the Boxcar, Leslie Honey: Or, Don't Cry for Me, Madonna, Just Pass the Milk: Steinbeck and Sentimentality." *Beyond Boundaries: Rereading John Steinbeck.* Ed. Susan Shillinglaw and Kevin Hearle. Tuscaloosa: U of Alabama P, 2002. 11–33.

Shamir, Milette, and Jennifer Travis, eds. *Boys Don't Cry?: Rethinking Narratives of Masculinity and Emotion in the U.S.* New York: Columbia UP, 2002.

Shane. Dir. George Stevens. Perf. Jean Arthur, Brandon De Wilde, Van Heflin, Alan Ladd, and Jack Palance. 1953. Paramount, 2000. DVD.

"She Wants to Be a Cowboy." *New York Times*, October 23, 1888: 6.

Shell, Marc. *Children of the Earth: Literature, Politics, and Nationhood.* New York: Oxford UP, 1993.

Shillinglaw, Susan, and Kevin Hearle, eds. *Beyond Boundaries: Rereading John Steinbeck.* Tuscaloosa: U of Alabama P, 2002.

Shindo, Charles J. *Dust Bowl Migrants in the American Imagination.* Lawrence: UP of Kansas, 1997.

Silverman, Kaja. *Male Subjectivity at the Margins.* New York: Routledge, 1992.

Simmonds, Roy. *John Steinbeck: The War Years, 1939–1945.* Lewisburg: Bucknell UP, 1996.

Slotkin, Richard. *The Fatal Environment: The Myth of the Frontier in the Age of Industrialization, 1800–1890.* 1985. New York: Harper Perennial, 1994.

———. *Gunfighter Nation: The Myth of the Frontier in Twentieth-Century America.* New York: Harper Perennial, 1992.

———. *Regeneration through Violence: The Mythology of the American Frontier, 1600–1860.* 1973. New York: Harper Perennial, 1996.

Smith, Henry Nash. *Virgin Land: The American West as Symbol and Myth.* 1950. Cambridge: Harvard UP, 1978.

Smith, Paul. *Clint Eastwood: A Cultural Production.* Minneapolis: U of Minnesota P, 1993.

Smith-Rosenberg, Carroll. *Disorderly Conduct: Visions of Gender in Victorian America.* New York: Oxford UP, 1986.

Speirs, Kenneth. "Writing Self (Effacingly): E-race-d Presences in *The Life and Adventures of Nat Love.*" *Western American Literature* 40.3 (Fall 2005): 301–20.

Spilka, Mark. *Hemingway's Quarrel with Androgyny.* Lincoln: U of Nebraska P, 1990.

Stein, Gertrude. *The Autobiography of Alice B. Toklas.* 1933. New York: Vintage, 1961.

Steinbeck, John. *Bombs Away: The Story of a Bomber Team.* 1942. New York: Paragon House, 1990.

———. *Cup of Gold: A Life of Sir Henry Morgan, Buccaneer, with Occasional Reference to History.* 1929. New York: Penguin, 1995.

———. *The Forgotten Village.* New York: Viking, 1941.

———. *The Grapes of Wrath.* 1939. New York: Penguin, 1999.

———. "Nobel Prize Acceptance Speech." 1963. *America and Americans and Selected Nonfiction.* Ed. Susan Shillinglaw and Jackson J. Benson. New York: Penguin, 2003. 172–75.

———. "To Carlton A. Sheffield." November 13, 1939. *Steinbeck: A Life in Letters.* Ed. Elaine Steinbeck and Robert Wallsten. New York: Viking, 1975. 193–94.

Stephens, Ann S. *Malaeska; or, the Indian Wife of the White Hunter.* 1860. *Reading the West: An Anthology of Dime Westerns.* Ed. Bill Brown. Boston: Bedford, 1997. 57–164.

Stewart, Matthew. "It Was All a Pleasant Business: The Historical Context of 'On the Quai at Smyrna.'" *Hemingway Review* 23.1 (Fall 2003): 58–71.

Stott, William. *Documentary Expression and Thirties America.* New York: Oxford UP, 1973.

Stout, Janis P. *Picturing a Different West: Vision, Illustration, and the Tradition of Cather and Austin.* Lubbock: Texas Tech UP, 2007.

———. "Willa Cather's Early Journalism: Gender, Performance, and the 'Manly Battle Yarn.'" *Arizona Quarterly* 55.3 (Autumn 1999): 51–82.

Stowe, Harriet Beecher. *Uncle Tom's Cabin, or, Life Among the Lowly.* 1852. New York: Modern Library, 2001.

Streeby, Shelley. *American Sensations: Class, Empire, and the Production of Popular Culture.* Berkeley: U of California P, 2002.

Strychacz, Thomas. *Hemingway's Theaters of Masculinity.* Baton Rouge: Louisiana State UP, 2003.

Susman, Warren I. "'Personality' and the Making of Twentieth-Century Culture." *Culture as History: The Transformation of American Society in the Twentieth Century.* 1973. Washington: Smithsonian, 2003. 271–85.

Szalay, Michael. *New Deal Modernism: American Literature and the Invention of the Welfare State.* Durham: Duke UP, 2000.

Taylor, Quintard. *In Search of the Racial Frontier: African Americans in the American West, 1528–1960.* New York: Norton, 1998.

Terada, Rei. *Feeling in Theory: Emotion after the "Death of the Subject."* Cambridge: Harvard UP, 2001.

Thurston, Michael. "Gender, Genre, and Truth in *Death in the Afternoon.*" *The Hemingway Review* 17.2 (Spring 1998): 47–63.

Tompkins, Jane. *Sensational Designs: The Cultural Work of American Fiction, 1790–1860.* New York: Oxford UP, 1985.

———. *West of Everything: The Inner Life of Westerns.* New York: Oxford UP, 1992.

Tonkovich, Nicole. "Guardian Angels and Missing Mothers: Race and Domesticity in *Winona* and *Deadwood Dick on Deck.*" *Western American Literature* 32.3 (1997): 241–64.

Torgovnick, Marianna. *The War Complex: World War II in Our Time.* Chicago: U of Chicago P, 2005.

Travis, Jennifer. *Wounded Hearts: Masculinity, Law, and Literature in American Culture.* Chapel Hill: U of North Carolina P, 2005.

Turner, Catherine. *Marketing Modernism: Between the Two World Wars.* Amherst: U of Massachusetts P, 2003.

Turner, E. S. *Boys Will Be Boys: The Story of Sweeney Todd, Deadwood Dick, Sexton Blake, Dick Barton, et al.* London: Michael Joseph, 1948.

Turner, Frederick Jackson. "The Significance of the Frontier in American History." *Does the Frontier Experience Make America Exceptional?* Ed. Richard W. Etulain. Boston: Bedford, 1999. 18–43.

Tuttle, Jennifer S. "Indigenous Whiteness and Wister's Invisible Indians." *Reading* The Virginian *in the New West.* Ed. Melody Graulich and Stephen Tatum. Lincoln: U of Nebraska P, 2003. 89–112.

"Vanity Fair's Own Paper Dolls—no. 5." *Vanity Fair* (March 1934): 29.

Walker, Don D. "Wister, Roosevelt and James: A Note on the Western." *American Quarterly* 12.3 (Autumn 1960): 358–66.

Warner, Michael. "What Like a Bullet Can Undeceive?" *Public Culture* 15.1 (2003): 41–54.

Watts, Sarah. *Rough Rider in the White House: Theodore Roosevelt and the Politics of Desire.* Chicago: U of Chicago P, 2003.

West, Mark I. "The Role of Sexual Repression in Anthony Comstock's Campaign to Censor Children's Dime Novels." *Journal of American Culture* 22.4 (Winter 1999): 45–49.

Wheeler, Edward L. *Deadwood Dick on Deck; or, Calamity Jane, the Heroine of Whoop-Up.* 1885. *Seth Jones by Edward S. Ellis and Deadwood Dick on Deck by Edward J. Wheeler: Dime Novels.* Ed. Philip Durham. New York: Odyssey, 1966. 97–188.

———. *Deadwood Dick, the Prince of the Road; or, the Black Rider of the Black Hills.* 1877. *Reading the West: An Anthology of Dime Westerns.* Ed. Bill Brown. Boston: Bedford: 1997. 273–358.

———. *Deadwood Dick's Claim; or, The Fairy Face of Faro Flats. Beadle's Half-Dime Library* 362 (July 1, 1884).

———. *Deadwood Dick's Doom; or, Calamity Jane's Last Adventure. Beadle's Half-Dime Library* 205 (June 25, 1881).

White, G. Edward. *The Eastern Establishment and the Western Experience: The West of Frederic Remington, Theodore Remington, and Owen Wister.* New Haven: Yale UP, 1968.

Will, Barbara. "The Nervous Origins of the American Western." *American Literature* 70.2 (1998): 293–316.

Williams, Raymond. "When Was Modernism?" *The Politics of Modernism: Against the New Conformists.* 1989. New York: Verso, 2007. 31–35.

Wilson, Edmund. *The Wound and the Bow: Seven Studies in Literature.* 1941. Athens: Ohio UP, 1997.

Wister, Owen. "The Evolution of the Cow-Puncher." 1895. *The Virginian: A Horseman of the Plains.* New York: Oxford UP, 1998. 329–44.

———. *Owen Wister Out West: His Journals and Letters.* Ed. Fanny Kemble Wister. Chicago: U of Chicago P, 1958.

———. *Roosevelt: The Story of a Friendship, 1880–1919.* New York: Macmillan, 1930.

———. *The Virginian: A Horseman of the Plains.* 1902. New York: Oxford UP, 1998.

Witschi, Nicolas. *Traces of Gold: California's Natural Resources and the Claim to Realism in Western American Literature.* Tuscaloosa: U of Alabama P, 2002.

Wolfe, Cary. *Animal Rites: American Culture, the Discourse of Species, and Posthumanist Theory.* Chicago: U of Chicago P, 2003.

———. "In the Shadow of Wittgenstein's Lion: Language, Ethics, an the Question of the Animal." *Zoontologies: The Question of the Animal.* Ed. Cary Wolfe. Minneapolis: U of Minnesota P, 2003. 1–57.

Work, James C. "Preface." *Shane: The Critical Edition.* By Jack Schaefer. Ed. James C. Work. Lincoln: U of Nebraska P, 1984. xiii–xvi.

Young, Philip. *Ernest Hemingway: A Reconsideration.* Revised ed. University Park: Pennsylvania State UP, 1966.

Index

Printed and bound by CPI Group (UK) Ltd, Croydon, CR0 4YY